Negotiating Learning and Identity
in Higher Education

Understanding Student Experiences of Higher Education

Edited by Paul Ashwin and Manja Klemenčič

As the number of students attending higher education has increased globally, there has been an increasing focus on student experiences of higher education. Understanding how students experience higher education in different national, institutional and disciplinary settings has become increasingly important to researchers, practitioners and policymakers.

The series publishes theoretically robust and empirically rigorous studies of students' experiences, including a broad range of elements such as student life, engagement in degree courses and extracurricular activities, experiences of feedback and assessment, student representation and students' wider lives. It offers a richer understanding of the different meanings of being a student in higher education in the twenty-first century.

Forthcoming in the series

Understanding Experiences of First Generation University Students, edited by Amani Bell and Lorri J. Santamaría
Everyday Mobilities in Higher Education, Kirsty Finn, Mark Holton and Kate Carruthers Thomas

Also available from Bloomsbury

Academic Identities in Higher Education, edited by Linda Evans and Jon Nixon
Reflective Teaching in Higher Education, Paul Ashwin

Negotiating Learning and Identity in Higher Education

Access, Persistence and Retention

Edited by Bongi Bangeni and Rochelle Kapp

Bloomsbury Academic
An imprint of Bloomsbury Publishing Plc

B L O O M S B U R Y

LONDON · OXFORD · NEW YORK · NEW DELHI · SYDNEY

Bloomsbury Academic
An imprint of Bloomsbury Publishing Plc

50 Bedford Square	1385 Broadway
London	New York
WC1B 3DP	NY 10018
UK	USA

www.bloomsbury.com

BLOOMSBURY and the Diana logo are trademarks of Bloomsbury Publishing Plc

First published 2017

© Bongi Bangeni, Rochelle Kapp and Contributors, 2017

Bongi Bangeni, Rochelle Kapp and Contributors have asserted their right under the Copyright, Designs and Patents Act, 1988, to be identified as Authors of this work.

British Library Cataloguing-in-Publication Data
A catalogue record for this book is available from the British Library.

ISBN: HB: 978-1-3500-0019-3
ePDF: 978-1-3500-0020-9
ePub: 978-1-3500-0021-6

Library of Congress Cataloging-in-Publication Data
A catalog record for this book is available from the Library of Congress.

Series: Understanding Student Experiences of Higher Education

Typeset by Deanta Global Publishing Services, Chennai, India
Printed and bound in Great Britain

To our students, whose stories have humbled and inspired us. We are deeply grateful for all we have learnt from your journeys.

Contents

Series Editors' Foreword   viii

Notes on Contributors   x

Acknowledgements   xii

Introduction : Conceptualizing Access, Persistence and Retention
Rochelle Kapp and Bongi Bangeni   1

1   Students' Negotiation of Learning and Identity in Working-class Schooling *Rochelle Kapp, Elmi Badenhorst, Bongi Bangeni, Tracy S. Craig, Viki Janse van Rensburg, Kate le Roux, Robert Prince, June Pym and Ermien van Pletzen*   17

2   'Closing the Gap': Three Mathematics Students Talk about their Transitions to and through their Undergraduate Degrees in the Sciences *Kate le Roux*   31

3   'Going Nowhere Slowly': A Longitudinal Perspective on a First-generation Woman Student's Withdrawal from University *Judy Sacks and Rochelle Kapp*   61

4   Humanities Students' Negotiation of Language, Literacy and Identity *Rochelle Kapp and Bongi Bangeni*   79

5   The Role of Religion in Mediating the Transition to Higher Education *Bongi Bangeni and June Pym*   95

6   A Longitudinal Account of the Factors Shaping the Degree Paths of Black Students *Bongi Bangeni*   109

7   Enabling Capabilities in an Engineering Extended Curriculum Programme *Tracy S. Craig*   133

8   The Impact of Previous Experiences and Social Connectedness on Students' Transition to Higher Education *June Pym and Judy Sacks*   155

Conclusion: Exploring the Implications of Students' Learning Journeys for Policy and Practice *Bongi Bangeni and Rochelle Kapp*   181

Index   189

Series Editors' Foreword

The 'Understanding Student Experiences in Higher Education' book series publishes theoretically robust and empirically rigorous studies of students' experiences of contemporary higher education. The books in the series are united by the belief that it is not possible to understand these experiences without understanding the diverse range of people, practices, technologies and institutions that come together to form them. The series seeks to locate students' experiences in the context of global changes to higher education and thereby to offer a rich understanding of the different global and local meanings of being a student in higher education in the twenty-first century.

Negotiating Learning and Identity in Higher Education is the first book to be published in the series and brilliantly exemplifies many of the things that we are trying to achieve in the series as a whole. In providing a qualitative and longitudinal lens on students' experiences of entering, studying and progressing through higher education, it provides a rich picture of the ways that students' identities and experiences intertwine. That the focus is on black, working-class students studying in an elite historically white South African university heightens the importance of answering the book's central questions of how these students can gain meaningful access to institutional and disciplinary discourses, how the existing knowledge and resources that students bring with them into higher education can be recognized and valued, and how to address the practices and structures that marginalize these students. The fine-grained and in-depth analysis of students' experiences in relation to these questions makes this a book that is concerned with the profoundly educational challenge of how we help all students to gain access to powerful forms of disciplinary and professional knowledge that can transform their understandings of the world and how they can change it. While these concerns have particular resonance for the South African context in which universities play a crucial role in addressing the legacy of apartheid, the book shows that addressing such concerns is equally important for higher education globally. The book makes an important contribution to the global discussion on access to higher education, students' persistence and progress, and how students from different backgrounds negotiate learning and identity. In providing such powerful accounts of students' individual and collective experiences of their learning journeys, *Negotiating Learning and Identity in Higher Education* makes an important and timely contribution to our understanding of contemporary higher education.

Paul Ashwin and Manja Klemenčič
Series Editors

Notes on Contributors

Elmi Badenhorst is Senior Lecturer in the Department of Health Science Education at the University of Cape Town, South Africa. She convenes an academic development programme for medical students and has extensive teaching and development experience in this field. She has published in the areas of academic development, student experience and cognition.

Bongi Bangeni is Senior Lecturer in the Centre for Higher Education Development, University of Cape Town, South Africa, and is a Mandela Fellow at the Hutchins Center for African and African American Research at Harvard University, USA. She has published in the areas of writing and identity, the development of discipline-specific literacies, and students' transitions from undergraduate to postgraduate spaces of engagement.

Tracy S. Craig is Senior Lecturer of Mathematics in the Academic Development Programme at the University of Cape Town, South Africa. She teaches mathematics in the Faculty of Engineering and the Built Environment and has published in the areas of mathematics education, engineering education and academic development.

Viki Janse van Rensburg has recently retired from the Education Development Unit of the Faculty of Health Sciences, University of Cape Town, South Africa, where she worked in the areas of student learning, curriculum development and staff development. She has published in the areas of teaching and learning, assessment and student experiences of the transition to higher education.

Rochelle Kapp is Associate Professor in the School of Education at the University of Cape Town, South Africa. She has extensive teaching and development experience in the fields of language and literacy education and has led a number of academic development projects. She has published in the areas of language and literacy practices, student experience and the politics of English.

Kate le Roux is Senior Lecturer in Language Development in the Academic Development Programme at the University of Cape Town, South Africa. Her research and teaching is located at the intersection of language, mathematics and the learning of disciplinary knowledge in science and engineering, with a particular focus on access, identity and power in the higher education context.

June Pym has recently retired as Associate Professor and Director of the Education Development Unit (Commerce) at the University of Cape Town, South Africa, and has extensive experience working with students from disadvantaged backgrounds. She has published in the area of first-generation student experiences of higher education and teaching and learning.

Judy Sacks lectures in the postgraduate teacher education programme in the School of Education at the University of Cape Town. Her research interests are in tertiary student experience, teacher development and language and literacy education.

Ermien van Pletzen is Associate Professor and Director of the Academic Development Programme at the University of Cape Town, South Africa. She has taught and engaged in educational development in the Humanities and Health Sciences Faculties and has published in the areas of language and literacy, public health and disability studies.

Robert Prince is Senior Lecturer in the Centre for Higher Education Development at the University of Cape Town, South Africa. He has extensive teaching and development experience in the fields of mathematics and quantitative literacy education as well as in educational testing and has published in the areas of quantitative literacy practices and educational testing.

Acknowledgements

This research was made possible by many years of collaboration across disciplinary boundaries with our research group colleagues who work tirelessly to ensure access for students from disadvantaged backgrounds: Moeain Arend, Elmi Badenhorst, Bonani Dube, Tracy Craig, Busayo Ige, Judy Sacks, Viki Janse van Rensburg, Kate le Roux, Robert Prince, June Pym and Ermien van Pletzen.

Longitudinal research requires stamina and the research group was fortunate to have the support of many friends and colleagues. Bonani Dube, Judy Sacks, Thobela Bixa, Sean Samson and Zulpha Geyer engaged in research assistance with sensitivity and enthusiasm. Glynis Lloyd provided superb editorial assistance and advice. Shirley Rix transcribed accurately and efficiently and kept reminding us of the importance of sharing the students' journeys. Cheryl Brown, Kay McCormick, Mugsy Spiegel and Kevin Williams helped us with data analysis. Veronica Twynam, Leigh Wentzel and Janine Peters fielded our many finance and administration requests with good grace. Jane Hendry decoded our obscure requests and provided the institutional statistics we didn't know we needed. We are particularly grateful to the following colleagues for their critical feedback and friendship over many years: Pam Christie, Brenda Cooper, Kathy Erasmus, Erica Gillard, Natasha Gordon-Chipembere, Lesley Greenbaum, Anne Herrington, Dave Johnson, Carolyn McKinney, Ian Scott, Suellen Shay, Crain Soudien, Lucia Thesen and John Trimbur. Camilla Erskine, Maria Giovanna Brauzzi, Paul Ashwin and Maria Klemenčič have all provided expert guidance.

This research would not have been possible without the financial support of the A.W. Mellon Foundation, the National Research Foundation and the University of Cape Town. We are indebted to Professor Stuart Saunders for his unflinching support of the research project.

Last, but not least, Bongi and Rochelle are grateful to their families for their unwavering support and love. Bongi thanks her mother, Nosipo, her sisters Nwabisa and Langelihle Nkabinde and Rochelle thanks her husband Kelwyn Sole and her parents, Rene and Eddie.

We gratefully acknowledge permission to republish: Kapp, R. and Bangeni, B. (2011), 'A Longitudinal Study of Students' Negotiation of Language, Literacy and Identity', *Southern African Linguistics and Applied Language Studies*, 29(2): 197–208 and to use material from: Kapp, R., Badenhorst, E., Bangeni, B., Craig, T.S., Janse van Rensburg, V., le Roux, K., Prince, R., Pym, J. and van Pletzen, E. (2014), 'Successful Students' Negotiation of Township Schooling in Contemporary South Africa', *Perspectives in Education* 32(3): 50–61.

Bongi Bangeni and Rochelle Kapp

Introduction: Conceptualizing Access, Persistence and Retention

Rochelle Kapp and Bongi Bangeni

Understanding learning journeys in context

Participation in higher education has increased globally, and in some projections will almost double by 2025 (Klemenčič and Fried 2007). Nevertheless, research across the globe has highlighted major inequalities in patterns of access of traditionally under-represented social groups, and globally, student retention and progress is a major source of concern (Burke 2012; Hall 2012; Chowdry, Crawford and Dearden 2013). This book provides a qualitative, longitudinal lens on the issues of access, persistence and retention and, in doing so, makes a contribution to the global discussion on how to widen access and facilitate meaningful participation in higher education through an analysis of various aspects of the learning pathways of black, working-class students at the University of Cape Town, a relatively elite, English-medium, historically white South African university.

South Africa is a particularly interesting case because in post-apartheid South Africa, considerable resources have been directed towards changing the racially skewed pattern of university participation. Nevertheless, the participation rates for African and coloured students (in the 20- to 24-year-old cohort) have remained 'persistently very low' (14% in 2011), and generally under a quarter of that of white students with 'under 5 per cent of African and coloured youth succeeding in any form of higher education' (Council on Higher Education 2013:15).[1] This pattern has in turn had a considerable impact on access to postgraduate studies for this demographic.

In addition, the 2015 and 2016 student uprisings in South Africa (which coalesced in movements such as #RhodesMustFall and #FeesMustFall) 'trended' internationally, focusing unprecedented attention on the lives of black students in higher education and announcing the sense of alienation and hitherto suppressed frustration and anger provoked by race, class and gender stratification within higher education institutions. However, both the statistics and the Twitter feeds contribute only to the headlines of the meandering journeys of many black, working-class South African students as they attempt to negotiate the labyrinth of higher education.

The participants in our research are part of a generation of young black people who have grown up in the new South Africa and are mostly first generation, working class and from single-parent families. They are bilingual or multilingual and English is generally a second or third language. Our research focuses on how this group negotiates new ways of 'saying-doing-being-valuing-believing' (Gee 1990: 142), that is, how they negotiate the discourses that characterize their new environment, and how they negotiate their senior years and their changing relationships to home discourses. Recent sociological studies of working-class township[2] youth have pointed out that there has been relatively little attention paid to youth agency: how South African youth interpret their educational and home contexts, strategize and take decisions and action (Soudien 2007; Bray et al. 2010). In post-apartheid South Africa, there is an almost daily outcry about educational failure and black, working-class youth are either described as failures or victims, characterized as the 'lost generation', 'disadvantaged' and 'marginalized' (see Swartz 2009: 13). This depiction of working-class youth is not unique to South Africa. Our work contributes to a growing body of international research which has pointed out that rather than addressing the complexity of lived experience, stereotypes such as these have the effect of reifying identity and contribute to the conceptualization of the presence of working-class students in higher education as an aberration (see Mann 2008; Fataar 2010; Reay et al. 2010; Janse van Rensburg 2011; Hall 2012; Case 2013; Soudien 2013).

This book conceptualizes learning as a journey. The commonly envisaged destination is graduation, but the journey there involves navigation of multiple places over time. Each place holds a set of expectations about what constitutes appropriate ways of learning and ways of being. The participants have to negotiate an intersection of (often conflicting) race, class, gendered and religious subject positions and while the institution provides a roadmap, it is fairly rudimentary, seldom sufficiently explicit and primarily based on normative (usually white, middle-class, English) assumptions about students, their ways of being, learning, home and schooling contexts. Consequently, black, working-class students are often faced with limited choices and are not necessarily made aware of alternative routes.

The chapters in this book foreground the participants' voices and their unfolding interpretations of their learning. We are interested in the consequences of students' interpretations of their school, home and academic environments for their learning and engagement. We argue that in order to understand how students gain meaningful access and *why* students persist, fail and/or leave, we need to understand their learning journeys in context. This entails understanding the ways in which institutional and societal structures and discourses enable and/or hinder their progress, as well as their agency: how they 'invest' in their learning, how they envisage their futures and when, where and why they engage (or disengage) with 'socially and discursively available resources as they cross borders and navigate boundaries' (Thomson 2009: 160).

Globally, higher education research has shown that in general, students struggle with the transition to higher education for a range of academic, linguistic, material and psycho-social reasons. Schooling socializes students into particular approaches to learning, ways of using language, attitudes and dispositions that are often at odds with what is required within higher education settings. In the field of higher education, there has been an important move away from generic research on approaches to learning towards understanding the way in which academic knowledge is socially situated and the consequences for teaching and learning (see for example Lea and Street 1998; Thesen and van Pletzen eds. 2006; Lillis and Scott 2007; Case 2013; Ashwin and Trigwell 2012). Such research has examined what counts as knowledge in particular disciplines; how disciplinary values, practices and ways of using language often remain tacit; how students draw on prior knowledge to interpret tasks and feedback; and how disciplinary knowledge is expressed in assessment tasks and in student writing. Importantly, research has highlighted the mismatch between lecturers' and students' understandings of their disciplines. While this work has sought to describe the characteristic features of individual disciplines, it has also foregrounded how the contestation within disciplines is often hidden from students.

Crucially, the research has critiqued the exclusive focus on individual attributes divorced from context (Haggis 2004: 2; Tinto 2006–7; Boughey 2009). It has also critiqued the deficit assumption that students will be passively assimilated into disciplinary discourses after they have been rehabilitated in adjunct, first-year courses without any changes to mainstream teaching practices and institutional culture (Haggis 2004; Boughey 2010; Pym and Kapp 2013). Researchers have increasingly attempted to understand the relationship between teaching and learning (Christie 2008; Ashwin 2012; Case 2013) and have focused on how to recognize, acknowledge and harness the resources that young people bring to higher education and how to transform the teaching and learning environment (Lillis and Scott 2007; Thomas and Quinn 2007; Walker 2010) and university policy and structures (Hall 2012).

There is also a growing body of international literature from various theoretical traditions in multiple higher education contexts which analyses the particular academic, linguistic and identity challenges faced by university students from second-language, first-generation, working-class, non-traditional backgrounds (see for example Thesen and van Pletzen eds 2006; Mann 2008; Reay, Crozier and Clayton 2010; Leibowitz, van der Merwe and van Schalkwyk eds 2012; Thomas 2012; Case 2013; Pym and Paxton eds 2013; Wilson-Strydom 2015). This research has highlighted the ways in which identity is central to learning and the ways in which students are often marginalized, stereotyped and alienated by the forms of 'cultural capital' valued within academia (Bourdieu 1991: 230). It has also been concerned with agency and student subjectivities, and the ways in which individuals invest in certain subject positions rather than others at particular times in relation to structures of power, interactions with others, emotions and opportunity (Norton 2000; Norton and McKinney 2010).

Much valuable research effort has gone into conceptualizing student experiences and academic literacy practices. However, with some notable exceptions (see Sternglass 1997; Herrington and Curtis 2000; Leathwood and O'Connell 2003 and Haggis 2011), there have been few qualitative studies that have traced students' experiences of learning, academic literacy and identity throughout their undergraduate years. Qualitative research on students' language and literacy attitudes and practices tends to be based on what students say in single interviews, and/or essays written within a short time frame. This has the effect of freezing experiences, language and literacy practices and identities in time and space and (ironically) reinforcing fixed, reified notions of identity. It is easy to assume a great deal of commonality in the experiences of second-language/ marginalized/disadvantaged/non-traditional learners across the world (as a great deal of research has done) if one treats school, neighbourhood and home contexts as background covered under the term 'research site' (see le Roux's discussion in Chapter 3 of this book; Thesen and van Pletzen eds 2006).

Our starting point is different. We ask: '*How and why is it that students persist despite coming from social backgrounds that do not seem to be conducive to learning?*' The qualitative longitudinal approach to this question foregrounds the centrality of context, enabling us to situate learning and identity in time and space (Thomson 2009; Thomson and McLeod 2015). We describe the participants' unfolding learning, literacy and numeracy attitudes and practices, and the ways in which they reassess their past and future trajectories in the light of their experiences in the academy and at home. Drawing on the evolving meanings participants attribute to their learning journeys over time and in the different spaces they inhabit allows us to explore how students' ability to be agentic is enabled and/or constrained by institutional structures at different times.

The chapters in this book illustrate in different ways that the school-to-university transition is neither linear nor universal. The participants in the research have to negotiate multiple identities and multiple transitions at various times in their degrees and cannot easily be categorized as alienated or assimilated. Whereas higher education research tends to focus on students' movement away from home, we illustrate the ways in which home remains central to the participants as they juggle multiple subject positions. English emerges as a key signifier. It is at once a portal for access and a potential gatekeeper, with connotations of loss and gain, whiteness and alienation, upward mobility and exclusion. The longitudinal perspective enables us to see that participants both resist and absorb institutional, disciplinary and home discourses and that they are able to be agentic in some spaces in some moments and not in others (Klemenčič 2015). We use Bhabha's (1994) work on postcolonial subjectivity to describe the participants' ambivalence as they straddle often conflicting discourses within their disciplines, within the institution and between home and the institution, and occupy multiple subject positions that are related to the boundaries and possibilities of place and time. We draw on a range of poststructuralist theories of identity, learning and language in the different chapters. This enables a multifaceted view on how the participants negotiate these subject positions by reframing and/or adjusting their understandings and practices, constructing coherence, developing situated identities and/or preserving 'face' in order to persist and achieve a sense of progress that is considered acceptable within multiple domains. Although our participants' journeys through the institution are by no means uniform, there are discernible patterns in their attitudes and practices that are intimately linked to their shifting understanding of disciplinary and home discourses, their increasing fluency in English, their use of resources and their changing sense of self over the course of their degrees.

Learning and identity in a time of institutional change

The research took place in a moment of convergence, as the University was opening access in partially realized and unevenly transformed ways. The research makes visible the considerable learning and identity challenges that black, working-class students face, particularly in a time of societal transition where historically dominant discourses are subject to overt contestation, but still hold real and intangible forms of power, resulting in Janus-faced institutional policy and practices.

Situated on the slopes of the majestic Table Mountain, the University is both the oldest in South Africa and rated first in Africa on key international ratings (such as the *Times Higher Education* World University Rankings 2016). Admission to study and work at the institution is highly competitive. It was designated for white students under apartheid, but small numbers of black students were permitted to study there under special government permit. Historically, the University has positioned itself as anti-apartheid and liberal in its ideology. However, it has also benefitted hugely from the unequal distribution of resources during apartheid. In post-apartheid South Africa, there has been government pressure to increase enrolment and graduation of black South Africans, to change the racial composition of staff, to change the structure and orientation of curricula and to engage in more socially relevant research. National policy commits the institution to improving teaching and learning practices in the mainstream and to improving retention rates, particularly of black students. Nevertheless, institutional ambivalence and concern with dropping standards is evident in the fact that efforts to achieve this tend to be sporadic, uncoordinated, and often reliant on the goodwill or leadership of particular individuals. State and corporate-sector funding has increasingly been directed towards redress-orientated teaching and learning activities, bursaries and research. In this context of shifting power relations, changing policies and, consequently, shifting resources, the institution's leadership has been anxious to shed its identity as an ivory tower, white university, while also attempting to increase its global status, marketability, credibility and reputation. Among many white academics and alumni, there has been considerable disquiet about a potential drop in standards, about the perceived challenge to academic autonomy, about the perpetuation of racial agendas, about having to expend time and energy on increasing administrative loads and 'weaker' students in a constantly changing policy environment, about their own career paths, and about pressure to engage in socially responsive research. Consequently, many of the changes have been instrumental and superficial in character (see Boughey 2009; Soudien 2013).

In a review of teaching and learning in five research-intensive South African universities, Boughey (2009: 33) presents an astute analysis of the consequences of this institutional positioning for constructions of students and student learning. She describes how students are constructed as 'a-social, a-cultural, autonomous beings'. Thus, the ability to succeed in higher education is viewed as 'dependent on factors inherent to the individual such as "motivation" and "potential"'. At the same time, student difficulties are attributed to contexts outside of the university, thus eliding 'social and cultural difference' (Boughey 2009: 34). In an interesting analysis of inequality in higher education, Hall (2012) makes a similar point about how the erasure of working-class student identities in British university systems perpetuates the fallacy of a level playing field.

The contestation about institutional identity and positioning is evident in the fact that discourses about promoting equity and those relating to excellence are routinely presented as antithetical (often unconsciously so), resulting in very little change in racial composition and institutional culture. Although the University has good financial aid and academic development systems and there are many initiatives underway to change the institution's profile and culture, the rate of change has been slow and the policy of accepting black students under special admissions remains contested. In addition, an emphasis on the University's research status has limited the number of black academics being appointed. In 2002, when our first cohort of participants arrived, 39 per cent of the University's undergraduate student population consisted of black South Africans, and 18 per cent of academic staff were black. By 2009, when the second cohort arrived, the percentage of black students had increased to 60 per cent, but the percentage of black staff had only increased from 2 per cent to 20 per cent.

As will be evident from our case studies, besides bridging the conventional gaps faced by students from marginalized backgrounds in terms of race, linguistics, social class and cultural issues, the students have also had to engage within an institution which had actively encouraged them to enrol, but was nevertheless ambivalent in its attitude to their presence. The felt effects of this structural context and its effect on agency are explored in this book.

Methodological considerations

This book is based on two collaborative qualitative longitudinal case studies conducted within the Academic Development Programme in the Centre for Higher Education Development at the University of Cape Town from 2002 to

2005 and from 2009 to 2012. The first study included twenty students from the Humanities Faculty. This study also traced the journeys of six students from this group who graduated and went on to register for postgraduate studies in the professional disciplines of marketing and law. The second study included 100 students from the Commerce, Engineering, Health Sciences, Humanities and Science Faculties. Both studies draw on background questionnaires, semi-structured interviews with students, students' written reflections on language and writing, as well as assignments selected by students.

The writers are academics who teach and undertake development work in faculty-based programmes (in Commerce, Engineering, Humanities and Science). These extended degree programmes are designed to induct black students from 'disadvantaged' home and school backgrounds into the discourse practices of their disciplines and to provide appropriate support. The models of academic development vary considerably across faculties, but in general, students who are deemed to have the potential to succeed at university, but who have not met the regular admissions' criteria because of structural disadvantage, are admitted to special programmes which extend the first year over two years and focus on building the foundations needed to proceed to mainstream courses. Students are taught in relatively small classes with constructivist approaches that aim to build the necessary conceptual foundations, provide space and time for the acquisition of the literacy and numeracy practices that characterize their disciplines, and provide various degrees of informal and/or formal psycho-social support.

While these special programmes are well established and successful in achieving good first-year results (relative to institutional and national statistics), unacceptably high numbers of students fail, underperform or withdraw after the first year when they enter the mainstream. Within the context of recent protests, the stigma associated with such programmes has come into focus. The work in this book explores the disciplinary, institutional and social structures and practices that prevail as students enter academic development programmes. In addition, the work examines those structures and practices students encounter as they transition into the mainstream. The researchers worked collaboratively to analyse the data and its implications for teaching and learning. The participants' meta-reflections provide a rich, complex and varied perspective on the ways in which these programmes helped and/or hindered their progress in the mainstream. The effect of repeated interviews was to allow us to see both continuity and change (Thomson and Holland 2003).

Our research does not assume that we can read off participants' identities from the interviews or establish an essential truth. Alongside other poststructuralist theorists, we are mindful of the positions from which participants compose, reconstruct, recontextualize and re-enact their identities in interviews as they review their past in the light of their present contexts and in the projections of possible futures (see Herrington and Curtis 2000; Sfard and Prusak 2005). We were interested in how the participants described their experiences, the issues and symbolic objects that they chose to foreground, and how they constructed a sense of self in relation to others in the different spaces they navigated over time.

Each chapter in this book focuses on the experiences of a small, typical sample of participants in order to provide an in-depth qualitative analysis of a particular aspect of students' pathways. The ways in which the authors approach this analysis vary, resulting in differences in the scope of individual chapters. Comparison is central to our methodology, and in those cases where we compare individual student pathways, the chapters are relatively lengthy in order to do justice to the complexity of participants' journeys. By exploring the implications of our findings for models of academic development and for teaching and learning interactions, the writers address questions that are central to the global higher education discussion about improving access and retention, namely: How do we facilitate meaningful access to institutional and disciplinary discourses? How can we recognize and draw on the resources that students bring into the academy? How can we transform discourses and structures that impede, exclude, marginalize and silence?

Chapter outlines

Written collaboratively by the research group, Chapter 1 provides an overview of the participants' learning experiences in working-class schools, providing context for the chapters which follow. The chapter draws on poststructuralist theories of identity, learning and language to analyse the subject positions in which the participants invested, as well as how they used resources. The writers argue that the increased vulnerability produced by this context is significant in terms of the participants' constructions of their learning identities and future possibilities. The data illustrate the ways in which the students had to carry the burden of navigating school contexts that were generally not conducive to learning and which did not prepare them for learning in higher education contexts. Nevertheless, the participants consciously positioned themselves as agents, working hard, finding opportunities to extend their learning and taking highly strategic adult decisions about their learning.

In Chapter 2, le Roux provides a nuanced analysis of three first-generation students who succeeded in majoring in mathematics against considerable odds. Using tools from critical discourse analysis and critical mathematics, she describes how they negotiated the transition from school mathematics to abstract university mathematics. Whereas the mismatch between school and university mathematics is considerable, an analysis of the students' talk over the course of five years reveals the extent to which race, social class position and language are given meaning and the extent to which a successful transition is shaped by an individual's unique, complex action to resist, reconfigure, accommodate, recontextualize and balance the subject positions on offer in these practices.

In Chapter 3, Sacks and Kapp examine the case of a coloured, working-class woman who withdrew from the university after successfully completing two years of her humanities degree. The writers draw on the work of gender education theorists and use narrative analysis of three interviews to describe the student's considerable agency and to show how she attempted to create a coherent sense of self by drawing on discourses of autonomous individual subjectivity and female empowerment as well as on her identity as a Muslim woman. In order to be accepted in multiple spaces and to create the semblance of functioning and progress, she created 'situational' identities (Renn 2004: 220). However, the emotion-work of dealing with structural constraints and living up to conflicting expectations eventually took its toll, causing her to withdraw from the university. The chapter focuses attention on the kind of psycho-social support that students from such backgrounds need.

During the course of the data collection, the researchers became aware of the significant role that religion seemed to play in the lives of the participants in the project. In Chapter 4, Bangeni and Pym illustrate that many participants turned to religion as a strategy to cope with stress and potential failure and to mediate areas of dissonance during their undergraduate years. Drawing on Gee's notion of discourse and on other sociological studies on the role of religion, the writers argue that religion provided an enabling framework which facilitated optimism, security and confidence. They argue that while this points to how religious beliefs largely function as a resource, the data also attest to the ways in which students' discomfort with academic discourse and its accompanying world views can be attributed to particular belief systems which sit uncomfortably alongside the ideologies evident in the course curricula of their academic disciplines. Based on these findings they argue that spaces need to be opened up for meta-reflection, where students can attempt to make connections between the curriculum and their world views and religious beliefs.

The focus of Chapter 5 is the participants' changing notions of language and academic literacy. Kapp and Bangeni draw on poststructuralist and postcolonial language, literacy and identity theory to describe and analyse students' shifts in language and literacy attitudes and practices and in constructions of self over the course of their undergraduate years in the Humanities Faculty. The chapter describes the students' ambivalence as they attempted to constitute appropriate subjectivity and become academically successful within the discourses of the academy, while retaining connections to home discourses. The participants used their linguistic resources and social science discourses to process, rationalize and neutralize their ambivalence. The chapter describes how they started off trying to maintain a notion of a single unified identity, but over time became adept at and self-conscious and less conflicted about shifting subject positions across contexts.

While preceding chapters offer insights into students' negotiations of learning and identity within their undergraduate disciplines and social environments, in Chapter 6, Bangeni tracks the progress of six students from undergraduate spaces of engagement into the postgraduate domain. She describes the degree choices that were available to them upon entry into the institution and the outcome of these choices when they graduated and proceeded to postgraduate studies in the Law and Commerce Faculties three years later. The chapter focuses on the factors that shaped degree choices: lack of access to their first choice of degree, the influence of the immediate family and wider home community on the choice process in later years, the challenges of accessing the job market, and the extent of the individual's personal investment in their first choice of degree. The longitudinal perspective allows for an understanding of the ways in which past constraints and affordances come to impact on students' disciplinary and emerging professional identities, as well as on decisions regarding the world of work.

In Chapter 7, Craig uses the lens of Sen's capability approach to evaluate a support programme in the Faculty of Engineering. The capabilities identified in the programme are compared to the capabilities articulated by fifteen engineering students over a five-year period. In the chapter, Craig examines the agreements and silences as well as the shifts in participants' perspectives on their learning and identities once they left the programme. The data highlight how the support provided in the first year was experienced by participants as enabling, and facilitated success in the form of relatively good pass rates. Nevertheless, there was a significant dropout rate. In their senior years, participants reflected on the ways in which some of the support in first year replicated school practices, consequently hindering their ability to become independent learners and contributing towards a sense of isolation within their disciplines. The writer engages with this dilemma, reflects on the nature of the academic and psycho-social support provided and discusses alternative ways to scaffold learning and develop the notion of a learning community.

Chapter 8 provides a longitudinal analysis of the experiences of five participants from multiple disciplines: Engineering, Science and Commerce. Pym and Sacks use Bourdieu's notions of *habitus*, *field* and *capital* to describe the positions assumed by the students when they entered higher education. The writers trace the changes in the students' attitudes towards their academic and career trajectories as they repositioned themselves in relation to their disciplines, peers and the institution over time. The students' sense of belonging and connectedness, their ability to access support and to deal with home circumstances are all raised as crucial issues that affected their well-being and academic progress. The writers discuss how a focus on student experiences might offer rich opportunities to rethink and reformulate academic practices and culture.

In conclusion, Bangeni and Kapp describe the key themes that have emerged from the longitudinal research and explore implications for policy and practice in terms of access, persistence and retention in South Africa and globally.

Notes

1   It is impossible to contextualize fully the imbrications of South African language and educational backgrounds without using the apartheid-era racial classification ('African', 'coloured', 'Indian' and 'white'). In this book we use the category 'black' inclusively to refer to 'African', 'coloured' and 'Indian' students.

2   In South Africa, the term 'township' is used to refer to underdeveloped urban living areas that are located on the periphery of towns and cities and were reserved for black Africans, coloureds and Indians under apartheid legislation.

References

Ashwin, P. (2012), *Analysing Teaching-Learning Interactions in Higher Education: Accounting for Structure and Agency*, London and New York: Continuum.

Ashwin, P. and Trigwell, K. (2012), 'Evoked Prior Experiences in First-Year University Student Learning', *Higher Education Research & Development*, 31(4): 449–63.

Bhabha, H. (1994), *The Location of Culture*, London: Routledge.

Boughey, C. (2009), *A Meta-Analysis of Teaching and Learning at the Five Research-Intensive South African Universities not Affected by Mergers*, Pretoria: Council on Higher Education, https://www.ru.ac.za/media/rhodesuniversity/content/politics/documents/, accessed 14 April 2016.

Boughey, C. (2010), 'Academic Development for Improved Efficiency in the Higher Education and Training System in South Africa', Report for the Development Bank of South Africa, Midrand, South Africa: Development Bank of South Africa.

Bourdieu, P. (1991), *Language and Symbolic Power*, Cambridge, MA: Harvard University Press.

Bray R., Gooskens, I., Moses S., Kahn L., and Seekings, J. (2010), *Growing Up in the New South Africa: Childhood and Adolescence in Post-Apartheid Cape Town*, Cape Town: Human Sciences Research Council Press.

Burke, P. J. (2012), *The Right to Higher Education: Beyond Widening Participation*, Abingdon: Routledge.

Case, J. (2013), *Researching Student Learning in Higher Education: A Social Realist Approach*, London and New York: Routledge.

Chowdry, H., Crawford, C. and Dearden, L. (2013), 'Widening Participation in Higher Education: Analysis Using Linked Administrative Data', *Journal of the Royal Statistical Society*, 176(2): 431–57.

Christie, P. (2008), *Changing Schools in South Africa: Opening the Doors of Learning*, Johannesburg: Heinemann.

Council on Higher Education, (2013), *A Proposal for Undergraduate Curriculum Reform in South Africa: The Case for a Flexible Curriculum Structure*, http://www.che.ac.za/sites/default/files/publications/, accessed 28 November 2013.

Fataar, A. (2010), 'Youth Self-Formation and the "Capacity to Aspire": The Itinerant "Schooled Career" of Fuzile Ali across Post-Apartheid Space', *Perspectives in Education*, 28: 34–45.

Gee, J. (1990), *Social Linguistics and Literacies: Ideology in Discourses*, London: Falmer Press.

Haggis, T. (2004), 'Meaning, Identity and "Motivation": Expanding what Matters in Understanding Learning in Higher Education', *Studies in Higher Education*, 29(3): 335–52.

Haggis, T. (2011), 'Where now? Questions about Assessment from a Five-Year Longitudinal Study into Learning in Higher Education', *Contemporary Social Science*, 6(2): 191–205.

Hall, M. (2012), *Inequality and Higher Education: Marketplace or Social Justice? Stimulus Paper*. London: Leadership Foundation for Higher Education. http://usir.salford. ac.uk/19491/1/Inequality_and_Higher_Education, accessed 3 January 2017.

Herrington, A. and Curtis, M. (2000), *Persons in Process: Four Stories of Writing and Personal Development in College*, Urbana, IL: National Council of Teachers of English.

Janse van Rensburg, V. (2011), 'Doing, Being and Becoming a First-Year Occupational Therapy Student', *South African Journal of Occupational Therapy*, 41:8–12.

Klemenčič, M. (2015), 'What is Student Agency? An Ontological Exploration in the Context of Research on Student Engagement', in M. Klemenčič, S. Bergan and R. Primožič (eds), *Student Engagement in Europe: Society, Higher Education and Student Governance*, 11–29, Council of Europe Higher Education Series No. 20, Strasbourg: Council of Europe Publishing.

Klemenčič, M. and Fried, F. (2007), 'Demographic Challenges and the Future of Higher Education', *International Higher Education*, 47: 12–14.

Lea, M. and Street, B. (1998), 'Student Writing in Higher Education: An Academic Literacies Approach', *Studies in Higher Education*, 23(2): 157–72.

Leathwood, C., and O'Connell, P. (2003), '"It's a Struggle": The Construction of the "New Student" in Higher Education', *Journal of Education Policy*, 18(6): 597–615.

Leibowitz, B., van der Merwe, A. and van Schalkwyk, S. eds, (2012), *Focus on First-Year Success*, Stellenbosch: Sun Press.

Lillis, T. and Scott, M. (2007), 'Defining Academic Literacies Research: Issues of Epistemology, Ideology and Strategy', *Journal of Applied Linguistics*, 4(1): 5–32.

Mann, S. J. (2008), *Study, Power and the University*, Maidenhead: Society for Research into Higher Education and Open University Press

Norton, B. (2000), *Identity and Language Learning: Gender, Ethnicity and Educational Change*, London: Longman.

Norton, B. and McKinney, C. (2010), 'Identity in Language and Literacy Education', in B. Spolsky and F. Hult (eds), *The Handbook of Educational Linguistics*, 192–205, West-Sussex: Wiley-Blackwell.

Pym, J. and Kapp, R. (2013), 'Harnessing Agency: Towards a Learning Model for Undergraduate Students', *Studies in Higher Education*, 38(2): 272–84.

Pym, J. and Paxton, M. eds (2013), *Surfacing Possibilities: What it Means to Work with First-Generation Higher Education Students*, Illinois: Common Ground.

Reay, D., Crozier, G. and Clayton, J. (2010), '"Fitting In" or "Standing Out": Working-Class Students in UK Higher Education', *British Educational Research Journal*, 32(1): 1–19.

Renn, K. (2004), *Mixed Race Students in College: The Ecology of Race, Identity and Community on Campus*, Albany: State University of New York.

Sfard A. and Prusak A. (2005), 'Telling Identities: In Search of an Analytic Tool for Investigating Learning as a Culturally Shaped Activity', *Educational Researcher*, 34: 14–22.

Soudien, C. (2007), *Youth Identity in Contemporary South Africa: Race, Culture and Schooling*, Cape Town: New Africa Education.

Soudien, C. (2013), 'Bearding the Capability Deprivation Machine: The Pedagogical Deal for Post-Apartheid Young South Africa', *Critical Studies in Teaching and Learning*, 1(1) 53–77.

Sternglass, M. (1997), *Time to Know Them: A Longitudinal Study of Writing and Learning at the College Level*, Mahwah, New Jersey: Lawrence Erlbaum Associates.

Swartz, S. (2009), *Ikasi: The Moral Ecology of South African Township Youth*, Johannesburg: Wits University Press.

Thesen, L. and van Pletzen, E. eds (2006), *Academic Literacy and the Languages of Change*, London and New York: Continuum.

Thomas, L. (2012), 'Building Student Engagement in Higher Education at a Time of Change', Final Report from the *What Works? Student Retention and Success Programme*, http://www.heacademy.ac.uk/retention-and-success, accessed 9 January 2013.

Thomas, L. and Quinn, J. (2007), *First-Generation Entry into Higher Education*, Berkshire: Society for Research into Higher Education and Open University Press.

Thomson, R. (2009), *Unfolding Lives: Youth, Gender and Change*, Bristol: Policy Press.

Thomson, R. and Holland, J. (2003), 'Hindsight, Foresight and Insight: The Challenges of Longitudinal Qualitative Research', *International Journal of Social Research Methodology*, 6(3): 233–44.

Thomson, R. and McLeod, J. (2015), 'New Frontiers in Qualitative Research: An Agenda for Research', *International Journal of Social Research Methodology*, 18(3): 243–50.

Times Higher Education World University Rankings, https://www.timeshighereducation.com/world-university-rankings/best-universities-in-africa-2016, accessed 9 June 2016.

Tinto, V. (2006–7), 'Research and Practice of Student Retention: What Next?', *Journal of College Students Retention*, 8(1): 1–19.

Walker, M. (2010), 'Critical Capability Pedagogies and University Education', *Educational Philosophy and Theory*, 42(8): 898–917.

Wilson-Strydom, M. (2015), *University Access and Success: Capabilities, Diversity and Social Justice*, London and New York: Routledge.

1

Students' Negotiation of Learning and Identity in Working-class Schooling

Rochelle Kapp, Elmi Badenhorst, Bongi Bangeni,
Tracy S. Craig, Viki Janse van Rensburg, Kate le Roux,
Robert Prince, June Pym and Ermien van Pletzen

Introduction

In this chapter, we draw on the perspectives of black, first-generation university students to provide an overview of their learning experiences in working-class township schools and of the ways in which they made use of resources and positioned themselves. These students were educated in post-apartheid South Africa and were part of the first cohort of Grade 12 learners who wrote the new National Senior Certificate (NSC) examinations in 2008, based on the highly contested principles of outcomes-based education.

The participants' home environments were characterized by domestic fluidity, overcrowding and high levels of poverty. Their parents had generally not completed their schooling and 63 per cent were raised in single-income, single-parent contexts by women, usually their mothers and/ or their grandmothers. Many participants moved between a parent and a relative's home as family circumstances changed, with consequent changes of neighbourhood and/or school. The students' perceptions and experiences provide an important context for the rest of this book which focuses on how students negotiate learning and identity in the university context. As we will show, the increased vulnerability produced by this context is significant in terms of participants' constructions of their learning identities and future possibilities.

Theoretical considerations

In this chapter we use the concept of *discourse* to describe the inextricable connection between norms, values, ways of using language and interacting that characterize and dominate particular social contexts and require individuals to take up particular subject positions within their ideological framework (Gee 1990).

We also draw on the notion of *investment* used by Norton (1997) and Thomson (2009: 160) in order to understand when, where and why individuals engage (or disengage) with 'socially and discursively available resources'. They argue that individuals invest in and defend certain subject positions rather than others at particular times, in relation to structures of power and opportunity. This process of identity construction entails negotiating who they are and who they want to be in relation to past and present interaction and, importantly, in relation to 'the desire for recognition, the desire for affiliation, and the desire for security and safety' (Norton 1997: 410). In this reasoning, educational success and failure are influenced by 'structures of opportunity' as well as individual agency, effort and the ability to reflect at a meta-level (Christie 2008: 8; see also Mann 2008; Luckett and Luckett 2009).

We use this theoretical lens to describe the discursive practices that characterized the participants' school experiences, as well as the ways in which they invested in and/or resisted expected subject positions by acting decisively and making purposeful use of resources. The data show that in their school contexts, the participants were highly agentic, taking adult decisions and finding learning resources and learning spaces in the absence of adequate schooling.

Methodology

The data for this chapter were collected in the first semester of the participants' first year of university in 2009. We analysed background questionnaires and semi-structured interviews with sixty-two students who were registered for extended degree programmes (see the Introduction). The programmes were designed to provide students with the foundations necessary to succeed in their course of study. The students were from the Faculties of Commerce, Engineering and the Built Environment, Health Sciences, Humanities and Science. They were asked to reflect on their home and school backgrounds after they had had some experience of the academic environment, in order to facilitate comparisons between contexts. Students were asked to describe their home, neighbourhood and school backgrounds; how they used resources and how they positioned themselves within these contexts.

We focused on a content analysis of general patterns and we used analytical induction to uncover categories and themes within the set of interview data. We assigned categories by clustering similar ideas and then assigning themes to the data (Boyatzis 1998; Ryan and Bernard 2003). The background questionnaires were used to compare and cross-check information in the interviews.

Gee (1990) argues that the transition from primary to secondary discourses facilitates meta-awareness, and we would add meta-reflection. In this chapter, we focus on the meanings that the participants attributed to their school experiences. In the words of Holland et al. (1998: 3): 'People tell others who they are, but even more importantly, they tell themselves.' We are interested in students' descriptions and explanations of their behaviour, beliefs and values; how they wished to be viewed and how they positioned themselves in relation to others in their school environment in the light of their transition to university. What is significant is the 'activity of identifying [within participants' narratives] rather than its end product' (Sfard and Prusak 2005: 17).

'Out of order': Students' perceptions of the school environment

Soudien (2007), Spaull (2013) and Southall (2016) all argue that South Africa effectively has two school systems, which bear the legacy of apartheid and in which the poor, mainly black population, receives a far inferior quality of education and performs worse academically. Spaull (2013: 6) illustrates: 'The smaller, better performing system accommodates the wealthiest 20-25 per cent of pupils who achieve much higher scores than the larger system which caters to the poorest 75-80 per cent of pupils.' His report shows that of every hundred pupils that start Grade 1, forty will pass the NSC examination and twelve will qualify for university. The participants' descriptions of their school learning experiences bear testimony to this context. They described their schools as poorly resourced in terms of basic infrastructure and learning resources such as textbooks, furniture, libraries and computers. Schools were frequently burgled and vandalized. Vuyokazi's[1] description of his school was typical:

> We would go [to computer class] once a month because there were few computers. … We had to share the textbook and the classes were so over-crowded that sometimes if you come in late in class, you don't have a desk and a chair to sit on … the windows were broken … some classes did not have doors and sometimes there were no boards. … In like 2007 … there was a break-in, so … when we came in the following day there were no computers in our school.

It seems that despite a great deal of attention being paid to the resourcing of schools since 1994, many of the efforts have been cosmetic and/or unsustainable. These infrastructural problems are often related to poor school management. Soudien (2007: 191) points out that there has also been little change in the substance of schooling, leaving intact a legacy of underprepared and often disaffected teachers. He argues, 'A child entering this kind of environment is entering a world of fragility where the social rhythms and regimens of a learning environment operate weakly and often capriciously.' This sense of instability and dysfunction was captured in the participants' characterization of their learning environment as 'out of order' and 'negative'. Participants referred to gang-related violence just outside or within the school, disruptive behaviour by fellow learners, limited career guidance and few opportunities to engage in sport and the arts. Many participants spoke of teacher absenteeism and frequent changes in the teaching staff and many had no teachers for long periods of time. Participants worked out at an early stage that they could not rely on teachers:

> I never depended on the teacher or what the teacher does because sometimes our teachers never came to classes so at the end of the day they are not the ones going to write the exams … (Mdudusi), and
>   the teachers would stay absent and we wouldn't know about them being absent and then we had to go to the office to find out, so then students would be waiting there and making noise (Josephine).

'Learning to pass': Teaching and learning in the classroom

The participants foregrounded difficulties with English and identified it as a major stumbling block in their transition from school to university. This is unsurprising. The language rights of the individual are enshrined in the Bill of Rights of South Africa's 1996 Constitution and the Department of

Basic Education's (1997) Language in Education Policy advocates teaching through the medium of the child's home language while they learn additional languages as subjects, or else teaching through the medium of two languages. However, this policy has largely been ignored and the reality is that the overwhelming majority of African language speakers study their subjects through the medium of English in the same way that English home language learners do, but they study the subject of English at a very basic, functional level as an additional language (for a more detailed explanation, see Probyn et al. 2002; Kapp and Arend 2011). Classroom-based research has shown that despite the emphasis on critical literacy in post-apartheid curricula, classroom practices have not changed from the mainly oral, rote learning, teacher-led practices described in the past, and while teachers are conscious of the requirements of the new curricula, they have been poorly trained, have weak subject knowledge and have had huge difficulties interpreting and mediating the shifting, often underspecified meta-languages of the new curricula (see Probyn et al. 2002; Chisholm 2005; Christie 2008; Hendricks 2008; Shalem and Hoadley 2009).

As a consequence of the challenges presented by English as medium of instruction, the under-resourced nature of the environment, as well as teachers' limitations in subject content, teachers engaged in elaborate compensatory practices. Students reported that their content subject lessons took place mainly in their home languages and teachers used code-mixing and code-switching to convey their subject matter orally (see Adler and Reed 2002; Probyn et al. 2002). Teachers circumscribed the information that their students needed in order to produce the requisite English to pass the externally set examinations in a process that is commonly called 'scope' in township schools (Kapp 2004). 'Scope' is achieved through summaries, worksheets and revision of past examination papers. In content subjects, like history and biology, this literacy practice precluded any need to engage with the readings themselves, or to engage in problem-solving and cognitively demanding writing.

With the benefit of hindsight, the participants described the limitations of their test-driven, formulaic school literacy practices which focused almost entirely on content. They had learnt in a manner which was superficial and which focused on getting the gist rather than on understanding, analysing and evaluating. In Fuad's words, 'You didn't really have to understand what you are reading because they didn't expect that of you actually.' Describing science report writing, Sakhile said, 'High school's reports were just a format in which you had to do something, you did it in that format and you hand it in.'

The participants described how the essays they wrote in English classes were mainly narrative and not factual or argumentative and how they copied their content subject essays from textbooks. Science students described how school mathematics appeared to be focused on formula-driven selection and substitution which involved a limited understanding. For example, Tebogo said, 'In school you just put in the formula, you just choose the right formula and put in the values, you got the answer ... so I was used to that school mentality, that if I study, if I memorize most of the things then I'll pass.'

The participants' descriptions of learning at school were often framed in terms of surface-level 'passing'. This characterization reflects the way in which results in the final Grade 12 examination have been constructed as *the* measure of the progress of the school system. It also reflects the fact that it is possible to pass with a very basic level of rote-learnt content knowledge, and that this minimal standard has been accepted as the norm in many black, working-class township schools (Kapp et al. 2014). The students in the study made a distinction between learning to 'understand' at university and 'learning to pass' (Zinhle) at high school, where in Tebogo's words, 'I was used to that school mentality, that if I study, if I memorize most of the things then I'll pass.'

Despite this critique, the participants' descriptions of their teachers reflected their sense of indebtedness to the custodial and pastoral roles many teachers had played in their lives in the absence of sufficient home resources. They described how teachers 'were trying' and often positioned teachers as victims of their circumstances, who had worked in solidarity with their students to enable them to overcome the barriers to learning in the environment: 'Teachers, *ja* [Afrikaans for 'yes'], teachers, *ja*, they were trying, some of them they were trying but ... there was nothing that they can do because there were no facilities.' (Phila) and 'They were good, they were good, they were trying to support, giving us work, allowing us to think critically, *ja*, by giving us researches and programmes.' (Zinhle) At the same time as Zinhle hailed her teachers for 'trying' to provide research-based projects, she spoke of the structural impossibility of implementing a meaningful inquiry-based approach to teaching and learning in her print- and digitally impoverished rural environment where class sizes averaged fifty-five learners. Like many students, Zinhle's descriptions of her teachers were complex and contradictory. In the same interview, she described how her teachers had attempted to limit her future by actively discouraging her from applying to university: 'They just told me that you are not going to make it.' Zinhle resisted this positioning both because of her personal circumstances: 'I'm the only one who has to change the situation of my family because it's poor,' and because she wanted to change the lives of physically disabled people in her poverty-stricken community: 'They don't have money to buy like wheelchairs, they don't have money to buy tools to adapt to the environments, so that's why I decided to do occupational therapy, so that at least people who are poor from my background ... can benefit from this type of provision.'

Zinhle graduated with a degree in Occupational Therapy. In her final year of study, she re-read her first interview and was able to analyse the subject position assumed by her teachers in terms of social class: 'They will expect good for people who are coming from quite nice backgrounds, good families who have like quite high status and they wouldn't really recognize us, just students coming from those poor families.' Throughout her studies, Zinhle reflected on and resisted the limiting and narrow subject position of victim and 'poor rural girl' assigned to her by others, and sought instead to construct herself as an agent of change (for more detail see Janse van Rensburg and Kapp 2014). Like most other participants, her descriptions of the differences between how she was taught at school and at university suggested significant problems that related to teaching and learning, as well as to the limiting ways in which learners' learning identities and futures were constructed by their teachers.

'Moving with the movers': Students' positioning in school

The participants succeeded in attaining the requisite level to pass Grade 12, despite their teaching and learning contexts. In order to do so, they invested in subject positions as hard workers in environments where many students drop out of school because of pregnancy, a lack of funds or because of involvement in crime (Kapp et al. 2014). For example, Luvuyo painted a vivid picture of the apathy, insecurity, ill-discipline and stasis that characterized his school experiences and in the process, distanced himself from the subject positions taken up by those around him:

> They [fellow students] want to finish Grade 12, it doesn't matter if they fail or pass as long as they are done with high school. *Ja*, so the majority is ... just going to school for the sake of going to school, so it is actually negative in some way because you will find out they are not well disciplined. ... They doubt their abilities in terms of passing, for example, when I used to ask ... fellow learners

'how do you think you are going to pass this year?', in March, and then they will say 'No, I don't know, we'll see.' With that kind of an attitude it's more or less certain that you won't pass because you are not sure about yourself.

The meta-level discourse about self-efficiency and personal growth in this quotation is evident in many students' narratives. The 'can-do' attitude it reflects has been described in a number of studies on youth identity (see Herrington and Curtis 2000; Thomson 2009; Marshall and Case 2010). It is significant that throughout his interview, Luvuyo made a clear distinction between the general mindset ('they') and his own sense of the value of self-belief and the need to be an agent of one's success. In the South African context, Bray et al. (2010: 252) write: 'In contexts where education is highly venerated, there is considerable symbolic, social and emotional value in adolescents maintaining a discourse that divides the world between those who are "on the right track" and those who are not.' They argue that young people can often achieve a sense of fulfilment and a bolstering of self-esteem by investing in such discourses which provide certainty and predictability in unstable circumstances. The participants were very clear about their investment in English and education as a tool for upward mobility and an escape from poverty. There are many examples where, like Luvuyo, the participants appeared to distance themselves from their peers, often covertly: 'When they are disruptive, *ja*, I may just laugh there in the background but I know that what I'm being taught is in my brain, I'm going to learn it' (Philile).

Some students spoke of sitting near the front of the classroom, where, in the words of Josephine, other students would not be 'in your face' and where it would be quieter and easier to connect to teachers who would otherwise not notice them. In Phiwe's words:

> In my school it was like if you determined, if you have courage, teachers were like helping you to like pass, pass and you would pass with flying colours. ... If you were like discouraged and de-motivated and not feeling like studying and you were not understanding the work and like you were failing your subjects you would go down the drain, it was like they moving with the movers. If you left behind, then you left behind, no one is going to care for you, no one is going to come and ask.

Phiwe's notion of teachers 'moving with the movers' is a common refrain in the townships alongside the refrain 'Teachers go with the students who are going.' Kapp (2004: 257) describes how the township teachers in her study coped with large, undisciplined classes by connecting to the students (usually in the front of the classroom) who were fluent in English and willing to learn. In such contexts, where academic success is not normative, the accepted notion seems to be that teachers will work with students who are self-driven and/or talented and have the potential for mobility beyond the confines of the township. This approach meant that many participants achieved affirmation from their teachers which enabled them to feel validated in the desire to learn and succeed. In this respect, learning theorists have long argued that processes of affirmation and recognition strengthen confidence and foster the development of learning identities (Thomson 2009; Ashwin and Trigwell 2012).

'Mentally I'm not there': Students' positioning outside of school

Many of the participants ascribed their success at school to the fact that they deliberately sought out peers who, like them, were serious, hard-working students, and formed study groups where their peers taught for long hours. A number of scholars have discussed the significance of peer relationships in identity formation, particularly in contexts where young people are placed in situations of extreme risk and vulnerability and where conventional support structures have broken down (Ramphele 2002; Bray et al. 2010).

The participants' strong sense of acting purposefully and directing their own future was often fostered by a source outside of schooling (Kapp et al. 2014). In the wake of difficulty, many students had turned to religion as an enabling framework that allowed them to 'stay positive' in the face of challenging home and school circumstances. Religion seemed to act as a 'sponsor' for their actions by offering a social identity which facilitated security, connection and agency, as well as a discourse of personal growth (Herrington and Curtis 2000: 369. See also Swartz 2009; Bray et al. 2010; Fataar 2010 and Chapter 5 in this book). In their study, Bray et al. (2010: 238) note, 'Adolescents who participated in church groups were significantly less likely to drop out of school.'

Students also sought out community organizations with specialized programmes, extra classes at other schools and fellow students from better resourced, middle-class schools. These sources provided them with alternative, generative ways of 'saying-doing-being-valuing-believing' (Gee 1990: 142) that countered the negative discourses that often characterized their schooling. Together with the fact that they had achieved at school, these discourses seemed to be the source of their sense of constructing future roles, careers and identities for themselves outside of the township. Luvuyo's case illustrates this point very well. Despite being a leader figure (president of the Student Representative Council) at his school, Luvuyo described how he had to distance himself (both mentally and physically) from school and from township culture in order to succeed. His particular coping mechanisms were to seek 'positive' stimulation and to find resources outside of the township through a range of workshops organized by community organizations:

> I didn't consider myself as a person who was living in this environment, although physically I was living there but my mind was not in that level of that environment because I related to outside things, to outside environments, so that's why I coped, because I didn't associate myself with the certain people that had this kind of behaviour and I always associated myself with people who would think positive. … I will go to school, then maybe go to a workshop or go to a meeting in some place, so my attitude was always, even though I lived there physically but mentally I'm not there, I don't live in that environment.

Luvuyo attributed his proficiency in English and his decision to apply to university to his engagement with community organizations. His sentiments about finding solace outside of the school and township were echoed by many comments that emphasized mobility through moving away as a route to success. Similarly, Kapp (2012) describes how participants in her study perceive English as a route to escape the township, and in the context of the UK, Reay (2001) describes how success in working-class education is similarly framed in terms of leaving, erasure and an escape from poverty. In subsequent chapters, we analyse how the tension between the desire to escape from home and the desire and pressure to retain home identities plays out in students' learning journeys.

Conclusion

In this chapter we have attempted to describe how a group of working-class, first-generation students experienced learning in their working-class school contexts. For most students, the classroom was not a space conducive to learning and joint construction of knowledge. Nevertheless, they invested in subject positions as hard workers and purposefully placed themselves in learning positions, distancing themselves from distraction. They were resilient and took strategic adult decisions. They generally took the decision to apply to university and chose the university without parental or school guidance. They were critical of dominant discourses and when their environments did not provide appropriate support and resources, they sought sponsoring discourses (Herrington and Curtis 2000: 369) which would provide enabling frameworks. These are all qualities and dispositions which are valued within the higher education context. As later chapters will show, this sense of agency is not necessarily harnessed within the university context. This is significant because as Reay, Crozier and Clayton (2009) and Marshall and Case (2010) all argue, the coping strategies developed in what is characterized as a disadvantaged social background could form useful resources for succeeding in higher education.

However, as many studies have shown, the superficial learning practices (e.g. rote learning or reading superficially) that dominate within such contexts are inappropriate for the higher education context (see for example Kapp 2004; Slonimsky and Shalem 2004; Van Schalkwyk 2007; Wilson-Strydom 2015). As the later chapters show, the participants' home and school discourses and identities are only minimally taken into account in higher education, and yet they form a bedrock for their academic practices and ways of being in the university setting. Many participants retained or reverted to ways of learning, and the use of time and resources which worked in their school environments, but which were not necessarily effective or appropriate within their disciplinary contexts. Understanding students' explanations of experiences and self provides a starting point for thinking through situated academic practices and for providing alternative learning models in order to facilitate the academic, linguistic and social transitions from school to university in appropriate ways.

In the chapters that follow, we describe and analyse how the subject positions and ways of learning that participants adopted in school impacted on their pathways over time.

Note

1   All participant names in this book are pseudonyms.

References

Adler, J. and Reed, Y. eds (2002), *Challenges of Teacher Development: An Investigation of Take-up in South Africa*, Pretoria: Van Schaik.

Ashwin, P. and Trigwell, K. (2012), 'Evoked Prior Experiences in First-Year University Student Learning', *Higher Education Research and Development*, 31(4): 449–63.

Boyatzis, R. (1998), *Transforming qualitative information*, Thousand Oaks, CA: Sage.

Bray, R., Gooskens, I., Moses, S., Kahn, L. and Seekings, J. (2010), *Growing Up in the New South Africa: Childhood and Adolescence in Post-Apartheid Cape Town*, Cape Town: Human Sciences Research Council Press.

Chisholm, L. (2005), 'The State of South Africa's Schools', in Daniel, J., Southall, R. and Lutchman, J. (eds), *State of the Nation: South Africa 2004-2005*, 201–26, Cape Town: Human Sciences Research Council Press.

Christie, P. (2008), *Changing Schools in South Africa: Opening the Doors of Learning*, Johannesburg: Heinemann.

Department of Basic Education, (1997), 'Language in Education Policy', http://www. education.gov.za/Portals/0/Documents/Policies/GET/LanguageEducationPolicy1997. pdf?ver=2007-08-22-083918-000, accessed 17 May 2016.

Fataar, A. (2010), 'Youth Self-Formation and the "Capacity to Aspire": The Itinerant "Schooled Career" of Fuzile Ali across Post-Apartheid Space', *Perspectives in Education*, 28: 34–45.

Gee, J. (1990), *Social Linguistics and Literacies: Ideology in Discourses*, London: Falmer Press.

Hendricks, M. (2008), '"Capitalising on the Dullness of Data": A Linguistic Analysis of a Grade 7 Learner's Writing', *South African Linguistics and Applied Language Studies*, 26: 27–42.

Herrington, A. and Curtis, M. (2000), *Persons in Process: Four Stories of Writing and Personal Development in College*, Urbana, IL: National Council of Teachers of English.

Holland, D., Lachicotte, W., Skinner, D. and Cain, C. (1998), *Identity and Agency in Cultural Worlds*, Cambridge, MA: Harvard University Press.

Janse van Rensburg, V. and Kapp, R. (2014), '"So I have to be Positive, no Matter how Difficult it Is": A Longitudinal Case Study of a First-Generation Occupational Therapy Student', *Journal of Occupational Therapy*, 44(3): 29–33.

Kapp, R. (2004), '"Reading on the Line": An Analysis of Literacy Practices in ESL Classes in a South African Township School', *Language and Education*, 8: 246–63.

Kapp, R. (2012) 'Students' Negotiations of English and Literacy in a Time of Social Change', *JAC*, 32(3–4): 591–614.

Kapp, R. and Arend, M. (2011), '"There's a Hippo on my Stoep": Constructions of Language Teaching and English Second Language Learning in the New National Senior Certificate', *Per Linguam*, 27(1): 1–10.

Kapp, R., Badenhorst, E., Bangeni, B., Craig, T. S., Janse van Rensburg, V., le Roux, K., Prince, R., Pym, J. and van Pletzen, E. (2014), 'Successful Students' Negotiation of Township Schooling in Contemporary South Africa', *Perspectives in Education* 32(3): 50–61.

Luckett, K. and Luckett, T. (2009), 'The Development of Agency in First-Generation Learners in Higher Education: A Social Realist Analysis', *Teaching in Higher Education*, 14: 469–81.

Mann, S. (2008), *Study, Power and the University*, Maidenhead: Society for Research into Higher Education and Open University Press.

Marshall, D. and Case, J. (2010), 'Rethinking "Disadvantage" in Higher Education: A Paradigmatic Study Using Narrative Analysis', *Studies in Higher Education*, 35: 491–504.

Norton, B. (1997), 'Language, Identity and the Ownership of English', *Tesol Quarterly*, 31(3): 409–30.

Probyn, M., Murray, S., Botha, L., Botya, P., Brooks, M. and Westphal, V. (2002), 'Minding the Gaps - an Investigation into Language Policy and Practice in Four Eastern Cape Districts', *Perspectives in Education*, 20(1): 29–46.

Ramphele, M. (2002), *Steering by the Stars: Being Young in South Africa*, Cape Town: Tafelberg.

Reay, D. (2001), 'Finding or Losing Yourself?: Working-Class Relationships to Education', *Journal of Education Policy*, 16(4): 333–46.

Reay, D., Crozier, G. and Clayton, J. (2009), 'Strangers in Paradise? Working-Class Students in Elite Universities', *Sociology*, 43: 1103–12.

Ryan, G. and Bernard, H. (2003), 'Techniques to Identify Themes', *Field Methods*, 15: 85–109.

Sfard, A. and Prusak, A. (2005), 'Telling Identities: In Search of an Analytic Tool for Investigating Learning as a Culturally Shaped Activity', *Educational Researcher*, 34: 14–22.

Shalem, Y. and Hoadley, U. (2009), 'The Dual Economy of Schooling and Teacher Morale in South Africa', *International Studies in Sociology of Education*, 19(2): 119–34.

Slonimsky, L. and Shalem, Y. (2004), 'Pedagogic Responsiveness for Academic Depth', in H. Griesel (ed.), *Curriculum Responsiveness: Case Studies in Higher Education*, Pretoria: South African Universities' Vice Chancellors' Association.

Soudien, C. (2007), 'The "A" Factor: Coming to Terms with the Question of Legacy in South African Education', *International Journal of Educational Development*, 27: 182–93.

Southall, R. (2016), *The New Black Middle Class in South Africa*, Auckland Park: Jacana and Konrad Adenauer Stiftung.

Spaull, N. (2013), 'South Africa's Education Crisis: The Quality of Education in South Africa 1994-2001', Report commissioned by the Centre for Development Enterprise, http://www.section27.org.za/wp-content/uploads/2013/10/Spaull-2013-CDE-report-South-Africas-Education-Crisis, accessed 15 November 2013.

Swartz, S, (2009), *Ikasi: The Moral Ecology of South Africa's Township Youth*, Johannesburg: Wits University Press.

Thomson, R. (2009), *Unfolding Lives: Youth, Gender and Change*, Bristol: The Policy Press.

Van Schalkwyk, S. C. (2007), 'Crossing Discourse Boundaries – Students' Diverse Realities when Negotiating Entry into Knowledge Communities', *South African Journal of Higher Education*, 21: 954–68.

Wilson-Strydom, M. (2015), *University Access and Success: Capabilities, Diversity and Social Justice*, London and New York: Routledge and Taylor and Francis.

2

'Closing the Gap': Three Mathematics Students Talk about their Transitions to and through their Undergraduate Degrees in the Sciences

Kate le Roux

The transition from school mathematics to advanced mathematics at university

'I'm used to maths as you know, you deal with numbers and stuff, but there is this other module, they do some weird stuff, … it's too theoretical, it is all about proofs and stuff, you don't even see digits there.' (Thabo, a mathematics student in his third year of undergraduate study). Thabo and his two university classmates, Luthando and Josephine, are the empirical focus of this chapter. When they applied to study at the University of Cape Town (UCT) in 2009 their school-leaving results and their self-reported personal information were used by the institution to identify them as having the potential to succeed as undergraduate science students but, on account of their home and school backgrounds, as requiring additional support to succeed. The three students were placed in an extended curriculum programme designed to provide the foundations for studying university science (see the Introduction). This student admission and placement strategy recognizes that opportunities to learn science in South Africa are influenced by a complex mix of race, class, language and geographical location (Soudien 2012) and that students carry their schooling with them to university. Indeed, as noted in Chapter 1, of the national cohort of students who started school with Thabo, Josephine and Luthando, only half made it to their final year of schooling and 12 per cent qualified to apply for university (Spaull 2013). Many of those who did not make it to the application process are likely to be Thabo, Josephine and Luthando's schoolmates from black, working-class schools.

The degree paths of Thabo, Josephine and Luthando required that they make the transition from the 'numbers' and informal, intuitive methods valued in school mathematics and first-year-level mathematics courses to second-year-level advanced mathematics courses. The last-mentioned courses, described by Thabo as 'too theoretical' and 'all about proofs', involve working with abstract mathematical objects that are deduced from definitions and axioms in theoretical proofs (Tall 1991, 1996). In this transition there is a change in knowledge criteria (Jablonka, Ashjari and Bergsten 2012) and in what it means to 'do' and to 'understand' mathematics (Hernandez-Martinez and Williams 2013:46). The three students' first-year-level mathematics course – referred to as 'extended' mathematics in this chapter – was run over two years, so they encountered advanced mathematics courses in their third year of study.

Statistically, these students' chance of successfully making the transition to advanced mathematics courses and graduating with a science degree with at least one advanced mathematics course was small. In South Africa 50 per cent of students complete an undergraduate science degree within five years, and the completion rate of white students is 50 per cent higher than that of African students (Thabo and Luthando's classification) and coloured students (Josephine's classification) (Council on Higher Education 2013). The University's Institutional Planning Department statistics (2015) show that of the 694 students who enrolled in the extended degree science programme between 2005 and 2009, 9 per cent (59 students) attempted the advanced second-year mathematics course and only a quarter of these (14 students) passed. Of the 2 per cent of students who attempted a mathematics major, only half (six students) passed. However, all three students in this study would be regarded as 'successful' by the University as they completed – albeit with lower third grade passes – the advanced mathematics courses required either to graduate or, in the case of Luthando, transfer to his original first choice of engineering.

Further complicating the transition to advanced mathematics is the fact that Thabo, Josephine and Luthando were part of the first cohort of South African students to complete their schooling in the post-1994 outcomes-based curriculum. This mathematics curriculum, which has since been revised to include a greater specification of content, was critiqued (see Engelbrecht, Harding and Phiri 2010) for providing poor preparation for the demands of university mathematics to all students, regardless of their home and school backgrounds.

Perspectives for viewing the transition

Statistics on who succeeds in mathematics do not offer explanations for differences in performance (Battey 2013) and have the potential to reify the mathematics performance of particular student groups (Gutiérrez 2013). Qualitative research in mathematics education has drawn on various theoretical perspectives to add context to these numbers with descriptions and explanations. For example, the transition can be viewed in terms of the 'fit' between mathematics practices (see Engelbrecht, Harding and Phiri 2010; Torenbeek, Jansen and Hofman 2010), the student's cognitive shifts from one mathematics practice to another (see Tall 1996), and the student's personal attributes like motivation, confidence and persistence (see Engelbrecht, Harding and Phiri 2010; Gibney et al. 2011). While these perspectives foreground differences between practices, they risk relying on a deficit view of the student either by assuming unproblematic knowledge transfer across practices or by locating the difficulties in the individual student. Other studies look beyond the individual to the home and school backgrounds of the student (see Frempong, Ma and Mensah 2012), but while such studies recognize the structural constraints on student transition, it is possible that constructs like race become reified and used in deterministic ways to explain performance (McGee and Martin 2011).

A growing number of researchers are using theoretical perspectives – mainly from poststructuralism, critical theory and critical race theory – to view student participation in mathematics as an interplay between individual action and wider social structure. These studies, in which interviews are a key source of data, may focus on school mathematics (see Berry 2008; Stinson 2008; Smith 2010) or on the transition from school to university mathematics practices (see Bartholomew et al. 2011; McGee and Martin 2011; Black and Williams 2013; Hernandez-Martinez and Williams 2013). These perspectives and methods have also been used in investigations of student participation in other disciplines at university (see Kapp and Bangeni 2011 on writing in the social sciences; Maunder et al. 2013 on psychology) and in studies that are not disciplinary specific (see Christie 2009; Reay, Crozier and Clayton 2009; Thomson 2009; Reay, Crozier and Clayton 2010). While these perspectives are regarded as productive for studying the experiences of historically marginalized students (Stinson 2008; Christie 2009), their use is not restricted to this group of students.

The study of Thabo, Josephine and Luthando's transition as mathematics students reported on in this chapter is located in this growing body of research. I use tools from the work of Fairclough (2001; 2003; 2006), the critical linguist, and Skovsmose (2005), the critical mathematics education researcher, to analyse student interviews: five each with Luthando and Josephine and four with Thabo. In particular, I ask:

1. How do the students describe the context of their transition to and through university as they talk about the past, present and future in longitudinal interviews? In particular, what subject positions do they identify as made available to them in this context?
2. How do the students describe the ways they take up these subject positions?

The answers to these questions offer a view of how 'systemic constraints become lived as individual dilemmas' (Walshaw 2013: 102). In particular, the interviews bring into view how these constraints and students' accounts thereof change over time during the transition (Thomson 2009). The chapter thus contributes to the small number of studies offering a longitudinal view on transition to higher education (see Black and Williams 2013 in mathematics education; Herrington and Curtis 2000; Leathwood and O'Connell 2003; Seider 2008; Kapp and Bangeni 2011; Birani and Lehmann 2013 in higher education research more generally). Like the works of Black and Williams (2013) and Haggis and Pouget (2002), this chapter focuses on the transition of students who did not gain direct access into their degree programmes of choice and were required to enrol for courses that extended the time to graduation. The data reveal the complexity and diversity of students' learning and identity challenges and highlight the need for the development of flexible degree pathways and appropriate support structures to mediate the transitions of traditionally under-represented students.

The research lens

Fairclough's three-level theory of the social world and language (2001, 2003 and 2006) provides a lens with which to view the relationships between social structure and individual student action, as well as the relationships between different practices. In Fairclough's (2003) terms, the context of this study can be described as a network of social practices. In this chapter I regard extended mathematics, advanced mathematics, the extended programme and school mathematics as practices, since each is a relatively stable, recognizable way of doing things that has material, language and psychological aspects. A practice mediates the meaning of abstract structural concepts like race, social class position, gender and languages like English, mediating for example, what it means to be a black or female advanced mathematics student.

Fairclough (2003) argues that practices are networked in relationships of recontextualization; features of one practice do not simply flow into another, but are actively 'filtered' (Fairclough 2003:139) by the recontextualizing practice. This process is not neutral but is shaped by histories and the power relations that control the boundaries between practices (Fairclough 2006), with some practices holding more value than others in an institution.

What happens in an event such as a mathematics lecture or research interview is constituted by two 'causal powers' (Fairclough 2003:22). Social practices (which mediate structure) shape what is possible for a student to do or say in an event by setting up subject positions. Yet an event is only 'partly' (Fairclough 2003:25) shaped by a practice; what happens may diverge from what is expected because the event cuts across different practices and student agency comes into play. Students 'do things, create things, change things' (Fairclough 2003:160), and give unique, personal meaning to the practices in which they act and the subject positions made available to them. Researchers have described the nature of this agentic action as accommodating, resisting, reconfiguring, absorbing, resignifying, reproducing and reusing (see Soudien 2008; Stinson 2008; Kapp and Bangeni 2011; Gutiérrez 2013), and I use these words where appropriate in this chapter. My use of the concept of agency, however, recognizes the power relations at work at the level of the event and the limits to which students can control the content of what is said and done, the language use, and the available social relations and subject positions in and across practices (Fairclough 2001).

Methodology

In this chapter I draw on van Leeuwen (2008: 3) who views the research interview as an instance of 'recontextualized social practice'. This recognizes, first, that a student's talk about a practice at a particular moment in the interview is filtered by the nature of the study and the power relations between interviewer and student. Second, in a longitudinal study the relationship between past, present and future is one of recontextualization, with the frame of reference for each

interview changing with time. To view how students use their interpretation
of past and future to give meaning to the present in an interview I draw on
Skovsmose's (2005) concepts of *background* and *foreground*. He argues that a
student's meaning in the present is related to his or her *background* – his or
her interpretation of past experiences – and, crucially, is related to the student's
foreground, that is, the student's interpretation of future possibilities.

When students talk in an interview they produce three types of meaning
(Fairclough 2003). First, they give meaning to a particular aspect of the world,
and this process is referred to as *representation*. Second, they enact relations
with other subjects and between texts in various practices, called *action*. Third,
they describe the self and others and are described by others, and this is called
identification. These three meanings are dialectically related. For example,
identification of oneself as a 'successful' mathematics student is relative to the
knowledge of the particular mathematics practice (representation) and, as noted
by Valero (2014), relative to other subjects (action).

The interview texts of Thabo, Josephine and Luthando were selected for this
chapter because they were the only participants in the 2009 longitudinal study
who completed the necessary advanced mathematics courses for their degree
purposes. Each student was interviewed separately by a trained interviewer
in the first half of each academic year. An interview was structured by a set
of questions pertinent to the particular year of study. Since my interest is in
what meaning a student ascribes to subject positions made available to them in
various practices rather than in any 'facts' about these practices, I used discourse
analysis to analyse the content and form of the interview texts. This analysis
involved working sentence by sentence through an interview text to identify the
lexical features (e.g. the naming of objects and participants) and the grammatical
features (e.g. the process verbs, the tense, the speech function and mood). These
textual features are a resource for producing meaning, with each feature serving
a particular function in terms of one or more of Fairclough's three meanings:
representation, *action* and *identification*. For example, process verbs identify a
student as doing material or mental work, and pronouns identify a student as
included in or excluded by a practice. When Thabo says, 'I just make sure when
I sit somewhere and people are talking, I just grasp the accent, the way they say
words and then I put them in my mind,' in this sentence 'sit' is a material process
verb and 'grasp' and 'put' (as in 'put in my mind') are mental process verbs.

I present the analysis of each student's interview transcripts below, one by
one, as a detailed case of transition to and through an undergraduate science
degree. This allows me to do justice to the scale of the interview data for each

student. It also allows me to present a 'thick' description – rather than aiming for 'saturation' – thus bringing into view the student's unique and complex meaning-making as he or she recontextualizes past, present and future in the moves between practices (Thomson 2009:25).

Thabo's transition

An award-winning mathematics student at a school that was lacking

Thabo grew up in a township of a major South African city, living in one of about 100 brick houses 'surrounded by shacks'. His mother, the head of the household, did not work and the family lived on maintenance from his father and money provided by Thabo's two older siblings. In his first interview as a university student Thabo represented his educational background by identifying what he lacked relative to others. The township was dangerous ('You can't go to school alone.'), and he was 'not even rich'. He represented his township high school as black ('I never went to a coloured school or a white school.') and when learning mathematics at school said, 'We don't talk English' but used 'our language' Sepedi. His school had a 'lack of materials' and a 'shortage' of electricity, books and chairs.

Thabo resisted taking up the subject position of a student from a school that was lacking by identifying himself rather as an award-winning student who was 'the best learner of the year'. This position was also set up for him by teachers who identified him as having university science in his foreground and by his peers who 'wanted to be like me, they wanted to know how I do things'. Being a top student involved teaching his peers and also enabled access to dedicated teachers, since 'only those who are clever would get those facilities first and then the rest will get the things after'. However, being 'clever' was also hard work, suggested by the repetition of and emphasis on 'study' in Thabo's description of his routine: 'study whole day, I would study during the class lessons when the teacher teaches other people, I would study. I would study after school, go home, eat, study.' Being 'clever' also meant being different from his peers, whom he identified as 'other people', 'the rest' and 'those who didn't know'. The difference was not just in his knowledge and study habits, but in how he dreamt about and loved the idea of higher education ('tertiaries'): 'Where I come from, it's not a tertiary environment that people would dream of going to tertiary one day, it's just that they only want Grade 12. ... They don't love tertiaries.'

A failing then passing extended programme mathematics student

Thabo was challenged in recontextualizing his subject position from top-school mathematics student to successful student in an extended mathematics programme at university, when he failed his first test. So in his extended mathematics course, Thabo wanted to be like the students who 'passed'. He resisted the subject position of failing mathematics student by approaching the successful students to 'figure out' what they did, by having success in his foreground, by telling himself he was not a failing student, by studying harder, and by repeating 'everything': 'I ... tell myself that next time I'm going to do better and study more and make sure I practise and do everything all over again, all over again.'

Thabo also explained his difficulties by reconfiguring his subject position as a mathematics student to include being a student learning mathematics in English. He emphasized that he was not comfortable with this reconfigured position: 'No, absolutely, no, I'm not.' He reluctantly linked his comprehension difficulties to the race and lecturing ability of his lecturers: 'I think this is my first time my [mathematics] teacher is a white guy, *ja* [Afrikaans for 'yes']. I don't normally do this but I think so. I don't blame him for being white but I just can't get the words.' The material and mental work Thabo did to become more comfortable learning mathematics in English involved sitting near people who were talking English, listening to 'the way they say the words' and then 'put[ting] them in my mind'. However, his discomfort with this reconfigured subject position was evident in all his interviews.

By the end of his first year of study Thabo was winning awards for his performance, something he achieved again in his second year of study when he took both extended and mainstream courses. As he had done at school, he identified himself as a successful mathematics student and the object of interest to his peers who 'want to put themselves close to me'. He represented both school and extended programme mathematics as being about 'numbers', with the calculations in the latter practice being 'more advanced' and requiring problem-solving skills. He linked his ongoing 'love' of mathematics to the fact that he was 'good with numbers'.

A failing advanced mathematics student

Having completed all his extended courses in his first two years of study as required, Thabo enrolled only for senior mainstream courses in his third year of study. He reported that he failed all his mainstream tests in the first term, including his first advanced mathematics test. Thabo distanced himself from the rest of the participants ('they') in advanced mathematics: 'I haven't figured it out yet because I'm used to maths as you know, you know you deal with numbers and stuff, but there is this other module, they do some weird stuff, … it is more, it's too theoretical, it is all about proofs and stuff, you don't even see digits there.' However, he resisted this positioning as a failing advanced mathematics student in an opaque practice, by reconfiguring the practice of advanced mathematics as not the 'numbers' of mathematics that he (and by assumption the interviewer, 'you') was 'used to' but rather as unnamed 'weird' modules involving 'proofs'.

Thabo further resisted this positioning by having the mental process of 'understanding' and the bodily feeling of being 'comfortable' with this practice in his foreground. He believed ('I am sure.') that he would occupy the subject position of successful advanced mathematics student in the new term by doing 'something'. He also supported this belief by recontextualizing his past subject positions as a student who likes mathematics ('I still enjoy maths.') and as a good student with a natural ability for solving problems: 'If your mind is in, if it is based on mathematics … you always find ways to solve problems.'

Thabo also resisted being positioned as a failing student by reconfiguring failure to mean 'close to the pass mark, but not really a pass' and resisting how the practice of assessment defined success in mathematics: 'You can't say you don't know something if you are not passing. … You have those people who can tell you answers if you ask them but they can't pass tests.' Yet Thabo took personal responsibility for his initial difficulties in his third year of study. He acknowledged that he had ignored the advice of his advisor to take fewer subjects, and explained his decision because of his difficulty accommodating the position of failing student in the present and future: 'I don't like dropping courses.'

Thabo passed all his senior mainstream courses in his third year, although with lower marks than he had achieved in his first two years. In his final interview he had graduating in his foreground, but accommodated being a student who 'gets 60 per cent or 65 per cent' by recontextualizing his subject position as a student with a particular background: 'I think it is a huge achievement, like from where I come from 50 per cent would mean a lot.' This accommodation was also enabled by his reconfiguration of what it means to be a mathematics student; a university degree was not just the 'academic side', but also gave him 'skills' like critical thinking, solving 'relevant problems' and communicating.

An extended programme student or not?

Thabo alternately accommodated and resisted being positioned as an extended programme student. Although initially he was 'happy' about this positioning and he configured it as a 'chance' to be at the UCT, his representation of the programme as designed 'to lift you up a bit, to take you into the new level, that mainstream' suggests that he described himself as lacking relative to students in mainstream courses. After a few months he resisted the subject position of extended programme student by recontextualizing his school subject position as a top student; he said the extended programme was 'not for him' as the pace was too slow and he resented not being able to move to the mainstream if he performed well. He did, however, accommodate being positioned as a student needing support in computer science, 'because I didn't do it at school'.

In his second year of study, Thabo's description of himself as someone who 'doesn't know anything', together with his interaction with mainstream students in some courses, led him to see value in the 'unlimited help' offered in the extended programme: 'Okay, in the [extended programme] they do like, I don't know how to put it, what can I say, they feel sorry for you, like they help you, you have unlimited help, … they know, they understand you, they take it that you don't know anything.' His difficulty with knowing 'how to put' this representation of the extended programme suggests his resistance to being positioned as someone the staff feel sorry for. However, a year later he admitted that the extended programme was 'actually a great place for me'. Accepting the positioning seemed to be enabled by his friendships rather than by the academic foundation he had obtained. He identified extended programme students as being given work that was done in lectures which was 'possible to do' and he represented the programme as 'spoon feeding'. In contrast, mainstream work required independent study and research: 'They give you something they know is going to give you hell, they give you something you know you are going to go and do research, go to the internet, Google it, study the whole book, understand and then try to solve it in your own way.'

As a mainstream student in his third and fourth years of study, Thabo celebrated his academic achievements and explained his difficulties by recontextualizing his subject position as someone who 'came here via the extended programme'. It seems that this identification signified his school and home backgrounds rather than the extended programme itself as his disadvantage. He attributed his personal discipline to being 'from the townships'; he identified himself, along with one 'white guy' as the only two students in the 'whole of the university' taking his combination of majors, and he quoted the words of university staff to describe this combination as 'tough' for someone with his background.

A student who is alone at university and resists non-academic subject positions

Thabo identified himself as lacking knowledge, which he relates to his subject position as a black, multilingual student: 'Most of the lecturers are white, so when they set the papers, they understand, they know how to write questions and you come there with your less knowledge of it and then you can't answer it well.' But he resisted being positioned as someone lacking knowledge by mainly acting alone. Because he believed that 'if you don't know anything, you can't ask', he did not approach a lecturer with questions straight after a lecture, but used the textbook and the internet to 'prepare what I'm going to ask'. He did consult tutors, but only after grappling with a problem for a week. In his third year of study he worked through the night to complete his assignments. Although he described himself as stressed, he lacked time to get help and dealt with stress alone. In fact, in his final interview Thabo attributed his progress to his personal effort: 'I have actually been doing everything alone.'

Thabo said he was at university 'to study'. Although at times he tutored school students, socialized with friends, had a girlfriend and was a residence dining-hall monitor, he resisted these roles 'When I'm busy, I'm very busy' studying. In his fourth interview, Thabo produced a picture of people 'performing drama' which he regarded a meaningful object. But his decision to pursue science rather than acting as a career seems to be related to the subject positions set up for him as a black student by his school teachers, family and community and the related material and symbolic power afforded by being a scientist. His school science teacher gave him 'this potential that you didn't see'; his family and the community identified him as 'successful' and 'intellectual'. Thabo said being a scientist was 'a faster way up the ladder' than acting and identified himself as a black person who cares for his family: 'We are black people, we have families we have to take care of and we need to go back home.' However, being a successful university science student involved, temporarily, resisting his position as a black family member by not thinking about home: 'Everything that happens at home, just stays there.'

Josephine's transition

An active top student at an 'average' school

Josephine described growing up with her working mother and her grandparents in a home in a working-class suburb of Cape Town. Her home language was English and she also spoke Afrikaans. As a first-year university student Josephine described the working-class public school she attended as 'average', 'alright' and 'okay'. While her school had material resources like classrooms, there was 'a lack' of or 'not many teachers'. Josephine used a selection of adjectives, sometimes modified by 'always' for emphasis, to represent the environment in some classes:

> I'd say it was rowdy, always busy and noisy, you would always have these disruptive students in class but … it depended whether or not we had teachers because the teachers would stay absent and we wouldn't know about them being absent and then we had to go to the office to find out, so then students would be waiting there and making noise.

While the collective, unnamed teachers 'would stay absent', the school management did not communicate this to students, leaving them to 'wait' passively. But Josephine and her friends ('we') resisted this positioning. They had no choice, but 'had to go and find out' from the school management. Josephine also resisted by joining a group of students who 'would get good marks', were in the same formal and extra classes, and were also friends. Being a top-school student involved working 'very hard', with this action enabling the social position of being 'popular'.

An extended programme student in science

Josephine applied to study medicine at the UCT, but her application was rejected and she was placed in the extended programme in the Faculty of Science. She downplayed the emotion related to being an extended programme student ('I was a bit upset') and, like Thabo, accommodated this new positioning by configuring it as a way of being 'accepted at the University'. She consistently configured the programme itself as differing from the mainstream in terms of duration, that is, four rather than three years. Unlike Thabo, she accommodated her new subject position throughout her first year of study. She participated in support activities in the programme and quoted unnamed university staff who in turn quoted mainstream students:

> Actually I'm glad I'm in here [the extended programme] because I can remember at the beginning of the year they told us that students would say, they would think we are like doing a bridging course or something, they would say 'Oh, you doing your three years in four years', but then they told us that those students that are actually in the mainstream, those are the students that will, that are going to come and crowd our classes.

Josephine consistently identified students as either extended or mainstream programme students. She attributed passing all her courses in her first year of study to being an extended programme student. Her second year of study was 'much more difficult, because I went into mainstream'. The length of time to graduation and the time available for studying featured prominently in her representations of the two programmes.

A student studying difficult advanced mathematics courses

Josephine represented university mathematics as 'difficult' and as 'much more' difficult as she proceeded through her degree. She said that compared to her earlier experiences of doing mathematics, advanced mathematics was 'more abstract', and required 'less calculating', 'more thinking' and 'doing a lot of proofs'. Josephine also represented the pedagogy in her advanced mathematics courses as constraining and identified lecturers impersonally: 'They didn't tell us about any books that were recommended.' Time and frequent changes in lecturers were a constraint in mathematics: Josephine measured the regular change of lecturers in weeks ('a lecturer per week or per two weeks'), and she used pace and load to compare courses. Doing first-year mathematics over two years in the extended programme was a constraint as she had to draw on work done 'two years back'.

Unlike Thabo, Josephine did not describe herself as being particularly passionate about mathematics and advanced mathematics in particular, or as having mathematics in her foreground. At times she used the word 'enjoy' in relation to working with 'numbers' and 'calculating', and she said the proofs in linear algebra were 'interesting'. However, she admitted she would not 'actually have gone down' the route of majoring in mathematics if it were not for her lack of enjoyment of certain other subjects, her performance in these subjects and timetable clashes.

Although Josephine identified a number of constraints in the discipline and pedagogy of advanced mathematics, she nonetheless succeeded in graduating with a major in mathematics. Next, I focus on her work in overcoming these constraints.

A student who learns more than 'academics' in mathematics

Josephine represented advanced mathematics as 'nothing related to anything that would help me'. Her response to an interview question about the relevance of university mathematics points to how she accommodated studying a subject that is not 'relevant' to her future career:

> I always answer this wrong, uhm, I think that it is, I think when you do study here, you not only learn things academically, you learn things in the classroom that are not related to academics, so I learnt to, you know, adjust to someone with a different accent, someone's set of notes, you know adapting to making my own and going to do my own research on a project.

First, Josephine said she was wrong about advanced mathematics being unrelated to her career. Second, like Thabo, she reconfigured what it means to be a mathematics student by foregrounding her learning as 'not related to academics', for example, doing independent research and 'adjusting' to the constraints of lecturers' accents and notes. In the interview she recontextualized representations of the utility of mathematics from popular discourse, that is, she suggested that it was useful 'just to have a mathematics background' and for calculating and measuring (e.g. 'when you want to purchase a house').

An active, resourceful and collaborative mathematics student

Josephine showed agency and moved away from being the passive beneficiary of a structured mathematics course, a position made available to her by the University, to being a more active student. 'So maybe like first year ... [in the extended programme] we got it all structured and easy to read, second year we got a whole set of notes and you have to go through it yourself and in third year you still trying to understand the lecturer and you know, and follow ....'

Josephine worked with this change, as well as the constraints of time, the discipline of mathematics and the mathematics pedagogy, by recontextualizing her subject position as an active school learner who interacts with authority and acts either individually or with her friends. She and her friends identified a classmate who is 'really, really smart', and asked him for help in ways that suited their needs: 'So then we were asking him about a tutor because there is another guy but he works with a group of six and we don't want the group to be too big also. So he is like okay, I will tutor you.' Josephine and her friends also joined extra classes offered to bursary students in a different faculty, an action that was represented as logical and simple: 'So we found out about it and we just joined in.' When lecturers did not identify the recommended books for the students, Josephine found resources in the library and shared these with her classmates. She also repeatedly watched explanations of mathematical concepts on YouTube videos.

A courageous extended programme student

In her third year of study Josephine failed one of her major subjects (not mathematics), thus extending her course length to five years. Although she felt 'sad' about being positioned as a student who 'had failed', she also thought about the two available subject positions – a student who just passes on a re-mark of her examination script or a student who repeats the course and passes with understanding:

> Okay, I was sad and I went back home ... and I was thinking about having my scripts remarked or rechecked and those things and then I was like okay, I can have it remarked and rechecked and have two marks added onto it or I can redo it where maybe I would get a better mark and then, because I am going to do [her major] the next year and I am going to need what I have done in second year, so I might as well redo it and then understand the work.

Josephine accommodated the subject position as a student who repeats a course, in a number of ways. First, she reconfigured what it means to repeat a course by representing this choice as taking 'a lot of courage'. Second, she had achieved a better mark and understanding in her foreground. Third, she represented the support of family and friends as assisting her to accommodate this subject position. Finally, Josephine recruited time (her age and time to graduation) and her subject position as an extended programme student to justify her choice to repeat the course: 'I only turned twenty-one this year, so if I would have graduated this year I would have been the same age as most mainstream students.'

Like Thabo, Josephine resisted being positioned as a struggling mathematics student by reconfiguring how success is defined; she reconfigured 'going well' to mean passing 'a difficult course'. In a few instances Josephine appeared to resist subject positions related to poor performance by simply not thinking about them: 'I don't want to think of that.'

A student who acts in non-disciplinary spaces

Josephine represented her academic studies as the reason for being at the University, but acknowledged that staying focused was 'difficult'. In fact, her home, university residence, friends, the university support services and leadership roles were foregrounded in her talk and in ways that suggested she belonged there rather than in disciplinary spaces. In this section I argue that Josephine worked in these non-disciplinary practices, either adopting different subject positions at different times or straddling different subject positions simultaneously, but all in the service of achieving her overall academic goal which remained present, but backgrounded in her talk.

Josephine identified her friends and her mother as key figures in supporting her to achieve her academic goals, but achieving academically meant that her interaction with these people varied over time. In her first two years at university Josephine's commute from home to campus each day reduced the time available for studying. Staying at home also constrained her opportunity to work with friends staying in university residences. Thus in her third year of study she moved into residence. Initially she did not 'like being there', went home 'every weekend' and studied alone on campus in the evenings. However, in her fourth year she seems to have balanced her roles as friend, daughter and student. In her interview in that year she identified her student card as a significant symbolic object, one that gave her access to residence. She represented residence as a place where she possessed the comforts of home: 'So I have a place, I have a bed to sleep on, I have food, I can come back to campus and all that.' Yet she also telephoned her mother regularly and went home on long weekends and during the vacation.

For Josephine, the demands of being a science student limited her long-standing participation in her local church. She worked with this by reconfiguring what it means to be a religious student, for example, she wore a piece of jewellery in the form of a religious icon more frequently on campus than when she stayed at home.

Josephine identified herself as a university student who needed and actively used the many support services at the institution. These practices, for example attending the life-skills programme in the extended programme, completing non-academic courses that help students adapt to university, accessing career services and attending extra classes were foregrounded in Josephine's talk. For example, she attended a voluntary lunchtime lecture on 'tips on how to survive university'. In her interviews Josephine named, using proper nouns, the places and/or people in these spaces and she quoted the subjects in these spaces to demonstrate her learning. For example, she named the manager of a campus centre who advises students on adaptation to university and used her words to discuss learning: 'She says that when you learn something new ... you have to first think about, first go from the brain to the heart and then back to the brain, so what you thought, how you felt and then what you learnt over all.' This differs from the collective, anonymous descriptions of lecturers in her disciplinary practices.

Although Josephine consistently used adjectives like 'smooth' and 'comfortable' to represent the extended programme, towards the end of her degree she represented the comfort of the programme as a constraint in her transition to the mainstream: 'I don't think they really explained it to you, that when you get into mainstream this is what is going to happen, because you are now so comfortable in your environment that when you come back the following year you are like, how do I cope?' The analysis so far points to how Josephine's individual action enabled her to 'cope' with this transition. She also acted to help other students 'cope' by joining various support programmes on campus and taking leading positions such as orientation leader, mentor, tutor and member of the residence outreach subcommittee. While she identified herself as belonging in these programmes, she remained focused on her studies.

Luthando's transition

A resourceful top student at a school with absences

Luthando talked about growing up in a 'township' where he lived with his mother, an aunt, his two brothers and a cousin. The language at home was Zulu. His teachers at the 'coloured' school he attended taught exclusively in English. In his first year at university he represented his school as 'coming right' in his final school years, but generally as lacking relative to what 'we should have had': 'too many learners' per class and no computers, science laboratory or mathematics teachers.

Luthando, like Thabo and Josephine, resisted being positioned as a student from a 'disadvantaged school' by identifying himself as a top student who 'never failed'. He foregrounded the importance of his teachers' encouragement 'that I am doing well' and his social standing among his peers who 'knew me by my marks' and came to him for help. Being a top student involved visiting the library 'a few kilometres up the road', identifying himself as different from 'other children' at the school, and studying alone: 'I just sit in the front and whatever the other children are saying I just cut it out and I just listen to the teacher.' When he did interact with his peers this was as someone who teaches students on Saturdays. In contrast to his peers who 'just thought they wouldn't make it to university' at all, Luthando was determined to attend the 'best' university in the country: 'I told myself I am definitely coming to UCT.'

An extended programme student or not?

Like Josephine, Luthando was not accepted for his first choice of degree at university, in his case engineering. He resisted his new subject position as extended programme science student by not finding out the reason for his placement. He identified extended programme students as lacking individual choice, using the third person pronoun 'they' to exclude himself from this group: 'Most students in [the extended programme], they don't like it because they feel they should be in a degree of choice because it's like they're choosing for you what to do.' While being a top-school student involved choosing to 'cut out' the talk of his peers, at university Luthando 'had to function alone' on account of an absence of social connections ('I didn't know anyone here.') and his lack of knowledge ('I had to learn how to use computers.').

A few months into his first year Luthando's interactions with others led him to reconfigure the subject position of extended programme student in science as an advantage: 'Everyone said "You are not going to cope there [engineering]."' He observed mainstream mathematics students who 'couldn't cope', who changed to his extended course and quoted these students' complaints about the workload, difficulty and pace of their mainstream courses.

In his fifth interview Luthando, like Thabo, appeared to accommodate the subject position of extended programme student for the social bonds it afforded:

> It is not something that we say that we want to go into, the extended programme, we are put in there and when we get there, we feel as if we went into the same thing and so we have that sense we understand what we are going to do, we are at the same stage, so we form a very strong bond in first year and extended programmes, so it was nice, I can't lie.

Although Luthando used the inclusive 'we' to identify himself as an extended programme student, he seemed less willing ('I can't lie') than Josephine to acknowledge the benefits of these social connections. Indeed in this fifth interview he identified being in the extended programme as a 'disadvantage' and as being 'babied'. While the social relationships with his peers were 'nice' and the content of his extended courses 'really relevant', this 'didn't really, really help' him when 'there is not time to play' in the 'totally different' mainstream courses. Thus, like Josephine, Luthando identified time as a key structural constraint. While he recognized the need for 'them to up the level' as he proceeded through his degree, he questioned whether the University had 'really covered the gap from first year [extended programme] to second year mainstream'.

A good/struggling mathematics student

In his first months at university Luthando was no longer a student for whom 'everything was a breeze'. He identified himself as someone who repeatedly 'struggles': 'You struggle and you struggle to submit, you submit late, deadlines every day and you struggle for a test.' He resisted this new subject position by not finding out what 'I did wrong' and reconfiguring the problem of performance as related to time constraints in tests and the lack of challenge offered by the course (he identified himself as needing a 'more difficult maths course').

In his second year of extended mathematics Luthando said he was 'doing good' at university. He related the mathematics in his extended mathematics course to the mathematics in his background, as 'stuff we've done but looking at it in a different way'. He recontextualized his school subject position as a student who 'loves' mathematics. Being a good extended mathematics student involved knowing 'my mistakes' and personally changing them ('I've changed them.'). It also involved reminding himself that he was someone who does not give up and seeking time-management advice from a relative who is a UCT Engineering graduate. In his second interview he represented time as only 'a little problem'. Luthando celebrated being a good student not just at any university but at one that he configured as teaching independence and preparing one for the deadlines of the workplace, and a place where 'the only way you can pass really well is if you study very, very well'. The latter requirement, he argued, proved 'too much' for some of his peers. However, the 'university maths' he encountered in the mainstream in his third year of study 'is just definitions, it's proofs' and 'sort of different' from the calculations one 'always' does in mathematics. He represented this new practice as opaque and identified himself as excluded from participation therein; 'like you cannot see what you doing, you absolutely cannot see what you are doing'.

Like Josephine, Luthando identified different subject positions made available to students in extended courses from those made available to them in advanced mathematics courses. In the former, the student passively followed the lead of the lecturer: 'He comes up with a topic, introduces the topic to you and he actually does the stuff with you and so it is not a lot of participation from us, it is just learn what he is telling us.' In contrast, he quoted an advanced mathematics lecturer as saying, 'I can't be helping you with everything.' Rather, the advanced mathematics student should bring mathematical knowledge to the discussion: 'They want you to tell them what you think.' Indeed, Luthando described his difficulty in adopting this active role, on account of his lack of knowledge and inability to enter the conversation:

> You sit there in class and the lecturer is bouncing ideas around and you don't know what the hell they are talking about and you get students, really smart students, students who really, really love maths and really do some research …, you get them interacting a lot with the lecturer and you are totally lost and they will be having a very nice conversation with the lecturer about the topic and you don't know jack, you don't know anything, you don't know what to say.

In this extract Luthando did not include himself with the students ('they') who 'really, really love maths'. He reconfigured his school and extended programme subject position from someone who 'loves' mathematics to someone who 'still likes' and 'enjoys' mathematics. This was reconfigured further in his fourth year of study when he identified himself as 'tired of just doing maths', failing one mathematics module and not having mathematics in his foreground: 'I didn't understand why I was doing maths.' He no longer asked questions in class nor sought help from the lecturer after class, and even stopped attending class. Nonetheless, Luthando completed enough mathematics to transfer to engineering in his fifth year at the University. Next I present the analysis of Luthando's work to achieve this goal.

A resourceful advanced mathematics student

Resisting the positioning as a failing advanced mathematics student, Luthando recontextualized his subject position as a resourceful student in his background. He revisited his notes, did his own 'research' using the internet or consulting textbooks in the library, and talked to friends in the same course. Like Thabo and Josephine, he reconfigured his degree programme as a 'difficult' combination of courses, in which 'people' in general 'tend to drop one or the other' and like Thabo, he questioned the assessment practices. His decision to engage in non-academic spaces or not – as a mentor to extended programme students or as a residence subwarden – involved thinking about and telling himself that his 'biggest responsibility here was to study'.

In his fourth interview Luthando chose as his significant symbolic object a definition of the word 'success': 'Coming from where I was brought up to being where I am now, like I didn't come from a very privileged background and my mom had to make do every day, so being where I am now is sort of success to me.' While Luthando believed that his own background was not as disadvantaged as some of his peers, he recontextualized his background to celebrate 'where I am now' and to make choices that accommodated his new subject position as a struggling mathematics student. For example, he replaced 'one of the harder' modules he failed with 'one of the easiest modules'. Also, he attributed his loss of interest in mathematics in his fourth year of study to his failure to secure the funding he needed for his studies.

Luthando, like Josephine, was emphatic that advanced mathematics was of no use: 'I have never had to use Maths 2 anywhere whatsoever.' Luthando appeared to accommodate being a student who studies a mathematics course with no perceived use value and regained his motivation to complete his final year of studies in mathematics. Indeed, completion of the course would secure his acceptance into engineering and he had being an engineer in his foreground. Once registered in engineering Luthando would need to be on 'top of' mathematics, but mathematics that involved 'numbers' and working out 'percentages and stuff'.

Privilege in the background and foreground

Although Luthando's interaction with others led him to downplay his subject position as lacking relative to others, his concern about his home and university finances recurred in his interviews. Initially, he identified university financial aid as enabling him as a UCT student: 'Sometimes I don't have the money to come back, but when I'm here [at UCT], *ja*, it's good because I get food allowances, book allowances.' Also, receiving this aid taught him to 'handle my finances very well'. He tried unsuccessfully for four years to secure a study bursary and represented his lack of success as an ongoing source of 'worry' for him and his family who could not support him. 'Finances are the last thing you should have to deal with as a student.'

Luthando resisted being positioned to ask for money, but accepted financial help from the qualified engineer in his family whom he identified as having overcome the constraints of his background: 'He has a house, he has a car, he has a child, he is sorted.' Indeed, Luthando used his past and present financial difficulties and the promise of having a 'great life' in his own and his family's foreground ('Look where you come from and where you want to go.') to motivate himself to complete the mathematics course necessary for engineering. Luthando's 'passion' for engineering appears to stem from his view that 'you don't really struggle financially', rather than from knowledge of an engineer's job ('I don't really know what is the life of a chemical engineer.'). However, like Thabo, who also looked forward to supporting his family when he graduated and got a job, there were times during his university career when Luthando had to resist his subject position as a family member who could provide 'answers'. Providing these 'answers', he suggested, was 'in conflict with my studies' and he had to 'separate my personal life from my studies'.

Discussion and conclusions

The cases of Thabo, Josephine and Luthando add context to the statistics on student success and failure by adding rich descriptions of students' experiences of the varied mediating practices and available subject positions in the past, present and future social context of their transition to and progress through university. These descriptions are 'patterned in systematic ways by location, common values, comparable resources and shared experience' (Thomson 2009: 9). Yet each student's material and mental action – involving a complex mix of resisting, reconfiguring, accommodating, recontextualizing and balancing representations of practices and the subject positions made available to them – is unique, situational and occurs at the intersection of social class position, race and language (Thomson 2009).

It is not possible, therefore, to generalize from the experiences of these three students. However, the particular in these cases can be used to understand the interplay between individual action and the social context more generally (Thomson 2009), and comparisons can be made with research about students in other university contexts (Wimpenny and Savin-Baden 2013; Maunder et al. 2013).

I end this chapter with comparisons between Thabo, Josephine and Luthando, with reference to other studies, and provide recommendations for practice and research.

Home and school backgrounds

Thabo, Josephine and Luthando used historical and socio-political binaries (Stinson 2008) to represent their home and school backgrounds as lacking – certainly in terms of material and human resources – relative to other students in the University. Yet each had particular, additional complicating factors: Thabo emphasized race and language, Josephine's geographical location was an issue and Luthando referred to his social class position.

Each student resisted being positioned as a student from a background that is lacking by identifying rather as a top mathematics student at school. They were able to position themselves as top students by referring to good results at school, loving mathematics, looking forward to positive outcomes and referring to their teachers' positive views about them (see Stinson 2008; Hodgen and Marks 2009; Ward-Penny, Johnston-Wilder and Lee 2011). Success required making a choice to distance oneself from the majority at school and to interact only with other top students (see the Introduction to this book; Stinson 2008; Reay, Crozier and Clayton 2009; Hernandez-Martinez and Williams 2013), and required doing considerable work – for example, studying hard and imagining being a science student in the future.

Alternating successes and failures at university

It is well documented that many students, and not just historically marginalized students, face a change from being a top-school student to being a struggling or failing university student (see Reay, Crozier and Clayton 2009; Wimpenny and Savin-Baden 2013). In this longitudinal study, the three students' placement in the extended science programme meant that they moved in and out of these subject positions as they negotiated shifts from school mathematics, to extended mathematics, and then to advanced mathematics in the mainstream. Thabo, Josephine and Luthando negotiated this movement by recontextualizing their school subject positions – for example, being academically strong, hard-working, independent and loving mathematics (Epstein, Mendick and Moreau 2010; Reay, Crozier and Clayton 2010; Hernandez-Martinez and Williams 2013) and by recruiting what others say about the new practices and subject positions (see Maunder et al. 2013). The affordances of this recontextualization varied across the three students and across mathematics practices.

The students represented extended mathematics in terms of continuity with the 'numbers' of school mathematics, only more challenging. This is significant, given that the course exists structurally to support students such as these in the transition from school to advanced mathematics. Just as students represent school mathematics pupils as compliant and lacking agency (see de Freitas 2008), Thabo, Josephine and Luthando identified an extended mathematics student as a passive receiver of knowledge. Making the transition from school to extended mathematics was not easy, but it was enabled by the similar knowledge criteria of the two practices and the students' recontextualization of their hard material and mental work as school students.

Being an extended mathematics student involved seeing oneself as different from mainstream students (see Haggis and Pouget 2003; Kapp and Bangeni 2011) and Josephine appears to have accommodated this new subject position more readily than Thabo and Luthando. Over time, all three came to represent the extended programme as a safe social space but as not mediating changing knowledge criteria, pedagogy and levels of independence in the transition to advanced mathematics. This longitudinal study thus brings into view the fact that neither the support offered to students nor research on this support should focus solely on the first few months at university (see Haggis and Pouget 2003; Jacklin and Le Riche 2009) or only on first-year undergraduate courses. Indeed, it is particularly in the three students' representations of advanced mathematics that we see where the challenge of transition lies. As in other studies, the practice of advanced mathematics is represented by the three students as totally different from preceding mathematics practices, as opaque and requiring independent study, and as having an exclusionary pedagogy (see Ward-Penny, Johnston-Wilder and Lee 2011; Hernandez-Martinez and Williams 2013).

Being an advanced mathematics student involved redefining the available subject positions in various ways. This included reconfiguring how assessments constitute success or even resisting assessment as a measure of ability (see Hodgen and Marks 2009). It involved recontextualizing the background subject position as lacking relative to others at university to understand and celebrate performance (see Aries and Seider 2007; McGee and Martin 2011), and recontextualizing popular representations of mathematics and the University as elitist and difficult (see Epstein, Mendick and Moreau 2010; Smith 2010). For Thabo it meant consistently recontextualizing his school subject position as a hard worker who works alone and relies on his own efforts (see Aries and Seider 2007; Reay, Crozier and Clayton, 2009), and as someone who loves mathematics (see Epstein, Mendick and Moreau 2010). Luthando, however, was not able to sustain the latter identification in the face of failure, but recontextualized his social class position to motivate himself and to explain his performance. Josephine's subject position as a mathematics major was serendipitous, yet she passed the course by recontextualizing her school subject position as someone who seeks out additional material and human resources (as does Luthando) and by taking up subject positions outside of mathematics. The talk of all three students was marked by a reluctance to seek help from lecturers (see Thomas 2002; Kapp and Bangeni 2011), in contrast to their relations to authority at school (see Stinson 2008). This reluctance was based on the perceived superior knowledge of lecturers, which for Thabo was deeply entwined with race and language use.

It is evident from this study that what is valued in advanced mathematics by the institution and how the institution understands what it means to be an advanced mathematics student need to be made explicit to students. Crucially, attention needs to be paid to how pedagogies in advanced mathematics courses – as well as support courses – mediate the transition from school to advanced mathematics. Institutional decisions about how to support students need to take into account that this transition is not just about acquiring disciplinary knowledge but about who one is and who one relates to (Christie 2009; Valero 2014). Attention needs to be paid to building inclusivity in disciplinary spaces, particularly for students like Thabo and Luthando who feel excluded from the norms of white, middle-class English ways of being in the institution, which constrains their access to resources, including their lecturers' expertise. Clearly, for the three students in this study, race, social class position, language, knowledge and geography affected them socially, materially and psychologically as they progressed through the institution (see Leathwood and O'Connell 2003; Soudien 2008; Kapp and Bangeni 2011).

These three cases highlight the complexity and uniqueness of student agency as they accept and resist the positions made available to them. Student ability to negotiate course content, language, social relationships and the subject positions made available to them is uneven. Students placed together in extended curriculum programmes cannot be placed in 'narrow boxes' (Erwin 2012: 97), with their backgrounds described in terms of student deficit (Kapp and Bangeni 2011). Rather, the institution needs to offer students flexible pathways.

Growing as connected, responsive students

The work required to focus on one's studies in difficult courses while also being an active family member, friend and community member featured in the talk of all three students. Thabo and Luthando resisted being a responsive family member. This 'denial' (Wimpenny and Savin-Baden 2013: 321) was not a critique of their background (see Kapp and Bangeni 2011), but about having academic success and the related material and symbolic rewards for them and their families in their foregrounds. It seems that Thabo and Luthando had to temporarily 'get out' of connections to home in order to 'get on' (Thomson 2009:7) with the university degrees in Science and Engineering which they viewed as ultimately improving these homes. It is possible that Josephine's support from her family and friends – which contrasts with Thabo and Luthando's concerns about the high expectations of family and the community – enabled her to accommodate being a student on an extended programme and one who gets lower marks, more easily and more consistently than Thabo and Luthando could. This accommodation opened the space for her to make use of the structural support offered by the institution.

While all three students felt alone when they first came to university (see Maunder et al. 2013), the sense of acting alone in the University space permeated all of Thabo's interviews. His sense of disconnection was represented, not as a personal choice, but as a function of his lack of disciplinary knowledge relative to others, his race and his difficulty learning mathematics in English. Thabo, therefore, seemed to have less control over social relationships (Fairclough 2003) at university than Josephine and Luthando, who were more likely to act with others in this space and who used their academic standing at a particular moment to make choices about these relationships.

Responding to the constraints they identified in the institution, both Josephine and Luthando positioned themselves within the University in order to make it more enabling for people from similar backgrounds, for example, by mentoring extended programme students (see Reay, Crozier and Clayton 2009). Drawing on the work of Ballet, Dubois and Mahieu (2007:187), it could be argued that the agentic action of Josephine and Luthando was 'strong' in the sense that they exercised responsibility towards others, while Thabo's action was 'weak' in that he focused on his personal goals. Overall, Josephine seemed to act with a more 'mobile' sense of belonging (Thomson 2009: 8) than Thabo and Luthando. This enabled her to balance being a mathematics student with being a family member, friend and mentor to other students.

Institutional responses to the challenge of supporting students in the transition from school to advanced mathematics must enable these students to grow, not as 'decontextualized cognitive subjects' (Valero 2004: 10), but as individuals who are connected to others in and outside the university, and who can work to help others to grow.

References

Aries, E. and Seider, M. (2007), 'The Role of Social Class in the Formation of Identity: A Study of Public and Elite Private College Students', *The Journal of Social Psychology*, 147(2): 137–57.

Ballet, J., Dubois, J-L. and Mahiue, F-C. (2007), 'Responsibility for Each Other's Freedom: Agency as the Source of Collective Capability', *Journal of Human Development*, 8(2): 185–201.

Bartholomew, H., Darragh, L., Ell, F. and Saunders, J. (2011), '"I'm a Natural and I do it for Love!": Exploring Students' Accounts of Studying Mathematics', *International Journal of Mathematical Education in Science and Technology*, 42(7): 915–24.

Battey, D. (2013), 'Access to Mathematics: "A Possessive Investment in Whiteness"', *Curriculum Inquiry*, 43(3): 332–59.

Berry III, R.Q. (2008) 'Access to Upper-Level Mathematics: The Stories of Successful African American Middle School Boys', *Journal for Research in Mathematics Education*, 39(5): 464–88.

Birani, A. and Lehmann, W. (2013), 'Ethnicity as Social Capital: An Examination of First-Generation, Ethnic-Minority Students at a Canadian University', *International Studies in Sociology of Education*, 23(4): 281–97.

Black, L. and Williams, J. (2013), 'Contradiction and Conflict between "Leading Identities": Becoming an Engineer versus Becoming a "Good Muslim" Woman', *Educational Studies in Mathematics*, 84: 1–14.

Christie, H. (2009), 'Emotional Journeys: Young People and Transitions to University', *British Journal of Sociology of Education*, 30(2): 123–36.

Council on Higher Education, (2013), *A Proposal for Undergraduate Curriculum Reform in South Africa: The Case for a Flexible Curriculum Structure*, http://www.che.ac.za/ sites/default/files/publications/, accessed 28 November 2013.

de Freitas, E. (2008), 'Critical Mathematics Education: Recognizing the Ethical Dimension of Problem Solving', *International Electronic Journal of Mathematics Education*, 3(2): 79–95.

Engelbrecht, J., Harding, A. and Phiri, P. (2010), 'Are OBE-Trained Learners Ready for University Mathematics?', *Pythagoras*, 72: 3–13.

Epstein, D., Mendick, H. and Moreau, M-P. (2010), 'Imagining the Mathematician: Young People Talking about Popular Representations of Maths', *Discourse: Studies in the Cultural Politics of Education*, 31(1): 45–60.

Erwin, K. (2012), 'Race and Race Thinking: Reflections in Theory and Practice for Researchers in South Africa and Beyond', *Transformation: Critical Perspectives on Southern Africa*, 79: 93–113.

Fairclough, N. (2001), *Language and Power* (2nd ed.), Harlow, England: Longman.

Fairclough, N. (2003), *Analysing Discourse: Textual Analysis in Social Research*, London: Routledge.

Fairclough, N. (2006), *Language and Globalization*, London: Routledge.

Frempong, G., Ma, X. and Mensah, J. (2012), 'Access to Postsecondary Education: Can Schools Compensate for Socioeconomic Disadvantage?', *Higher Education*, 63: 19–32.

Gibney, A., Moore, N., Murphy, F. and O'Sullivan, S. (2011), 'The First Semester of University Life; "Will I be Able to Manage it At All?"', *Higher Education*, 62: 351–66.

Gutiérrez, R. (2013), 'The Sociopolitical Turn in Mathematics Education', *Journal for Research in Mathematics Education*, 44(1): 37–68.

Haggis, T. and Pouget, M. (2002), 'Trying to be Motivated: Perspectives on Learning from Younger Students Accessing Higher Education', *Teaching in Higher Education*, 7(3): 323–36.

Hernandez-Martinez, P. and Williams, J. (2013), 'Against the Odds: Resilience in Mathematics Students in Transition', *British Educational Research Journal*, 39(1): 45–59.

Herrington, A. and Curtis, M. (2000), *Persons in Process: Four Stories of Writing and Personal Development in College*, Urbana, IL: National Council of Teachers of English.

Hodgen, J. and Marks, R. (2009), 'Mathematical "Ability" and Identity: A Sociocultural Perspective on Assessment and Selection', in L. Black, H. Mendick and Y. Solomon (eds), *Mathematical Relationships in Education: Identities and Participation*, 31–42, New York: Routledge.

Institutional Planning Department, University of Cape Town, (2015), unpublished data.

Jablonka, E., Ashjari, H. and Bergsten, C. (2012), 'Recognizing Knowledge Criteria in Undergraduate Mathematics Education', in C. Bergsten, E. Jablonka and M. Ramon (eds), *Proceedings of the Eighth Swedish Mathematics Education Research Seminar*, 101–110, Linköping: Swedish Society for Research in Mathematics Education.

Jacklin, A. and Le Riche, P. (2009), 'Reconceptualising Student Support: From "Support" to "Supportive"', *Studies in Higher Education*, 34(7): 735–49.

Kapp, R. and Bangeni, B. (2011), 'A Longitudinal Study of Students' Negotiation of Language, Literacy and Identity', *Southern African Linguistics and Applied Language Studies*, 29(2): 197–208.

Leathwood, C. and O'Connell, P. (2003), '"It's a Struggle": The Construction of the "New Student" in Higher Education', *Journal of Education Policy*, 18(6): 597–615.

Maunder, R. E., Cunliffe, M., Galvin, J., Mjali, S. and Rogers, J. (2013), 'Listening to Student Voices: Student Researchers Exploring Undergraduate Experiences of University Transition', *Higher Education*, 66: 139–52.

McGee, E. O. and Martin, D. B. (2011), '"You Would not Believe What I Have to Go Through to Prove my Intellectual Value!": Stereotype Management among Academically Successful Black Mathematics and Engineering Students', *American Educational Research Journal*, 48(6): 1347–89.

Reay, D., Crozier, G. and Clayton, J. (2009), '"Strangers in Paradise?" Working-Class Students in Elite Universities', *Sociology*, 43(6): 1103–21.

Reay, D., Crozier, G. and Clayton, J. (2010), '"Fitting in" or "Standing out": Working-Class Students in UK Higher Education', *British Educational Research Journal*, 36(1): 107–24.

Seider, M. (2008), 'The Dynamics of Social Reproduction: How Class Works at a State College and Elite Private College', *Equity & Excellence in Education*, 41(1): 45–61.

Skovsmose, O. (2005), 'Foregrounds and the Politics of Learning Obstacles', *For the Learning of Mathematics*, 25(1): 4–10.

Smith, C. (2010), '"Sometimes I think Wow I'm Doing Further Maths…": Tensions between Aspiring and Belonging', in U. Gellert, E. Jablonka and C. Morgan (eds), *Proceedings of the Sixth International Mathematics Education and Society Conference*, 437–446, Berlin, Germany: Freie Universität Berlin.

Soudien, C. (2008), 'The Intersection of Race and Class in the South African University: Student Experiences', *South African Journal of Higher Education*, 22(3): 662–78.

Soudien, C. (2012), *Realising the Dream: Unlearning the Logic of Race in the South African School*, Cape Town: Human Sciences Research Council.

Spaull, N. (2013), 'South Africa's Education Crisis: The Quality of Education in South Africa 1994-2011', Report commissioned by the Centre for Development Enterprise, http://www.section27.org.za/wp-content/uploads/2013/10/Spaull-2013-CDE-report-South-Africas-Education-Crisis, accessed 14 July 2015.

Stinson, D. W. (2008), 'Negotiating Sociocultural Discourses: The Counter-Storytelling of Academically (and Mathematically) Successful African American Male Students', *American Educational Research Journal*, 45(4), 975–1010.

Tall, D. (1991), 'The Psychology of Advanced Mathematical Thinking', in D. Tall (ed.), *Advanced Mathematical Thinking*, 3–21, Dordrecht: Kluwer.

Tall, D. (1996), 'Functions and Calculus', in A. J. Bishop, K. Clements, C. Keitel, J. Kilpatrick and C. Laborde (eds.), *International Handbook of Mathematics Education*, 289–325, Dordrecht: Kluwer.

Thomas, L. (2002), 'Student Retention in Higher Education: The Role of Institutional Habitus', *Journal of Education Policy*, 17(4): 423–42.

Thomson, R. (2009), *Unfolding Lives: Youth, Gender and Change*, Bristol: The Policy Press.

Torenbeek, M., Jansen, E. and Hofman, A. (2010), 'The Effect of Fit between Secondary and University Education on First-Year Student Achievement', *Studies in Higher Education*, 35(6): 659–75.

Valero, P. (2004), 'Socio-Political Perspectives on Mathematics Education', in P. Valero, and R. Zevenbergen (eds), *Researching the Socio-Political Dimensions of Mathematics Education: Issues of Power in Theory and Methodology*, 5–23, Boston: Kluwer Academic Publishers.

Valero, P. (2014), 'Cutting the Calculations of Social Change with School Mathematics', in P. Liljedahl, C. Nicol, S. Oesterle and D. Allan (eds), *Proceedings of the Joint Meeting of PME 38 and PME-NA 36*, 1: 73–7, Vancouver, Canada: PME.

Van Leeuwen, T. (2008), *Discourse and Practice: New Tools for Critical Discourse Analysis*, Oxford: Oxford University Press.

Walshaw, M. (2013), 'Post-structuralism and Ethical Practical Action: Issues of Identity and Power', *Journal for Research in Mathematics Education*, 44(1): 100–18.

Ward-Penny, R., Johnston-Wilder, S. and Lee, C. (2011), 'Exit Interviews: Undergraduates who Leave Mathematics Behind', *For the Learning of Mathematics*, 31(2): 21–6.

Wimpenny, K. and Savin-Baden, M. (2013), 'Alienation, Agency and Authenticity: A Synthesis of the Literature on Student Engagement', *Teaching in Higher Education*, 18(3): 311–26.

3

'Going Nowhere Slowly': A Longitudinal Perspective on a First-generation Woman Student's Withdrawal from University

Judy Sacks and Rochelle Kapp

Introduction

In this chapter we analyse the case of Roshni, a first-generation, coloured, working-class South African undergraduate student who withdrew from the University after successfully completing two years of her social science degree. We draw on three years of data gathered from 2009 to 2011 to show how Roshni attempted to negotiate the conflicting subject positions made available to her by home and disciplinary discourses. Drawing on poststructuralist understandings of identity and discourse, we argue that an intersection of gendered, class and cultural expectations had a considerable effect on Roshni's attitudes, behaviour and decisions. We describe how she attempted to create a coherent sense of self by drawing on discourses of autonomous individual subjectivity and female empowerment (Walkerdine 2003; Fraser 2013), as well as on her identity as a Muslim woman. In order to be accepted in multiple spaces and to create the semblance of functioning and progress, she created 'situational' identities, foregrounding 'different identities at different times' (Renn 2004: 220) and in different places. However, the emotion-work of dealing with structural constraints and living up to conflicting expectations eventually took its toll, causing her to withdraw from the university in her third year.

There has been a great deal of statistical focus on the low retention and graduation rates of black South African students (see the Introduction). Nevertheless, at a national level, no one has tracked the patterns of black undergraduate women in terms of retention and withdrawal. Significantly, of the cohort who first registered at the university in 2009, 30 per cent of black women dropped out or failed within five years. Importantly, 10 per cent (ninety) of these dropped out in good academic standing, compared to 6 per cent (forty-four) of black males. Similarly, while there is a considerable body of valuable qualitative research on the experiences of undergraduate black, working-class and/or first-generation students in higher education in South Africa (see for example Thesen and van Pletzen 2006; Firfirey and Carolissen 2010; Leibowitz, van der Merwe and van Schalkwyk 2012; Case 2013), this research has not tended to disaggregate the experiences of men and women, and with the exception of Breier's (2010) work on financial dropout, it has not focused on students' perspectives on withdrawal.

Engaging in the longitudinal analysis of a single case enables us to examine the complex interplay between agency and structure, in order to understand how the 'specifics of context and history translate in dynamic and unstable ways into multiplicity and difference in the lives of situated individuals' (Haggis 2004: 337). We are interested in the meanings Roshni attributed to her experiences in different spaces at different moments in time, how she made use of resources within and outside of the institution and how home and institutional discourses enabled and/or constrained her progress. While a single case cannot address the complexity of why first-generation black women students are gaining access, but are failing or withdrawing, we argue that Roshni's experiences and perceptions have considerable resonance with those of other women participants in our longitudinal studies (see Chapter 4, this book; Janse van Rensburg and Kapp 2014) and with working-class women and/or first-generation students in the UK (see, for example, Lucey, Melody and Walkerdine 2003; Thomas and Quinn 2007; Reay, Crozier and Clayton 2010). We will draw on this body of research, insights from Roshni's case and our experience of student and academic development work to suggest issues that need to be considered to ensure that working-class women succeed in the academy.

Theoretical framework

Tinto (2006-7: 2) points out that when student retention first appeared as an issue within higher education studies more than forty years ago, student attrition was typically viewed through the lens of psychology: 'Lack of student retention was seen as the reflection of individual attributes, skills and motivation.' However, recent theory has pointed out that while identity is central to learning, idealized descriptions of the 'good' student which remove individuals from the complexities of their contexts fail to take into account the many reasons why students struggle and often withdraw. In particular, students from marginalized backgrounds are often unable to engage with or resist engaging with institutional norms and values (Haggis 2003: 98; Thomas and Quinn 2007; Mann 2008). This is relevant to the South African context where first-generation, black students are entering previously white, English-medium, relatively elite institutions which have taken-for-granted dominant discourses which often generalize black working-class experiences and cast home discourses that are different in deficit terms (Boughey 2009; Pym and Kapp 2013).

Fraser (2013: 140) emphasizes the fluidity and complexity of social identities. She shows that the category 'woman' intersects with other identities in relation to context:

> Social identities are knitted together from a plurality of different descriptions arising from a plurality of signifying practices. Thus, no-one is simply a woman; one is rather, for example, a white, Jewish, middle-class woman, a philosopher, a lesbian, a socialist and a mother. Because everyone acts in a plurality of social contexts, moreover, the different descriptions comprising any individual's social identity fade in and out of focus ... in some contexts, one's womanhood figures centrally in the set of descriptions under which one acts; in others, it is peripheral or latent.

Fraser (2013), Christie (2008) and Thomson (2009: 154) argue that individual lives are both 'constrained' and 'agentic'. Individuals position and re-position themselves, make decisions and take action in relation to their past and present experiences and their desires for the future, but the degree to which they are able to take action and reconstruct who they are is regulated by the extent to which they are able to access the material, linguistic, social and cultural resources that are valued within dominant discourses (Norton 1997). Nevertheless, a number of gender, literacy and education theorists have written very powerfully about how neo-liberalism and popular media have appropriated radical discourses about empowerment and equity and have constructed the notion of an autonomous individual subject with free choice. Thus Lucey, Melody and Walkerdine (2003: 285) write: 'Discourses of endless possibility for all girls circulate freely, although tempered and regulated by the kind of meritocratic principles that can explain any failure to "achieve" and to "have" as a personal one.'

In Chapter 1 we described how in working-class communities, success in education is often constructed as the means to free choice and upward mobility and an escape from poverty and working-class life. Reay (2001) and Lucey,

Melody and Walkerdine (2003) point out that working-class parents often invest in these notions of upward mobility and escape, which entail distance from home discourses (dis-identification), but also expect their children to retain identification and affiliation with home. They describe the consequent pain and loss for individuals that often accompany class transition (see also Read, Archer and Leathwood 2003; Bangeni and Kapp 2005; Thomas and Quinn 2007; Soudien 2008). In this chapter we argue that Roshni's withdrawal from her studies resulted from her failed efforts to sustain multiple, incommensurable discourses, as well as from the very real structural constraints of her putative academic path and the pressure to conform to gendered domestic roles.

Methodology

We used qualitative longitudinal analysis (Thomson and Holland 2003) to explore Roshni's perceptions and lived experiences. Thomson (2009: 16) argues that whereas single interviews of participants tend to reify identity, multiple interviews capture the 'subject in process' and enable one to see how individuals reflect, re-position themselves and are positioned in particular times and places. The exploration of a single case illuminates the particular, multifaceted complexity of an individual's experiences (Herrington and Curtis 2000). Roshni's case was purposively selected from the larger case study of 100 students because we wanted to understand why she dropped out after a seemingly successful transition to university.

The data we used consisted of three individual semi-structured interviews, a written reflection on Roshni's language and mathematics history and self-selected essays, tests and assignments from her first two years. The data were analysed manually and inductively. For the purposes of this chapter, we focused on the two interviews conducted in her first two years of study (2009 and 2010) and the interview conducted after she had withdrawn (2011). We were interested in how she described and reconstructed her experiences, the issues that she chose to foreground, and how she constructed a sense of self in relation to others in the different spaces she navigated over time. Her narrative was not linear. This was particularly evident in her second and third interviews when she was dealing with difficult issues. Re-examining the data from the first two years in the light of her withdrawal caused us to reassess many of our earlier assumptions. We represent Roshni's positioning and re-positioning by drawing on narrative methodology and critical discourse analysis to analyse how subject positions, experiences and contexts are constructed in her narratives through repetition, contrast, evaluations, pronouns, silences and contradictions (Fairclough 1995; McCormick 2005). We draw attention to the multivocality and intertextuality in Roshni's narratives – her speech is replete with conceptual framing, metaphors, idiomatic expressions and clichés drawn from religion, popular media and the discourses on identity and gender in her social science courses. Through a close analysis of her speech, we show how she draws on these disparate images to facilitate the enactment of situational identities, as well as to construct a coherent sense of her future self.

'I want to do something with my life'

In Roshni's first interview, she foregrounded her working-class identity and her identity as a Muslim woman. She repeatedly characterized her neighbourhood environment as 'corrupt' and described in some detail the generalized sense of imminent danger and unease occasioned by the proximity and frequency of large, and small-scale crime, violence and noise: 'In the mornings, like not even on the week-end, there are drug lords a few houses away in my road, there are gang fights ... there are robberies ... there are people on the corners that are unemployed, there are alcoholics ... arguing probably four o'clock in the morning and the police are often in my neighbourhood.' Drawing on the discourse from a humanities course, she used Thornton's (1988) metaphor of 'boundaries' to describe how she and the female members of her family had learnt to navigate the violent neighbourhood where police are bribed and 'No-one steps out of bounds.' She described the need for a physical and emotionally boundaried existence in defence against the 'corruption' outside: 'If you keep to yourself and you don't let whatever is happening around you enter your home, then it won't affect you.'

In this respect, Roshni ascribed 'innocence' to her own household and attributed this to the values, attitudes and behaviour that characterized her Muslim upbringing. Nevertheless, she also characterized her family background as 'very complicated' because her father had two wives living with their children in two separate townships, which she described as 'kind of accepted' within her religion. Her father's salary supported his first wife's family and Roshni's mother, a nurse, was the sole breadwinner in her home. Roshni's household included her sister, who suffered from schizophrenia, her aunt and occasionally her two step-sisters. Whereas Roshni mentioned her father three times in her three interviews, her mother was constantly invoked as a point of reference in her descriptions of everyday life at home, as a sounding board for the articulation of her desires, as a role model for her resilience and as the person from whom she sought affirmation.

Roshni portrayed her high school in similar terms to her neighbourhood, characterizing it as 'corrupt', plagued by overcrowding and violence, a weak culture of teaching and learning, and teachers who were poorly qualified, indifferent and often absent. There were often vacant teacher posts at the school. In her final year at school, Roshni had no mathematics, accounting or Afrikaans teachers for most of the year as a consequence of teacher resignations. Teaching practices were highly reproductive and mainly oral. Although English was the official medium of instruction, classes were mediated in a mixture of English and Afrikaans, which Roshni labelled '*Kombuistaal*' (kitchen language), which signalled its proximity to her description of her home language ('broken Afrikaans mixed with broken English put together') and its distance from the formal expression that characterizes academic proficiency.

In her first interview, Roshni recounted that she had been determined to succeed at school despite the conditions and that she had told her mother that, 'I want to do something with my life.' She identified herself as a hard worker (classified by others as part of a group of 'super-nerd children'). Like many of the participants in our study, she formed a study group at school who continued working despite the lack of teachers. In each of her three interviews, she emphasized her desire for upward mobility, to escape the expected path that, 'After school you go work in a factory, after school you go work in a shop.' The expectation that women with a high school education would be breadwinners, but in low-paying assistant, service or care-giving roles like teaching or nursing was common to most female participants in the study. In contrast to male students, female students were often actively discouraged from applying to the university by teachers who told them that they would fail (see Chapter 1).

As was the case with most of the first-generation participants in our study, Roshni's decision to go to university was taken independently from her parents and teachers (see also Thomas and Quinn 2007; Lubben et al. 2010). Although she grew up just twenty-three kilometres from the University, Roshni had not heard of it until her final year of school, when a friend invited her to attend an open day for prospective students. Roshni was enthralled by the atmosphere of excitement about learning and by the beauty of the environment. She applied, but her application was rejected on the basis of her final school-leaving marks. Her response was indicative of the agency that characterized both her schooling and university life. She appealed to the University, including a letter of support from her former headmaster, and was consequently accepted for an extended degree programme in Social Science, a degree designed to provide augmented and extended support for students from disadvantaged educational backgrounds.

'You see the ladder'

Because Roshni's parents did not want her to stay in university accommodation, she commuted for around three to four hours every day between home and the University. In order to navigate the overcrowded public transport system, she rose at half past four each morning and was expected to be home by sunset to engage in domestic chores such as cooking and cleaning. Because home was not conducive to academic work, and she worked part-time at a local shop on weekends, all her academic work had to be completed on campus during the week.

Roshni's first two years at the University were marked by high levels of enthusiasm, passion and active engagement with her studies, her peers and lecturers. While many participants in our study described their motivation to study in predominantly instrumental ways (see Kapp and Bangeni 2009; Pym and Kapp 2013), Roshni set about creating a strong 'learning identity' (Christie et al. 2008: 569), following the advice offered by her mentor and other lecturers in her extended programme. She attended all her classes, made herself highly visible and situated herself socially in her disciplines through participation and engagement. Most of the students in our larger study participated in small-group tutorial discussions, but were generally too unconfident to speak in large lectures because of their insecurity about their ideas, the speed of the interaction and/or their levels of English fluency. They also generally refrained from individual consultations with lecturers. By contrast, Roshni was outspoken in lectures from her first year: 'I usually ask a lot of questions and I usually let myself be heard, if I don't understand.' She battled with the academic literacy expectations and consulted her lecturers often, made use of available resources such as the Writing Centre and engaged in research beyond the prescribed texts.

The campus was also a site of 'institutionalized moratorium', where Roshni consciously tried out different roles and options, as many in late adolescence do (Adams, Berzonsky and Keating 2006: 87). In each interview, Roshni drew from the language of her academic subjects (in particular psychology), to describe how she saw herself engaged in a process of self-discovery and reinvention. In her second year, she described her first year as a process of 'finding my identity, developing who I am'. She spoke of choosing a range of courses because 'I really want to explore what university is really about.' She stated that she chose courses that 'made me grow more, personally and individually and socially' and spoke enthusiastically about the University as a place that had expanded her horizons. This seemed to have literal and figurative connotations. She often referred to the physical beauty of the University campus and to being entranced by the perspective and magnitude of the 'views' from the University, situated on the side of the mountain. In her first interview, she spoke excitedly of her surprise and pleasure at meeting people from outside South Africa:

> It's the first time I meet someone from overseas because I'm usually just in my neighbourhood, I only know those people, I'm only clustered around those people, I have never met someone from abroad, that was the first encounter I had. ... I met people from England, Julian and I met someone from Japan, Alicia, and China and all those places and I was like – OK, so the world isn't that small after all.

This quotation signals the residual geographic separation of apartheid that was successful in isolating communities on the basis of race and class and is still evident in South Africa today. Roshni again invoked Thornton's (1988) metaphor of boundaries to describe her belief in the need to 'look past all the boundaries ... and go straight for it'. Unlike many participants in the study who embraced a notion of benign multiculturalism in theory only, Roshni practised her faith and was an active member of the Muslim students' organization, while she also purposefully spoke to people and made friends across conventional boundaries of race, religion, nation and class. She even attended a church with an American friend who later joined her at a mosque. She saw the University as a place which had opened up new ways of understanding and connecting, but also of previously unimagined possibilities and free choice. Roshni seemed to experience very little sense of the shock and alienation described by many scholars (see for example Christie et al. 2008) and by other participants in our study.

When asked (in her second year) about the highlights of her first year, Roshni said the following:

> Basically meeting people and setting goals for yourself, setting living standards, because to me, I come from a poor background ... you don't see any goals there, the highest would be like – I want to be a teacher, I want to be a bus driver, I want to work after Matric, so when you come here and you will be like, Oh my gosh, he is studying robotics, Oh my word, he is studying engineering, how in the world does he do that, Oh my word he is inventing something, he is a master's student, so you see the ladder you *want* to climb, you see that you *want* to have honours, you see that you *want* your master's, you see you *want* this and you want that, you *want* to study, you *want* to be someone. [our emphasis]

This statement is highly significant because it illustrates in quite literal terms how Roshni started to view the world, as she envisaged the 'ladder' and the possibilities it offered for choosing a future very different from life in the township. This statement of her desires ('wants') contrasts sharply with her reaction (in the same interview) to the tedium, entrapment and subservience entailed in her part-time job as a cashier, which enabled clarity about the subject position she did not want to occupy: 'You tell yourself, *I don't want* to earn this, *I don't want* to be treated like this.' A number of participants spoke in similar terms about how university life helped them to project a positive future and to construct desires, whereas working-class township life existed only in the present characterized by lack and negativity (le Roux 2013).

Roshni's declaration that 'I want to be someone' is telling. The pronoun 'someone' connotes a desire to be special, resonating with her earlier statement that, 'I want to do something with my life.' However, it also signals Roshni's lack of sense of direction, what Sfard and Prusak (2005: 18) call a 'designated identity', which they argue, gives 'direction to one's actions and influences one's deeds to a great extent'. Although Roshni always desired upward mobility and an escape from her working-class life, her goals for the future remained ephemeral. When asked (eight months into her first year) about why she chose organizational psychology as a subject, she replied:

> I can't say for sure but human resource management is something I might look into. This is going to sound really cheesy but HR [Human Resources], you in an office right? You in your own office, and I've always like when I grew up I always played this game, 'housey-housey' where I'm sitting in an office

and I have my bag and stuff, ... so I thought OK maybe that would be a nice profession for me man, because while I grew up I always like imagined my life in an office.

While it seems that Roshni was being somewhat self-ironic, as evident in the comment about being 'cheesy', it is significant that she cast her future in terms of a physical, materialist and girlish image of herself (playing 'housey-housey' with a 'bag') rather than by drawing on an image of what she might do, how the knowledge from organizational psychology had influenced her thinking or how she could make meaning from her experiences. Her fairly nebulous notion of her future was also reflected in her attempt to solicit confirmation from the interviewer that human resources work takes place in an office. While Roshni felt that her horizons had broadened, the ways in which media images, together with her social positioning as a working-class woman influenced and circumscribed her notion of the future are evident in this statement. This statement is also interesting because in the same interview, Roshni signalled that she chose courses that foregrounded gender issues 'because in my religion males are practically dominant'.

Roshni's attempt to create coherence from the disparate subject positions made available by home and the academy was evident in a more concrete notion of a possible future when she decided to major in Arabic in her second year:

Because Arabic is what I'm supposed to know as a Muslim, I'm supposed to know it ... and that's personal and it's also beneficial because I can go to the United Arab Emirates or any Arabic country. As a woman, you don't have anything, but if you have knowledge you can go far because you have Arabic and in that country you can do teaching.

Here she endeavoured to conjure a future where it would be possible to embrace her faith, to conform to the conventional subject position of Muslim woman, to achieve upward mobility and to escape geographical and class boundaries. In her everyday life at university, she situated herself by engaging in a lively social life that existed exclusively in the day time, using the University campus as a base. She would leave the campus between lectures to frequent a nearby cinema or malls with friends, but always wore her scarf and partook in none of the activities that would be considered sinful for a Muslim woman: 'I don't party, I don't dance.' Within her home and community environment, she maintained a respectful, self-effacing silence: 'You respect their opinion when you have your own ... you never show what you have.'

'Suffer in silence'

The extent to which Roshni managed to maintain a 'situated' (Renn 2004: 220) sense of self became apparent in a crisis she experienced towards the end of her first year which she narrated in her second interview. She had to take over the household's domestic duties and care for her sister while her mother went on pilgrimage to Mecca. During that time, her sister ran away and Roshni exhausted her budget, which forced her to take on further employment after her father refused to help her, saying 'I don't have, I don't want to give, it's up to you, you are your mommy's child.' Roshni narrated her acceptance of her fate thus: 'So every day after campus I would go home, cook, clean ... make sure everybody is happy. ... I need to pray. ... I need to make sure that ... I need to plan for her [mother's] return. ... It was up to me to make sure we had funding ... I have to make sure.'

Despite the fact that Roshni repeatedly emphasized that she felt at home on campus, that she had many friends and that coming to university was a 'stress reliever' she dealt with these additional burdens in silence, telling no one on campus:

> You come to campus you fake it, you don't show anyone your problems, you smile, you don't cry, you make sure that you strong, no one sees you cry ... because you are firm, because you are a woman you can take it ... that's what you supposed to ... say that over and over to yourself to motivate to go on the next day ... you are your mommy's child, you are a woman ... you are a rock, you are supposed to handle this ... you are your mommy's child.

In both of the above statements, Roshni foregrounded the roles and duties that were expected of her. In this respect, Thomas and Quinn (2007: 86) describe 'how family dispositions of to "do" rather than to "be" are highly formative in the educational trajectory' of the first-generation participants in their study who often went against their own desires and interests in order to preserve family financial security and harmony.

In Roshni's second statement, the switch to the second person 'you', has the effect of creating distance. She appropriated her father's dismissal and turned it into a motivating mantra: 'you are your mommy's child'. She also recontextualized anti-apartheid feminist struggle discourse 'woman you are a rock', thereby simultaneously critically analysing, confirming her silent entrapment and preserving face by 'faking it'.

The practice of maintaining a semblance of coping and respectability, and not soliciting help when in trouble (particularly in relation to finances) is commonplace in our data and is a feature of working-class life documented by a number of researchers (see Walkerdine 2003; Soudien 2007; Firfirey and Carolissen 2010). Roshni adopted a similarly intellectual critique, yet a passive stance in relation to the young man she started dating in her second year. She spoke of the 'stereotypical' expectation that she would 'need' a boyfriend: 'Now everybody, ... [from]my cultural background would be like, "oh my gosh, soon you will be twenty-one and then what is going to happen to you?"' While Roshni seemed to construct the relationship as an additional burden which entailed fulfilling many social engagements and being on call for her partner's constant text messages, her parents encouraged the relationship. She spoke of how 'you feel pressured' by the community and family: 'I assumed Mommy and Daddy like him so much, it's best that this go on like this, suffer in silence, some would say.' Despite these considerable challenges, she passed her courses and maintained a narrative of progress, asserting in her second year that 'I am more open to be who I am, instead of conforming. I stand on my own two feet. I know who I want to be and where I want to be and I have goals.'

'I don't have proper direction'

Roshni became mentally ill early in her third year and was advised by a doctor to withdraw from her studies. In the interview conducted after she withdrew from university, she attributed her crisis to the difficulty of trying to juggle three lifestyles – her home life, her student life and her relationship with her boyfriend. The stress seemed to take its toll particularly because of the substantially increased academic workload and conceptual demands in the third year when she was no longer the recipient of support from the extended degree programme. In her third interview, Roshni spoke for the first time about feeling ambivalent about her identity as a student and about her future direction: 'The comfort in first year was definitely felt and in second year it was there ... third year, it was more about finding the right shoes to step into, finding the direction where you want to study in, so being comfortable doesn't necessarily mean you know where you're going, why you are studying there, so it's a bit of both.'

Roshni lamented her lack of a career path in her third year of university and the very real possibility that she could end up unemployable: 'Basically I was stumbling ... as to which direction I wanted to study because now you rethinking everything ... where am I going to fit in, am I going to have a sustainable job or a sustainable income?' Whereas she had previously viewed academia as opening up 'horizons' and enabling mobility, she now described her sense of stasis. 'I'm going nowhere slowly and I don't have proper direction.' Ironically, the statistics presented in a community development course made her aware of the reality of unemployment that university graduates face. In her third interview, Roshni emphasized her determination to return to her studies and characterized her withdrawal as temporary. She still maintained her desire to be an autonomous individual with free choice, 'to be my own person', and also drew heavily on social science discourse to evaluate her sense of self. She spoke of the project of 'remodelling' herself and of how she needed this time out of studying for 'seeing the patterns' she had been following and for 'personal growth'. The University appeared to provide her with a readily available discourse to analyse her situation and construct a narrative of reinvention, but not with the tools to chart a possible way forward. Roshni, who so readily made use of available academic resources in her first two years of study, chose not to ask for help or advice within the institution during her crisis.

Conclusion

The data illustrate a set of experiences that would otherwise remain invisible. An intersection of gendered, class and cultural expectations had a considerable effect on Roshni's behaviour, experiences and decisions. She succeeded in gaining entry to university through her own agency and passed her first two years despite considerable structural obstacles. She was an engaged, critical, hard-working motivated student with high levels of commitment to her studies. In this respect, her case does not fit the decontextualized indicators outlined by many large-scale analyses of student dropout. Roshni's failure is not an individual failure to work hard or be motivated, but rather illustrates the ways in which the discourses and notions of appropriate subjectivity of home and the institution worked both to 'enable' and 'constrain' her path (Thomson 2009:154).

Roshni attempted to reconcile difference, to create a narrative of a coherent sense of a future self in which she could maintain allegiance to her religious faith and her home identity as a dutiful Muslim woman, as well as to fulfil her desire for upward mobility, vocal social engagement and respite from the demands and constraints of working-class life. To achieve this, she had to temper her voice and create situated identities. She conformed to the expectations of womanhood in her home and also embraced the discourse of empowerment of women offered by academic and popular discourse. She drew on poststructuralist conceptions of multiple identities, as well as popular, neo-liberal notions of free choice and self-realization to rationalize the ways in which she situated her identities in both places. The longitudinal perspective enables one to see the emotion-work and preservation of face involved in negotiating subjectivity and a sense of belonging. Many of our participants adapted to the situated sense of self entailed in conforming to the subjectivity required at home and within the institution (see Chapter 4). However, the combined pressures on Roshni of doing domestic work at home, travelling long distances, maintaining a demanding relationship and managing an increased academic workload made the situation unsustainable.

Walkerdine (2003) points out the importance of not pathologizing (and we would add romanticizing) the discourses of working-class families. The challenge is to acknowledge that home discourses continue to play a huge role beyond students' initial transition from school to university, to understand their significance and to support students appropriately. The longitudinal perspective allows us to see that in trying to make sense of their experiences, students negotiate multiple transitions. And yet, higher education institutions tend to put their energies into ensuring that students are successful in their first year with the assumption that they will cope thereafter.

Reay, David and Ball (2005: 85) write powerfully about how students from middle-class backgrounds in their study live out pathways that are anticipated beforehand and are strongly supported by their families and schools, whereas the pathways of students from working-class backgrounds to higher education often involved 'a process of finding out what you cannot have, what is not open for negotiation and then looking at the few options left, or a process of self-exclusion'. (See Bangeni's analysis in Chapter 6 of how this issue of constrained choice unfolds in the postgraduate space.) The longitudinal perspective shows how the discourses of the social sciences provided Roshni with new ways of conceptualizing and critically evaluating, but offered no concrete guidance as to possible pathways. Roshni's ability to look beyond the instrumental, to choose courses in order to explore a sense of self is a commendable, 'prized objective of the higher education process' (Soudien 2008: 663). Nevertheless, it leaves her stranded, 'going nowhere slowly' in terms of developing possible future trajectories.

The data also highlight the temporal and spatial nature of agency. Although Roshni appeared to feel comfortable within the institution, her silence and maintenance of a facade in the time of her crisis tell a different story. In admitting Roshni, despite her poor school-leaving results, the institution recognized her considerable agency. However, the failure to create an adequate, sustained support environment left her with very few resources to harness and sustain that potential to ensure that she could continue to be agentic and to succeed.

References

Adams, G. R., Berzonsky, M. D. and Keating, L. (2006), 'Psychosocial Resources in First-Year University Students: The Role of Identity Processes and Social Relationships', *Journal of Youth and Adolescence*, 35(1): 81–91.

Bangeni, B. and Kapp, R. (2005), 'Identities in Transition: Shifting Conceptions of Home by Black South African University Students', *African Studies Review*, 48(3): 1–19.

Boughey, C. 2009, *A Meta-Analysis of Teaching and Learning at Five Research-Intensive South African Universities*, Higher Education Quality Committee Report, https://www.ru.ac.za/media/rhodesuniversity/content/politics/documents/, accessed 14 April 2016.

Breier, M. (2010), 'From "Financial Considerations" to "Poverty": Towards a Reconceptualisation of the Role of Finances in Higher Education Student Drop-Out', *Journal of Higher Education*, 60(6): 657–70.

Case, J. M. (2013), *Researching Student Learning in Higher Education: A Social Realist Approach*, London and New York: Routledge.

Christie, H., Tett, L., Cree, V., Hounsell, J. and McCune, V. (2008), '"A Real Rollercoaster of Confidence and Emotions": Learning to be a University Student', *Studies in Higher Education*, 33(5): 567–81.

Christie, P. (2008), *Changing Schools in South Africa: Opening the Doors of Learning*, Johannesburg: Heinemann.

Fairclough, N. (1995), *Discourse Analysis*, London and New York: Longman.

Firfirey, N. and Carolissen, R. (2010), '"I Keep Myself Clean... At Least When You See Me, You Don't Know I Am Poor": Student Experiences of Poverty in South African Higher Education', *South African Journal of Higher Education*, 24(6): 987–1002.

Fraser, N. (2013), *Fortunes of Feminism: From State-Managed Capitalism to Neoliberal Crisis*, London: Verso.

Haggis, T. (2003), 'Constructing Images of Ourselves? A Critical Investigation into "Approaches to Learning" Research in Higher Education', *British Educational Research Journal*, 29(1): 89–104.

Haggis, T. (2004), 'Meaning, Identity and "Motivation": Expanding what Matters in Understanding Learning in Higher Education', *Studies in Higher Education*, 29(3): 335–52.

Herrington, A. and Curtis, M. (2000), *Persons in Process: Four Stories of Writing and Personal Development in College*, Urbana, IL: National Council of Teachers of English.

Janse van Rensburg, V. and Kapp, R. (2014), '"So I have to be Positive, no Matter how Difficult it Is": A Longitudinal Case Study of a First-Generation Occupational Therapy Student', *Journal of Occupational Therapy*, 44(3): 29–33.

Kapp, R. and Bangeni, B. (2009), 'Positioning (in) the Discipline: Undergraduate Students' Negotiations of Disciplinary Disciplines', *Teaching in Higher Education*, 14(6): 589–98.

le Roux, K. (2013), '"I Just Make Sure that I Go for It": A Mathematics Student's Transition to and through University', in M. Berger, K. Brodie, V. Frith, K. le Roux (eds), *Proceedings of the Seventh International Mathematics Education and Society Conference Cape Town*: ME7: 360–9.

Leibowitz, B., van der Merwe, A. and van Schalkwyk, S. eds (2012), *Focus on First-Year Success*, Stellenbosch: Sun Press.

Lubben, F., Davidowitz, B., Buffler, A., Allie, S. and Scott, I. (2010), 'Factors Influencing Access Students' Persistence in an Undergraduate Science Programme: A South African Case Study', *International Journal of Educational Development*, 30: 351–58.

Lucey, H., Melody, J. and Walkerdine, V. (2003), 'Uneasy Hybrids: Psychosocial Aspects of Becoming Educationally Successful for Working-Class Young Women', *Gender and Education*, 15(3): 285–99.

Mann, S.J. (2008), *Study, Power and the University,* Maidenhead, Society for Research into Higher Education: Open University Press.

McCormick, K. (2005), 'Working with Webs: Narrative Constructions of Forced Removal and Relocation', in M. Baynam and A. De Fina (eds), *Dislocations/Relocations: Narratives of Displacement*, 144–69, Manchester and Northampton: St Jerome.

Norton, B. (1997), 'Language, Identity and the Ownership of English', *TESOL Quarterly*, 31(3): 409–30.

Pym, J. and Kapp, R. (2013), 'Harnessing Agency: Towards a Learning Model for Undergraduate Students', *Studies in Higher Education*, 38(2): 272–84.

Read, B., Archer, L. and Leathwood, C. (2003), 'Challenging Cultures? Student Conceptions of "Belonging" and "Isolation" at a post-1992 University', *Studies in Higher Education*, 28(3): 261–77.

Reay, D. (2001), 'Finding or Losing Yourself?: Working-Class Relationships to Education', *Journal of Education Policy*, 16(4): 333–46.

Reay, D., Crozier, G. and Clayton, J. (2010), '"Fitting In" or "Standing Out": Working-Class Students in UK Higher Education', *British Educational Research Journal*, 36(1): 107–24.

Reay, D., David, M. and Ball, S. (2005), *Degrees of Choice. Social Class, Race and Gender in Higher Education*, Stoke-on-Trent: Trentham Books.

Renn, K. (2004), *Mixed Race Students in College: The Ecology of Race, Identity and Community on Campus*, Albany: State University of New York.

Sfard, A. and Prusak, A. (2005), 'Telling Identities: In Search of an Analytic Tool for Investigating Learning as a Culturally Shaped Activity', *Educational Researcher*, 34(4): 14–22.

Soudien, C. (2007), 'The "A" Factor: Coming to Terms with the Question of Legacy in South African Education', *International Journal of Educational Development*, 27: 182–93.

Soudien, C. (2008), 'The Intersection of Race and Class in the South African University: Student Experiences', *South African Journal of Higher Education*, 22(3): 662–78.

Thesen, L. and van Pletzen, E. eds (2006), *Academic Literacy and the Languages of Change*, London: Continuum.

Thomas, L. and Quinn, J. (2007), *First-Generation Entry into Higher Education*, Berkshire: Society for Research into Higher Education and Open University Press.

Thomson, R. and Holland, J. (2003), 'Hindsight, Foresight and Insight: the Challenges of Longitudinal Qualitative Research', *International Journal of Social Research Methodology*, 6(3): 233–44.

Thomson, R. (2009), *Unfolding Lives: Youth, Gender and Change*, Bristol: The Policy Press.

Thornton, R. (1988), 'Culture: A Contemporary Definition', in E. Boonzaier and J. Sharp (eds), *South African Keywords: The Uses and Abuses of Political Concepts*, 18–29, Cape Town: David Philip.

Tinto, V. (2006–7), 'Research and Practice of Student Retention: What Next?', *Journal of College Students Retention*, 8(1): 1–19.

Walkerdine, V. (2003), 'Reclassifying Upward Mobility: Femininity and the Neo-Liberal Subject', *Gender and Education*, 15(3): 237–48.

4

Humanities Students' Negotiation of Language, Literacy and Identity

Rochelle Kapp and Bongi Bangeni

Introduction

In this chapter, we analyse shifts in language and literacy attitudes and practices and in constructions of self, of students in the social sciences who participated in a longitudinal study over the course of their undergraduate years. We focus on twenty participants who were first registered for undergraduate social science degrees in the Faculty of Humanities in 2002. They were (with the exception of one student) the first in their family, sometimes the first in their community, to attend university. Sixteen of the students identified English as an additional language and their home languages included Xhosa, Zulu, Sotho, Tswana, Swati, Afrikaans and Chinese. Four of the coloured students identified English as the main medium of communication in their homes, but they spoke a mixture of English and Afrikaans as is common in many coloured neighbourhoods on the Cape Flats.

We draw on poststructuralist theories which view language and literacy attitudes and practices in multilingual contexts as being embedded in larger social, political, economic and historical discourses (see the Introduction; Gee 1990; Pavlenko and Blackledge eds 2004; Norton and McKinney 2010). We show how students used their linguistic resources and social science discourses to process, rationalize and neutralize their own ambivalence as they attempted to reconcile conflicting home and institutional ways of using language and ways of identifying. We illustrate how they began their undergraduate journeys trying to maintain a notion of a single identity, but over time adopted a notion of 'situational identity', foregrounding 'different identities at different times' (Renn 2004: 220). Language was a primary tool for their positioning. Over time, they became adept at and self-conscious and less conflicted about shifting identity and languages in order to fit into particular contexts.

Methodology

We use qualitative longitudinal analysis to analyse our participants' shifts in language and literacy attitudes and practices. Thomson (2009: 150) describes interviews as 'snapshots of particular times and places', and argues that whereas single interviews tend to freeze participants' images in particular times and places, multiple interviews enable snapshots 'to be articulated, providing a timescape' that enables one to see how individuals reflect and position themselves.

Our twenty research participants were all registered for an academic literacy course designed for students considered academically at risk on the basis of their performance on an entrance test and their school-leaving results. They were taught by us in two separate classes in their first semester in 2002. They volunteered to participate in our study in March of that year and all remained active participants from 2002 to the end of 2004. We held at least four individual interviews with each student, as well as two focus group sessions and two informal gatherings. Our interviews were semi-structured, in order to facilitate comparisons within each student's corpus over time, as well as comparisons across the group. The questions covered the areas of students' literacy and language development, their attitudes to language and academic literacy, their relationships to their chosen disciplines, their experiences of institutional culture and their relationships to home. However, we always also asked individual questions based on prior interviews and on our analyses of the students' essays. When the students were in their first year, our interviews were relatively short, probably influenced by our position as their lecturers at that time. Over time, the interviews became longer as participants spoke more, often reflecting on past interviews. A number of interviewees commented that they valued the opportunity to discuss their experiences and the participants discussed issues raised within the interviews informally among themselves.

In addition to the interview data, we collected biographical questionnaires, three essays written for our literacy course and essays from the students' other courses (collected each semester and chosen by the students). We kept journals which documented our classroom observations, informal interactions and conversations with the participants and between ourselves. Towards the end of their undergraduate studies, we asked our participants to write reflection papers on their undergraduate writing. We made our portfolios of their undergraduate writing available to them and we asked them to draw on this corpus to analyse the changes in their writing and ideas over three years. We asked about their relationship to their disciplines. We also asked about their writing strategies and tried to access their notions of good writing. We compared these sources of information with what they said in their interviews at different stages.

We used Clark and Ivanič's (1997) theory on writer identity to trace the participants' shifting representation of self – the conflict between what Clark and Ivanič (1997: 134) refer to as 'their former selves and their becoming-selves'. Clark and Ivanič (1997: 136–52) identify three (often overlapping) aspects of writer identity, which they describe as the 'discoursal' self, the 'authorial' self and the 'autobiographical' self. The 'discoursal' self refers to a writer's awareness of the discipline in which they are writing. The 'authorial' self refers to the writer's authority, the extent to which writers take ownership of their writing and the 'autobiographical' self refers to the extent to which writers draw on their personal histories.

Tracing patterns, exceptions, silences and contradictions has been essential to our data analysis. We have used the different sets of data to try to distinguish 'between how people think they ought to behave, how they say they behave, and how they are observed to behave' (le Page and Tabouret-Keller, 1985: 207). In this way we have been able to trace their shifts in language and literacy practices as they position and re-position themselves in relation to institutional discourses and home over the course of their undergraduate years.

Negotiating new discourses

From the moment of entry into the institution, the students in our study felt themselves marked as different. For example, Andrew, a coloured, Afrikaans-speaker was verbally abused on his first day on the campus when he asked a white man the time. This left him wary of speaking to white people. Students were also silenced by the level and speed of the English spoken in class, and by early experiences of being judged as second-language speakers and consequently stigmatized. For example, two students spoke of being accused of not doing their own work because they had produced fluent essays.

Our data also reflect the students' shock at the dominance of the English language in the University's social environment – in the words of Noluthando, a Tswana-speaker, 'It's white and you don't get to speak your language very easily here.' Woolard (as cited in Pavlenko and Blackledge 2002: 121–2) argues that 'ideologies of language are rarely about language alone, but are socially situated and tied to questions of identity and power in societies'. It was evident that at this stage, in their first semester, English, power and material resources were conflated with whiteness in the students' minds. Because the majority of our participants grew up in geographically separate townships, they would have had minimal contact with white people, and then only in situations where whites were in control of the exchange both linguistically and materially. This conflation of English, power and material resources with whiteness is therefore an unsurprising reflection of an undifferentiated sense of otherness that characterized the students' first encounters with a new, essentially foreign culture. The only exception to this was Yandisa, who had attended an exclusive private school and hardly spoke his home language in the everyday university environment.

For the participants from working-class township schools, the transition represented their first encounter with black people from middle-class backgrounds. When they first arrived, the students were surprised to discover that some African language speakers were using English in the informal social environment. Vuyani, a Xhosa-speaker, spoke of his fear of speaking English 'in a large crowd of whites and those blacks called "coconuts".'[1] Noluthando expressed anger about how 'white some black people are'. She narrated an incident where she and a friend were rebuked by a Xhosa-speaker for laughing 'on top of our voices, saying, "Stop being so black."' In their first interviews, the students spoke of how they felt intimidated when using English among African language speakers from English-medium schools. For these students, black students from relatively elite English-medium schools also came to be associated with whiteness (see de Kadt, 2005, for a similar observation).

The data cited above illustrate the emotionally charged nature of the participants' early experiences in the institution. Norton (2000: 5) argues that it is through language that 'a person negotiates a sense of self within and across different sites at different points in time, and it is through language that a person gains access to – or is denied access to powerful social networks'. Wenger (1998: 149) describes identity formation as 'negotiated experience': 'We define who we are by the ways we experience our selves through participation as well as by the ways we and others reify our selves.' Unsurprisingly, the students reacted defensively to these hostile verbal encounters which often had the effect of silencing them in class. Both in their early interviews and in their first essay on 'Language and Identity', they expressed a strong need to retain organic connections to home and home identities. Identity was generally articulated in terms of a singular, consistent ethnicity/race threatened by possible contamination and loss/'forgetting' in the white environment of the University. Language and ethnicity were often conflated. The students' mission was articulated as an instrumental need to succeed at university in order to return to contribute to the development of their communities.

Alongside their expressions of alienation from the institution which often included feeling alienated from fellow black students, our participants expressed a strong investment in the University, (describing it as an 'excellent' institution), in English as the medium of instruction and in the discourses of the institution and the 'new' South Africa about the importance of embracing diversity. For example, Sisanda, a working-class student who had attended a middle-class, English-medium school, wrote of her strong Zulu identity in an early essay on 'Language and Identity': '[The Zulu language] tells the other person who I really am, no matter where I am or what I do I still remain *umZulu* as I want to be recognized as that only and nothing else.' However, in an interview with Bongi a few weeks later, Sisanda spoke of how she had been influenced by a classroom discussion of Thornton's (1988) notion of a common culture which enabled her to see culture from a broader perspective than tradition and ethnicity. She intended to take this new perspective back to her community. She spoke of her perception of the environment as being 'kind of a free environment, people are more friendly; it is flexible, moving and active'. She said that she felt that she fitted in: 'They like share the same values as I do, to learn, most of the time.' Nevertheless, these assertions did not seem to temper her continued subsequent assertions of Zuluness nor ameliorate her feelings of alienation from faculty and peers from class and ethnic backgrounds other than her own.

The multiple subjectivities apparent in the students' early essays and interviews are evidence of their struggles to find a place to be as they negotiated their transition. While this may appear to be an individual battle, their consciousness mirrors a new South African political ideology that is drawn from models of multiculturalism within global capitalism. This ideology suggests that apartheid's policy of ethnic division and related linguistic and geographic separateness and difference should be overcome in the interests of nation-building and connecting to global markets, but also that separate cultures should be preserved and accepted under the banner of one rainbow nation (see Thornton's 1988 critique of multiculturalism).

Our participants experienced daily reminders at the University of their own financial and linguistic disadvantage. Both their academic and social environments were foreign and they started to describe the limitations of their own backgrounds in terms of access to resources and the concomitant 'cultural capital' (Bourdieu 1991: 230) offered by the institution. Nevertheless, as is evident in the quotations given above, they saw the institutional environment as a microcosm of the transition of the broader society and retained the belief, reflected also in surveys among black working-class South Africans (see Seekings and Nattrass 2005), that they and the institution were engaged in a process of transformation.

Another feature of the data presented above is the students' nascent critique of their own upbringing and prior notions of culture as fixed and static. For many of the participants, the notion that social and cultural boundaries are constructed and can be transgressed was liberating. Both in class and in his first interview, Garth, a coloured student revealed that he had been taught to despise black [African] people by his white grandmother who had raised him in his rural village: 'I remember that my grandmother used to say blacks stink, they never wash and you are not supposed to eat [food that comes] out of their hands.' In an early essay, Garth wrote: 'Coming to [the University] represented a lot of things that I was socialized against .... I am proud to say that ... I can freely cross the boundaries of another culture and find commonness within that culture with which I can communicate .... Culture does indeed change, because it is not organic but social, which means it can be unlearned and redefined.'

The participants' struggles with identity are visible in their early writing, albeit in emphatic or conversational tones. However, their 'autobiographical' and 'authorial' selves very quickly receded in response to negative feedback in their early essays about what is considered appropriate in academic discourse in terms of values and register. Fear of failure loomed large. They decided that in order to pass, they needed to set aside their primary discourses in favour of an uncritical mimicking of the discourse. In Sizwe's words, 'I simply reproduced what the tutors taught me about the subject, my writing was largely shaped by tutors' ideas, mine were scarce.'

Our participants learnt that academic discourse is circumscribed, that they had to argue within the confines of a limited range of subject positions and that their arguments had to be modulated. For example, Belinda learnt that the 'feminist tone' she had developed in the Gender Studies courses was considered inappropriate by a lecturer in the Department of Classics. The participants also learnt that personal experience is valued in some disciplines and not others. For example, Andrew's first reflective essay for his Social Work course was highly confessional, as he attempted to use the theory to analyse deeply traumatic episodes in his own life. The feedback he received suggested that he should learn to use a 'broader vocabulary' to express emotions and that he should consider exploring some of the issues he had raised in his essay, in a therapeutic relationship. By the time he wrote his Psychology essay, he used the first person just once (as a structuring device) and wrote of 'misconceptions in the community out there'.

As the participants spent more time at university, they started to separate out their notions of who they were and what they valued, from academic discourse. They were writing to achieve personal mobility and contribute to their communities. This is reflected in Babalwa's impatience with the academy: 'You keep on debating [in philosophy] because there's no answer.... They [academics] say they don't look at the outcome, but in a way you are because you are using education as a means to go.' The students' uncritical, and in some cases, instrumental attitudes to their academic writing contrasted starkly with their excitement (described in interviews) about the lively debates with black, mainly working-class peers outside of the classroom environment.

Negotiating home

As a number of theorists have shown (Read, Archer and Leathwood 2003; de Kadt, 2005; Walker 2006), the process of acquiring increasing access to and fluency in a range of institutional discourses of the academy also entails loss of connection to home. Evidence of the participants' growing alienation from home was present from their second interviews in the second semester of their first year. In some cases, their increasing distance from home was the result of their growing critique of home discourses, their increasing use of English and shifts in their tastes. For example, Vuyani, who in his first interview described African language speakers from former white schools as 'coconuts' was shocked to find himself labelled in this way when he returned home for the vacation: 'Back home they now say I am a coconut, they have changed their attitude towards me.' This was because he had substituted *Umhlobo Wenene*, an African language radio station, for the more urban, multilingual Metro FM, 'and as you know it's English'. Many participants spoke of how their everyday conversation and perspectives had been influenced by the discourse of the academy: Noluthando said: '[My friends] think I'm not on their level anymore and some of them think I'm snobbish because now I'm out of the circle, I can look at them and I can now analyse them.'

The participants often cast their home culture in terms of boredom, stasis and confinement (because of violence) in contrast to the University environment which offered choice, freedom and a lively and safe social environment. For Sizwe, the University represented the future, where 'we talk about positive things', whereas in the township, many of his friends were unemployed and/or had become gangsters and talk was confined to 'things that affect you negatively like girls and drink'.

The participants' growing sense of distance from home was exacerbated by the fact that their efforts to reconnect within their neighbourhood communities were often rejected.[2] Like Vuyani, they found that they were labelled 'elitist' and/ or 'white' by virtue of their enrolment at the University. Andrew's description was typical: 'People stigmatize and label you ... they label you that you think you are better than them.' The University became a refuge from the township, but also remained a site of alienation. In Andrew's words, 'When I'm here, I want to be there and when I'm there, I want to be here.' Bhabha's (1994: 44) notion of the postcolonial subject as *unhomed* captures the sense of occupying an ambivalent space, of 'being in two places at once' that was evident in our data. As in Walker's (2006) research our data are replete with metaphors of travelling as the students tried (and failed) to reconcile conflicting pulls on their sense of self into a single space.

Straddling multiple discourses

Despite all the evidence to the contrary, when we asked the participants (towards the end of their first year) whether they believed they had changed, the stock response was to assert that they had not changed, but they had 'grown'. Newkirk (as cited in Herrington and Curtis 2000: 359) writes that students entering university, '... have a psychological need to view their lives as progressive narratives. ... The literature of self-direction suggests that this future is claimable if there is sufficient personal will. It protects against fatalism, helplessness, and determinism. It transforms that which is disagreeable and painful into strategically placed obstacles that both teach and strengthen.' This discourse of achievement through personal effort and motivation is also evident in the public media in post-apartheid South Africa. Interestingly, American talk show hosts Oprah and Dr Phil were as strong a point of reference for our participants as Nelson Mandela.

The students in our study also seemed to derive a sense of direction from their membership of Christian organizations (see Chapter 5). Most belonged to an evangelical Christian organization, 'His People', which has a 'cell' in many of the student residences. Membership extends beyond conventional racial and ethnic boundaries. The sermons deliver strong messages about agency, self-direction and upward mobility, and the organization seemed to provide a sense of community and belonging in the face of loneliness in their first year. For a student like Sisanda, religious affiliation was also in part a response to the death of seven people in her family during her first year and the fact that she was unable to attend some of the funerals because of financial constraints. The 'His People' church organization performed many of the traditional cultural rituals that would conventionally be provided within an extended family.

All of the participants passed their first year of study. From the students' second year onwards, there were noticeable differences in their confidence levels, their choices of lifestyle habits and of dress codes, as they attempted to fit into the environment.[3] Many had part-time jobs and were able to acquire social goods such as cell phones, computers and brand name clothing, and concomitant social habits which would have been inaccessible previously. S'busiso's comment is typical:

> When I came here first I didn't worry about getting the clothes, like maybe the Levis, jeans and maybe e-h-h, Soviet, now I wear Soviet. You know, but something like this, gents, like they never said change your outlook but they influence. Like these guys, my friends, they influence. It changed my thinking because but now I think about what guys go for (S'busiso, interview 5).

In their senior years, the participants started using English more in their everyday social environments and became more confident and outspoken. Although they still mainly mixed with other black students, this now included students from a range of ethnic and class backgrounds and there seemed to be a slow, but visible re-alignment as distinctions between 'whiteness' and 'Englishness' were made.

By his second year, Vuyani said: 'I think it's crazy this year most of the time I am using English ... even with fellow Xhosa-speakers this year, *ja* [Afrikaans for 'yes'].'

Although the participants used English more, they also deliberately code-mixed and switched between English, Afrikaans and Xhosa, interspersing their talk with Kwaito-derived slang. Kwaito is a local music form which Nuttall (2004: 433) describes as 'a potent blend of city and township sound that emerged after the democratic transition in 1994, mixing up the protest dancing and chanting known as *toyi-toyi* with slow-motion house, local pop ("bubblegum") and a dash of hip-hop'. In Sizwe's words, 'People use it as some sort of in-between language. People are using English but a certain style of English, they are sort of Africanizing it.' Interestingly, Andrew described the code as '*Backstage* language'. *Backstage* is a South African television soap opera which makes use of extensive code-mixing and switching and cultivates the notion that cross-cultural mixing is trendy and desirable, a notion that has become commonplace in the media since 1990. Nuttall (2004) has similarly described emerging hybrid cultures among black South Africans as they signal township and city identities. It seems that this shared code allowed the participants to feel comfortable using English because they were also signalling their Africanness. It also enabled them to feel comfortable connecting across both conventional ethnic/language barriers and perceived class differences.

Negotiating new spaces

Over time, the discourse of the academy came to seem natural and commonplace to the students (Althusser 1971). In their senior years, their reflection papers and interviews revealed an intellectual 'investment' (Thomson 2009: 60) in their academic disciplines which was certainly not evident earlier. In an unsolicited preamble to his reflection paper in his final year, Andrew wrote:

> I am in an academic discourse where it is required of one to act/or to be the discipline, this is what I have come to realize over these past years. It is one thing to be in the discipline and another 'to be' the discipline. And each day I find more and more evidence within myself that I am at that point where I moved from being in my discipline, to where I am my discipline. This is evident in my speech, thought, and ways I approach certain things, whether in an academic or formal setting.

Andrew's analysis, as well as the language in which it is expressed, reflected a growing awareness that he was not only learning the skills and content of the discipline, but was also entering into new subjectivities (see Johns 1997; Herrington and Curtis 2000).

Nevertheless, the students' paths were by no means straightforward and linear. In her first year, Babalwa had expressed impatience with critical debate and the academy, 'because there's no answer'. In her second year, the desire for clear answers and truth was still evident. This is made explicit in a review of a book (for Political Studies) about Idi Amin. Babalwa demonstrated critical awareness by drawing attention to the fact that the writer's account was based on anonymous personal experiences. She explained that the sources were anonymous because the people feared for the lives of their families in Uganda. However, she concluded that the information provided was 'reliable' and 'true' purely because it was written during the time that Amin was in power. In the review itself she treated the material as 'factual' and showed no meta-awareness about the authorial narrative. In her final year reflection paper, she wrote:

> I have grown to realize that what I have been taught about God, females and males, the world is not necessarily what it is and that what I believe in is not necessarily true or wrong – not everything is black and white. ... I have learnt that human beings are not passive; they question things, its roots and how things become universally accepted (the norm).

This statement suggests a significant shift. However, in their interviews in their final year, while Babalwa and other female students spoke of learning to question gender identity through academic discourse, they also spoke of how they had to resume passive, gendered roles when they went home. In a focus group interview in his second year, Andrew used the discourse of one of his first-year social science courses to speak of 'alternating [identity] back and forward all the time'. The students spoke openly to each other and to us about the situated nature of their identities as they switched within and between contexts as they negotiated competing ideologies.

Renegotiating voice

By the end of the participants' final year, this process of careful negotiation of multiple subject positions seemed to play out in their writing identities. They had moved away from the reproduction that characterized their early writing, but there was very little sense of taking authorial ownership (Clark and Ivanič 1997). An example is Babalwa's final-year Political Studies essay in response to the question 'What were the crucial socio-political events in Rwanda which subsequently enabled an environment or realm that led to civil war in 1994?' The essay was well structured and researched. She contextualized the problem through careful detailing of historical factors and through the exploration of theories of political violence which look at socio-psychological factors. Unlike the second-year review of the Idi Amin book which showed no meta-awareness of authorial perspective, she identified opposing viewpoints and contrasted the views of two different writers on whether or not the ethnic differences served as a catalyst for the war. However, she relied heavily on the content and authority of secondary sources and tended to limit an engagement in critical analysis. She signalled her agreement with Mahmoud Mamdani's view (that the issue at stake was more related to the questions about what constitutes indigenization) by quoting him extensively. However, she did not actually show *how* this questions the ethnicity argument nor *why* this is a more valid argument.

Another feature of the senior writing of our participants is their use of excessively careful modality. In a Social Anthropology essay entitled 'Redefining Culture? Or dispensing with the term?', David wrote:

> Ngugi's (1993) main argument is that language is the sole carrier of people's culture and history and that if their language is systematically suppressed, so too will their culture, history and values be suppressed. This would be the case if language as an explicit form of communication determined what people know and how they could learn these things. As Bloch points out though, it is taken as a given fact 'that culture is thought and transmitted as a text through language (only), or that culture is ultimately "language like", consisting of linked linear propositions' (Bloch 1991:184).

David used careful modality: 'This would be the case if …' rather than the bold assertions of his early writing. When certainty is expressed, it is articulated via authority ('As Bloch points out; it is taken as a given fact'). The passive voice embedded within the statement ('it is taken') expresses the writer's caution and deference. Unlike Babalwa, David engaged beyond the level of content in his essays and analysed the 'chains of reasoning' and rhetorical moves made by the authors in quite sophisticated ways (Geisler 1994: 92). However, David's own 'authorial' presence is carefully marshalled through the voices of others, through comparisons of sources, using one source to critique another.

Most of the participants' senior essays engaged at the level of content. Although their 'authorial' voices were discernible, they were effaced, often appearing only towards the end. This deference seemed to play a large part in preventing them from achieving upper-second or first-class passes. For the most part, the primary feedback on their writing came in the form of ratings on marking grids developed by departments. Our participants tended to score average or above-average marks on content categories (relevance to the essay question, grasp of core concepts, comprehensiveness), as well as in the areas of coherence and planning. However, lecturers often critiqued the descriptive nature of the essays and the lack of critical or analytical engagement with theory. The participants were judged 'weak' in areas related to creativity, originality, critique and personal insights. In their reflections, they accounted for their failure to achieve higher marks in terms of their struggles with English, but although 'lack of precision in language' was often noted in the feedback, this seemed to be a fairly minor and sometimes non-existent category for assessment in most departments.

The participants' deference to authority reflected an insecurity that was also visible in their tendency to consult tutors rather than lecturers and in their hesitation to participate in class. Andrew, who wrote in his reflection paper 'I am the discipline', did not become 'at home' in the classroom despite his intellectual commitment to the values of the discipline and his increasing fluency in the discourses of the discipline. In his final-year interview Andrew spoke of his insecurity about participating in class. Drawing on the discourse of psychology, he names it 'the fear of the child':

> This soft guy if I may put it, is still there hey, it is still there, and I was trying to change and ... but it is still a barrier ... It becomes more visible also when I find myself in a position to say something .... You are eager to speak, it just takes me a moment and I will talk and in the same time it will come to my mind ... you are talking in front of people now and I would start shaking and words won't come out of my mouth and I'll have this expression on my face and I will turn red.

Conclusion

Our data show that the changes in the participants' language and literacy attitudes and practices over their undergraduate years were intricately related to social roles and boundaries. The students were always responding to multiple, and often conflicting, expectations of what constitutes appropriate subjectivity

(George 1996). By tracing the students' experiences over time and focusing on their experiences of university and home, we are able to illustrate that their relationships with and levels of attachment to both the University and home were characterized by fluidity, ambivalence and change. They both resisted and absorbed the discourses of the academy. Their relationship to their disciplines shifted from the instrumental, but they were still cautious and deferential in taking ownership. In order to be recognized as successful in the academy while retaining a connection to home discourses, they had to reposition themselves constantly. They were not at home in either place, but they became less conflicted about this situation over time, rationalizing the shifts they had to make as a function of living in a transitional time and in a diverse context.

Significantly, all twenty of the participants in this cohort graduated and were awarded first degrees, compared to 62 per cent of their (mainstream) cohort in the Faculty of Humanities. On the surface, these students were very successful in the eyes of the institution and of their families. However, the fact that they achieved lower-second marks rather than upper-seconds or firsts prevented them from being accepted into the honours degrees of their choice.

In more recent years, universities have become quite good at facilitating access for students from disadvantaged backgrounds and providing the necessary academic structures and mentorship programmes to help them at the first-year level. However, as also highlighted in chapters 2 and 3 in this book, there is still a lack of support at senior levels and a continuing underlying perception that students need to be provided with a quick-fix skills package so that universities may continue on the same path (Rose 1990). The transition of the students in our study enabled them to question and critique firmly held beliefs. However, institutional transformation remains mainly symbolic – facilitating access, renaming buildings and using multiple languages in institutional communication. The academy itself has a long way to go in terms of finding ways to enrich the social science debate by acknowledging students' 'autobiographical' voices and experiences, as well as engaging critically with the effects of its discourses (see Clark and Ivanič 1997; Thesen 1997; Janks 2010). Academia continues to perpetuate a form of colonization in that excellence which is measured by norms set by the metropole, even though the very different South African socio-political context renders this a fiction (see also the Introduction to this book). The social environments in which our participants grew up are of interest to and are researched by academics within the institution, but their students are not viewed as knowledgeable. The message to black, working-class students is that if they wish to succeed, they need to subscribe to the values and the circumscribed range of subject positions made available within discourses of the academy. Thus, the possibility of looking within the country to enrich the academy and the international debate is lost.

Notes

1 This is originally an American term used to refer to a black person who is perceived as acting white.
2 In the case of five of our participants whose families were starting to straddle class positions, this hostility was not evident.
3 One of the participants, Sisanda, stands out as an exception in our data because she maintained her strong allegiance to 'Zulu' culture and language and resisted consumerism on an intellectual level and in practice. For a detailed analysis, see Bangeni and Kapp (2005).

References

Althusser, L. (1971), *Lenin and Philosophy and Other Essays*, trans. Ben Brewster, London: New Left Books.

Bangeni, B. and Kapp, R. (2005), 'Identities in Transition: Shifting Conceptions of Home by Black South African University Students', *African Studies Review*, 48(3): 1–19.

Bhabha, H. (1994), *The Location of Culture*, London: Routledge.

Bourdieu, P. (1991), *Language and Symbolic Power*, Cambridge, MA: Harvard University Press.

Clark, R. and Ivanič, R. (1997), *The Politics of Writing*, London: Routledge.

de Kadt, E. (2005), 'English, Language Shift and Identities: A Comparison between "Zulu-Dominant" and "Multicultural" Students on a South African University Campus', *Southern African Linguistics and Applied Language Studies*, 23(1): 19–37.

Gee, J. (1990), *Social Linguistics and Literacies: Ideology in Discourses*, London: Falmer Press.

Geisler, C. (1994), *Academic Literacy and the Nature of Expertise: Reading, Writing, and Knowing in Academic Philosophy*, Hillsdale, NJ: Erlbaum.

George, R. (1996), *The Politics of Home: Postcolonial Relocations and Twentieth-Century Fiction*, Berkeley: University of California Press.

Herrington, A. and Curtis, M. (2000), *Persons in Process: Four Stories of Writing and Personal Development in College*, Urbana, IL: National Council of Teachers of English.

Janks, H. (2010), *Literacy and Power*, New York and London: Routledge.

Johns, A. (1997), *Text, Role and Context: Developing Academic Literacies*, Cambridge: Cambridge University Press.

le Page, R. and Tabouret-Keller, A. (1985), *Acts of Identity: Creole-Based Approaches to Language and Identity*, Cambridge: Cambridge University Press.

Norton, B. (2000), *Identity and Language Learning: Gender, Ethnicity and Educational Language*, London: Longman.

Norton, B. and McKinney, C. (2010), 'Identity in Language and Literacy Education', in B. Spolsky and F. Hult, (eds), *The Handbook of Educational Linguistics*, 192–205, West-Sussex: Wiley-Blackwell.

Nuttall, S. (2004), 'Stylizing the Self: The Y Generation in Rosebank, Johannesburg', *Public Culture*, 16(3): 430–52.

Pavlenko, A. and Blackledge, A. (2002), 'Introduction', *Multilingua*, 21(2/3): 121–40.

Pavlenko, A. and Blackledge, A. eds (2004), *Negotiation of Identities in Multilingual Contexts*, Great Britain: Cromwell Press Ltd.

Read, B., Archer, L. and Leathwood, C. (2003), 'Challenging Cultures? Student Conceptions of "Belonging" and "Isolation" at a Post-1992 University', *Studies in Higher Education*, 28(3): 261–77.

Renn, K. (2004), *Mixed Race Students in College: The Ecology of Race, Identity and Community on Campus*, Albany: State University of New York.

Rose, M. (1990), *Lives on the Boundary*, New York: Penguin.

Seekings, J. and Nattrass, N. (2005), *Inequality in South Africa*, New Haven: Yale University Press.

Thesen, L. (1997), 'Voices, Discourse and Transition: In Search of New Categories in EAP', *Tesol Quarterly*, 31(3): 487–511.

Thomson, R. (2009), *Unfolding Lives: Youth, Gender and Change*, Bristol: The Policy Press.

Thornton, R. (1988), 'Culture: A Contemporary Definition', in E. Boonzaier and J. Sharp (eds), *South African Keywords*, 17–28, Cape Town: David Phillip.

Walker, M. (2006), '"First-Generation" Students in England: Social Class Narratives of University Access and Participation', unpublished paper, School of Education, University of Sheffield.

Wenger, E. (1998), *Communities of Practice: Learning, Meaning and Identity*, Cambridge: Cambridge University Press.

5

The Role of Religion in Mediating the Transition to Higher Education

Bongi Bangeni and June Pym

Introduction

In this chapter we present a longitudinal account of the role that religion played in our research participants' lives as they made the transition into higher education. We draw on data which address two of the sub-questions of the project. One of the sub-questions seeks to understand the strategies which our research participants used to cope at the University of Cape Town (UCT). A related question seeks to understand the individual and institutional resources which enabled them to progress within the institution during their undergraduate years. In addressing these questions, we foreground the threads that emerged over a four-year period (2009–12) that relate to how the students used religion to mediate areas of dissonance and how religion provided an enabling framework which facilitated optimism, security and confidence within the academic environment. The data show that the participants often turned to religion and associated structures as a way of dealing with stress and potential failure, as they negotiated the transition into new discourses which require taking on unfamiliar ways of thinking, believing and being (Gee 1996). Of equal significance is the sense of belonging and community that religion offered the students, who found support and guidance within religious groups and organizations both on and off campus.

While these findings point to how religion largely functions as a resource, the data also attest to the ways in which the participants' discomfort with academic discourses and the accompanying world views can be attributed to particular aspects of their religious beliefs which sit uncomfortably alongside the ideologies within the course curricula of their academic disciplines. In his article, which describes the tensions evident between African value systems and those outlined in the National Plan for Higher Education, van Niekerk (2004: 123) writes about how 'the holistic nature of African rationality' implies that issues within formal education cannot be seen in isolation from factors such as an individual's religious beliefs, due to the intertwined nature of faith and reason within African religious systems. The data highlight how this particular world view finds meaning in formal learning spaces where students attempt to reconcile religious beliefs with course curricula, some with more success than others.

Our focus on religion and the role it plays in students' lives within the institution stems from our analysis of the first two years of data yielded by the project and of the findings of a longitudinal study which tracked twenty students in the Faculty of Humanities over the course of their undergraduate studies (see Bangeni and Kapp 2005). In both studies, the findings reflect how the participants foregrounded the importance of religion, particularly Christianity, in their initial years at the institution, often perceiving it as a resource on which they could draw in pressured times. Based on this, we took the decision to address the issue directly in the interviews we conducted with our participants, during their third academic year. We asked the students whether they had experienced clashes between the curricula of their majors and their religious beliefs. We also asked them to reflect on their first and second years at the institution. Part of this reflection entailed a discussion of the highlights and lowlights of the previous year and how they had dealt with adversity in their lives during this time. Walsh (2003) argues that religious beliefs impact on the way adversity is managed, and provide convictions and practices that nurture the individual's and community's sense of well-being. While theorists such as Bangeni and Kapp (2005) and Swartz (2009) have discussed the importance of religion in the lives of young South Africans, there has been no in-depth analysis of *how* religion functions in the academic and personal lives of students within the higher education context.

The role of religion, particularly Christianity, in South Africa

The data show that the participants conceived of religion as a resource and this can be linked to its role in the broader societal context. Many theorists have demonstrated that religious beliefs (in particular Christianity) are central to the lives of 'the relatively and absolute poor, centered in the poorest parts of the world' (Walls 1998: 14). For example, recent research has pointed to the fact that religion forms one of the main building blocks of personal identity in black people's lives in post-apartheid South Africa (see Bangeni and Kapp 2005; Swartz 2009; Bray et al. 2010).

Religious organizations and religious leaders played a critical role in both supporting and opposing apartheid. African churches 'staked out a distinctive religious terrain in the power relations of South Africa' (Chidester, Tobler and Witten 1997: 12) and are defined by their independence from white ecclesiastical control (Kiernan 1990). In the context of dehumanizing conditions caused by the legacy of apartheid, crippling poverty and unemployment, members of African-initiated churches have found a space that enables a sense of cohesive community and identity, and facilitates hope and celebration (Kiernan 1990). This reflects how, for many black South Africans, religion represents a way of being in the world (Conroy et al. 2013).

Identity and religion

We draw on a poststructuralist notion of identity in order to describe and explain the role that religion plays in the lives of our participants. For poststructuralist scholars such as Bhabha (1994), identity is multifaceted, fluid and contradictory, rather than fixed. In viewing identity in this way, poststructuralism embraces the multiple interpretations which individuals attach to their experiences. As researchers approaching the notion of identity from this theoretical perspective, it is of particular importance to us that we acknowledge the precarious task of attempting to engage with an aspect of identity (religious identity) which typically finds meaning outside of the academic space. The enactment of identity within the institution is characterized by its connectedness to the range of investments that students bring with them from home and other environments and these in turn directly affect how students (dis)engage with learning. Students from the school and home backgrounds described in the Introduction of this book are usually invested in studying at institutions such as UCT in pronounced ways that are often linked to socio-economic factors and the aspirations of family members back home (Bangeni and Kapp 2005). In most cases, these socio-economic factors and influences from families have a direct impact on factors such as choice of degree (see Chapter 6) and, consequently, on students' engagement with the various facets of higher education. We therefore find it necessary to situate our attempts at meaning-making *alongside* those of the research participants. This entails understanding how they negotiate various aspects of their personal and academic identities in particular settings, and how religion informs these negotiations.

Research methodology: Attempting to hear the student voice

We draw on the data yielded by semi-structured interviews conducted with each student over a four-year period. In doing so we attempt to shed light on the various ways in which the participants drew on their religious beliefs and the ways in which their religious beliefs positioned them in relation to institutional culture and course curricula. In the following sections we present the themes which were yielded by our content analysis. These include the ways in which religion functions as an individual resource for students in challenging times, the role of campus religious organizations in informing how students negotiate the self and the institution, and lastly the impact of course curricula on students' religious beliefs. We foreground the participants' voices to shed light on how they positioned themselves in relation to disciplinary and religious discourses.

Religion as an individual resource

The participants in our study began their university careers feeling fairly confident in themselves, largely with an identity that had been developed around being 'an achiever' in their high schools and communities and being accepted into a relatively elite higher education institution. In her first interview, Dineo, a student from a rural background, stated: 'In my village not so many people are educated. I am the first person in my family and in my village to be in a prominent university' (interview 1, 2009). The data show that our participants' sense of optimism was often fuelled by particular religious convictions. Religion seemed to act as a 'sponsor' for their actions by offering a social identity which facilitated security, connection and agency (Herrington and Curtis 2000: 369, see also Bray et al. 2010). Lunga, a confident student in the Faculty of Humanities, for example, described the security she gained from fellow Christians who provided a support system for her after she lost three members of her immediate family within the space of a year: 'In terms of my spirituality I can say that I have grown quite a lot in my faith and you know I have had people around me to help me with that and to support me and you know I guess that is what helped me through, you know, my loss and stuff like that'. The quotes from the interviews over the three years also illuminate the roles they saw God playing as saviour, protector and enabler, for example: 'I've overcome much trials and tribulations in my life through God' (Lunga, interview 1, 2009); 'What I am is a gift from God and what I become is a gift to God' (Isaac, interview 2, 2010) and 'God is the sole person I put all my trust in' (Dineo, interview 3, 2011).

Despite the positive influence of religion outlined above, however, the majority of students in this study experienced significant crises that related to academic and linguistic difficulties, affective issues and particularly an erosion of identity, because their experiences within the institution were not in harmony with their home and school backgrounds and contexts. Our data show how, in this instance, religion was once again used as a 'sponsoring discourse' (Herrington and Curtis 2000: 369) to enable them to handle difficult and hugely traumatic events in their lives. These events ranged from adapting to a very different environment, coping with English as the language of learning, challenges with course work, facing potential academic failure for the first time in their lives, financial challenges, and a range of problems and worries related to family 'back home'. The phrase 'You don't have to pay to pray', uttered by one student, aptly captures the solace that religion provided to these students who have experienced great vulnerabilities in their lives.

It is significant to note that our research participants turned to religion before seeking help or support from the institution. Bray et al.'s (2010: 238) study of the lives of adolescents growing up in various locations around the Fish Hoek area in the Western Cape indicates how 'personal faith plays a very special role in providing an alternative framework for understanding failure'. As with the youth in that study, for our participants, religion was often the first port of call before they attempted to solve problems. This is evident in the statements from the interviews, for example: 'I pray and then I just handle it' (interview 2, 2010). It emerged later in the interview that 'just handling it' included phoning home for family support and getting advice from close friends: 'When things get very hard, I just pray, and call my mom, it has always been my mom and prayer.' It is important to note that many of these students have lived in contexts 'in which it was virtually impossible not to believe in God' (Taylor 2007: 3) and have now moved to the University where 'faith, even for the staunchest believer, is one human possibility among others' (ibid). This presents various options: entrenching one's religious convictions; engaging in identity work to sustain one's faith or making quite different choices. What is evident in the data is how the participants sought refuge in religion and prayer rather than in institutional resources. In general, the data show that religion is pivotal in providing a framework for the strong focus on the meaning of life and the need for self-actualization.

Religion at an institutional level

Scholars have argued that formalized religion offers a way for individuals to share their experiences and be part of a group support system (e.g. see Fukuyama and Sevig 1999). Religion also provides opportunities for forming communities and social networks, where individuals engage with people who share similar values, beliefs and needs. In their first three years, the students in our study frequently experienced contexts and situations within the institution that directly challenged their religious beliefs. In some ways, not being in a familiar context foregrounded the participants' consciousness of the ways of being that characterized their home environments. This often further contributed to their sense of alienation in their new environment. In order to address this alienation, affected students sought out like-minded fellow students with whom they could engage in dialogue, as expressed in the following statement by Lunga: 'Having people that pray for you such as in our prayer groups, that you can pray with is great, you can just knock on your friend's door and like just pray together' (interview 2).

It seems that religious organizations on and off campus, such as the campus Student Christian Society and community fellowship groups, are fertile ground for providing a network of social contacts and a sense of belonging. Engagement in these religious organizations seemed to play the role of increasing the participants' self-esteem and confidence. Moreover, participants who started their university life already connected with religious organizations seemed to increase their involvement over time, often taking on leadership positions.

While most students in our study seemed to find both solace and a sense of belonging in these organizations, some students spoke of the dissonance in the style of worship and doctrines between the religious practices at university and those back home. In response to a question which sought to access the participants' views of religious organizations on campus, Isaac, a staunch Christian, responded:

> My church [back home] is a black church and the one here is a white church. …
> The music is different ….Back at home, it's the Benjamin Dube stuff [a black gospel singer who is also a pastor], I really miss that music. I didn't know much about different doctrines but then when I came here I came to know about different doctrines and some of these concepts I am very uncomfortable with that is why I just ignore them. (interview 3)

Isaac made a distinction between his individual notion of 'God' and what seemed to constitute acceptable norms of behaviour within Christian circles:

> Some Christians here don't have a problem with alcohol. … I had to really decide what's right before God now that I'm alone. It hasn't been easy because I'm seeing new things regarding alcohol and sex which I am the first time exposed to so I have to wait and see whether God really approves of me engaging in it or not. (interview 2)

This statement from Isaac shows how religion provided a strong moral compass for students who found themselves in a different context with a variety of challenges relating to alcohol, sexuality and ways of being. In the next section we discuss how our participants carved out spaces for their religious beliefs in the process of negotiating their course curricula.

The impact of course curricula on students' religious beliefs and practices

In the third interview, the participants were asked to comment on instances where their course curricula clashed with their religious beliefs, if at all. There was a significant difference in the data from students in the Faculty of Science and those in the Faculty of Humanities.

The responses to the above question from participants in the Humanities were typically framed around either benefitting from or being negatively affected by the presence of different views of religion and God in their curricula. For some, the impact of course curricula on their religious beliefs and practices was perceived as invaluable in the affirming role it played. This perception was prominent in data elicited from interviews with Roshni, a humanities student. While Sacks and Kapp (Chapter 3) illustrate the complexity in Roshni's attempts to reconcile family and institutional expectations, her interview data particularly reflect how she viewed the topics discussed in her courses as providing a platform for her to 'conduct research' into her Islamic faith. In her second-year interview, in response to a question which sought her reflection on her own development, she said: 'I think in responsibility I have grown, in wanting to know and [take] control of my future. Religion-wise, yes because I'm doing research on my own religion, so now it's like wow I didn't know this.' She also described how topics on gender in one of her first-year courses had encouraged multiple interpretations of gender roles and relations within her religion: 'I enjoyed the gender essays because in my religion males are practically dominant so *ja* [Afrikaans for 'yes'], that's the thing, I like seeing different views on how to see that perspective.'

For Lunga, course topics on gender encouraged multiple interpretations and understandings of gender roles in religion, in the context of her attempts to reconcile her Christian identity with her identity as a feminist, an identity which seemed to have been generated by her Gender Studies major, and one whose aspects she was still in the process of negotiating:

> I was actually thinking about it just yesterday because my lecturer was just saying how there isn't much literature on Christian feminism, if you know, such a thing exists and I actually thought about it and I am like – I am a Christian, yes, but I also have feminist ideas and I call myself a feminist but I haven't quite comfortably settled into the different categories of feminism. It has been a bit challenging because you know there are certain elements of Christianity that are very oppressive toward women. But then I was listening to this Muslim lecturer and she was talking about how, inasmuch as we say that women are not represented in our religions, it does not mean that they were not active, it just means that their stories were not told, they were not put into the Bible or the Koran, and it hit me just because stories aren't there does not mean that they don't exist and just because, similarly to Africans, just because our stories weren't told does not mean that they never existed, that we were never strong, we were never spiritual, you know. So this all just made me think about that and really challenge myself as a Christian and how I see things because sometimes we always take religion as it is, we don't question it. (interview 3)

Lunga's reflection points to how her questions around religion were addressed within an aspect of the curriculum, which resulted in a strengthening of her religious identity. This phenomenon of course curricula and formal lectures providing a platform from which to speak out about or against religious practices which were previously unquestioned is also evident in Kapp and Bangeni's

(2009) study on students' negotiation of various aspects of their identities within the institution. While their study did not specifically set out to examine the role of religion to the extent we have done in this chapter, the findings similarly reflect how some courses resulted in their participants questioning the gendered enactment of religious practices in their home communities.

While the intersection of curricula and religious beliefs was seen as empowering by students such as Lunga, it was not viewed in this positive light by all. For Isaac, a deeply religious student from the province of KwaZulu-Natal, the questions posed in one of his courses about the existence of God resulted in an introspective exercise which saw him asking more questions:

> There were problems in my Ethics course, especially something that was said by Pascal that contradicted my understanding of Christianity. He said 'I will wager if God exists or not, the outcome of my wager will be that God exists because should he exist and I live my life as though he does not exist then I am doomed for eternal punishment. But if he does not exist and I live as though he exists, I haven't really lost anything in life but should he exist and I have lived as he exists I will enjoy eternal reward'. But I don't really agree with believing in God as a wager. According to my Christian faith you believe in God fully and you live life accordingly, not as a wager, *ja*, so that for me was a contradiction. (interview 3)

Isaac's lengthy explanation of his disagreement with Pascal's philosophy reflects his attempts to remain true to his religion within an environment which he perceived as having the potential to lead him astray: 'My life is in the hands of God, He has trusted me enough to place me here, trusting that I will be capable to keep our fellowship and relationship intact' (interview 3). Apart from demonstrating the extent of Isaac's devotion and trust in his religious beliefs, this statement also illustrates how he attributed his ability to be agentic and to engage with his new environment, to his relationship with God. In this understanding then, God was not only seen to be responsible for his presence at the UCT but was also entrusted with the role of sanctioning his actions there.

For some students in our study, course curricula served as a catalyst to questioning connections between material affluence and the conferring of leadership positions within community churches back home. This is reflected in the following quote from Lunga:

> Due to some of my courses I've learnt to look at things in a different way from my church back home. There you find that priests always mock people within the congregation and one is judged by the fact that – oh, you know Mr, So and So has a nice car, so he has to be given a position in the church, not because he

> grows the congregation or preaches the Word, but because of the material things
> that he has. For me faith is a huge issue so I needed a church that would let me
> express who I was. I needed people to share the Word with and grow my faith,
> and I found that here. (interview 1)

Lunga uttered the above statement during a period in which she had abandoned
her family religion in favour of a more charismatic church which has a branch
on the campus. This questioning is therefore important as it seemed to provide
guidance during times of change.

It would appear that, unlike some of the students in the Humanities, most of
the science students in our study kept their personal religious beliefs separate
from their engagement with the curriculum. In his third interview, Luthando
remarked:

> In our high school Bio class, we were told to forget about our religion for the
> section we were doing on evolution, we were told, 'Ok, just forget about religion
> for now, we are going to do this section and then finish it, and then after that you
> can get back to your lives.' I believe that there are things that you cannot explain
> religiously and some of the things you cannot explain scientifically.

Luthando's quote points, first, to how the participants' views about knowledge
continued to be shaped by those instilled in them in high school. Secondly, the
quote offers a picture of the nature of school practices and ways of engaging with
knowledge. The schools in which the majority of our participants matriculated
are characterized by a lack of critical engagement with knowledge which places
them at a distinct disadvantage (see Chapter 1). There were also statements
made by the participants which pointed to their attempts to make sense of the
various paradigms and schools of thought within and outside of their courses.
The following statement from one of the science students, Chris, reflects this:

> In philosophy there is an argument: 'What is the existence of God?' but I think
> the only problem there, there is a theoretical part and a practical side and they
> are using the theoretical which is obviously going to fall on their side of the
> argument which says that God does not exist. But when it becomes practical
> then it is something else.

Unlike Isaac, who felt personally affronted by this questioning of God's existence
in the Philosophy course, Chris's statement shows how he attempted to make
sense of the above question by considering the theoretical and practical sides
of the question asked, rather than by personalizing it. A possible explanation
for the nature of the science students' responses would be that they, unlike

the humanities students, are directly confronted with the creationism versus evolution debate because of the nature of the subjects they encounter in their degrees. Their perspective on this issue is therefore less personal.

A number of studies have sought to understand how science students come to reconcile their religious beliefs with a scientific world view (see for example Fleener 1996). These studies revealed that students tended to experience considerable clashes between these two world views. The findings of our investigation, however, revealed the ways in which some of our students' responses to this issue were less straightforward. For example, in her third interview, one of the students, Josephine, maintained that the courses for which she was registered did not significantly impact on her religious beliefs. Yet the following statement attests to her efforts at making a clear distinction between two diverse approaches in her Biology course:

> No [there isn't a clash], not really. But I know in biology last year, we did Darwin's theorem. I didn't think it actually clashed with my beliefs as a Christian, but there is that aspect of biology that … that I am drawn to and that aspect of my religion which is part of me. But I think that … I have to set a boundary like … there is some limit between the two of them. So I do believe in some aspects of Darwin's … and I do believe in creation. I think it's a more religious approach for the beginning of the world … than the scientific approach would be the beginning of human kind like how they can go back to how it all started with some embryotic process. I think I do believe that theory of evolution. But then for like the beginning of creation, I do believe in Christianity and Christ was born and that's how everything was. … So I don't think there's actually really a clash in me, but I think I do believe in both too, sometimes. (interview 3)

It seems that in negotiating a place for the world views introduced by their curricula, the science students in the study attempted to make sense of this process by compartmentalizing – by making distinctions between theory and practice in Chris's case, and between creation and evolution in Josephine's. Josephine's attempt at locating a space for herself within these two approaches was, at best, ambivalent. While she made it clear that for her, the beginning of the world can be explained in religious terms, she found it necessary to ascribe certain aspects of the creation of the world to either religion or science. Fysh and Lucas's (1998) study of religious beliefs in the science classroom goes some way in providing insights into the nature of these responses. These authors argue that students' attitudes to the science versus religion debate are more often than not, complex and contradictory and should, therefore, not be viewed from a one-dimensional perspective. This is evident in the tentative manner in which Josephine ended her explanation. It is therefore highly likely that, in another context outside the classroom, the students in our study would have positioned themselves differently.

Interestingly, the theme of compartmentalizing extended into how some of the science students positioned themselves within the institution. Philisani, for example, described his life within the institution in terms of a process where he 'divides [himself] into different parts' (Interview 3) in an attempt to successfully engage with institutional demands. In describing their research participants' attempts at adapting to various aspects of university life, Kapp and Bangeni (2011) reference Renn's (2004:220) notion of *situational identity*. This notion signals the fluid nature of identity, as the participants in their study similarly came to be strategic in terms of which identity they chose to foreground at a specific time.

Conclusion

Our study's findings point to how religion functioned as a powerful resource for some of the students in our study. The findings highlight the fact that we cannot work with students in a diverse society without taking cognisance of the integral nature of religion in their lives. The findings also highlight the dual role played by institutional religious organizations in affording students opportunities to engage, socialize and critique but at the same time symbolizing difference and conflict for some. These findings point to the need for student support structures to be put in place in spaces such as residences, to acknowledge the role that religion plays in students' processes of familiarizing themselves with institutional culture, both within and outside of the classroom. This means that a holistic engagement with students is necessary so that opportunities are created for them to feel a sense of social connectedness and belonging.

In considering students' negotiations within the classroom, our findings show how course curricula serve to change, challenge and support existing beliefs and religious practices. The new discourses that students encounter as they enter the academy are embedded in taken-for-granted ideological frameworks. Students thus not only have to learn to negotiate values, attitudes and beliefs that are different from their home discourses, both within the institution and their disciplines, but sometimes experience considerable clashes with their sense of themselves and ways of being in the world. Roth and Alexander (1997) maintain that conflict between religious and scientific discourses is likely to impact negatively on the extent to which students are able to learn the subject matter of their curricula. In an attempt to address the findings pertaining to students' negotiation of their course curricula, we believe that spaces need to be opened up for meta-reflection, where students can attempt to make connections between the curriculum on the one hand and their world views and the religious beliefs which guide their understandings on a daily basis on the other. Students need to feel empowered enough to critically examine the ways in which the dominant discourses of the institution affirm or refute their religious beliefs. In pointing to this need, it is important to state that a key objective of higher education is, quite rightly, the challenging of students' norms and values so that they are able to engage in an ongoing re-evaluation of these and their place in contemporary society. However, it is equally important that the institution does this from a position of understanding students' investments and how these impact on their engagement with course curricula and institutional culture as a whole. This will hopefully result in a situation where students do not feel silenced by dominant discourses within curricula and can engage with them in legitimate learning spaces rather than in isolated reflections.

References

Bangeni, B. and Kapp, R. (2005), 'Identities in Transition: Shifting Conceptions of Home among "Black" South African University Students', *African Studies Review*, 48(3): 1–19.

Bhabha, H. (1994), *The Location of Culture*, London: Routledge.

Bray, R., Gooskens, I., Khan, L., Moses, S. and Seekings, J. (2010), *Growing Up in the New South Africa: Childhood and Adolescence in Post-Apartheid Cape Town*, Cape Town: Human Sciences Research Council Press.

Chidester, D., Tobler, J., and Witten, D., (1997), *Christianity in South Africa*, Westport: Greenwood Press.

Conroy, J. C., Lundie, D., Davis, R. A., Baumfield, V., Phillip Barnes, L., Gallagher, T., Lowden, K., Bourque, N. and Wenell, K. (2013), *Does Religious Education Work? A Multi-Dimensional Investigation*, London: Bloomsbury.

Fleener, M. J. (1996), 'Scientific World Building on the Edge of Chaos: High School Students' Beliefs about Mathematics and Science', *School Science and Mathematics*, 96: 312–20.

Fukuyama, M. A. and Sevig, T. D. (1999), *Integrating Spirituality into Multicultural Counselling*, London: Sage Publications.

Fysh, R. and Lucas, K. B. (1998), 'Religious Beliefs in Science Classrooms', *Research in Science Education*, 28(4): 399–427.

Gee, J. (1996), *Social Linguistics and Literacies: Ideology in Discourses* (2nd ed.), London: Taylor & Francis.

Herrington, A. and Curtis, M. (2000), *Persons in Process: Four Stories of Writing and Personal Development in College*, Urbana, IL: National Council of Teachers of English.

Kapp, R. and Bangeni, B. (2009), 'Positioning (in) the Discipline: Undergraduate Students' Negotiations of Disciplinary Discourses', *Teaching in Higher Education*, 14(6): 587–96.

Kapp, R. and Bangeni, B. (2011), 'A Longitudinal Study of Students' Negotiation of Language, Literacy and Identity', *Southern African Linguistics and Applied Language Studies*, 29(2): 197–208.

Kiernan, J. P. (1990), *The Production and Management of Therapeutic Power in Zionist Churches within a Zulu City*, Lewiston, NY: Edwin Mellen Press.

Renn, K. (2004), *Mixed Race Students in College: The Ecology of Race, Identity and Community on Campus*, Albany: State University of New York.

Roth, W. and Alexander, T. (1997), 'The Interaction of Students' Scientific and Religious Discourses: Two Case Studies', *International Journal of Science Education*, 19(2): 125–46.

Swartz, S. (2009), *Ikasi: The Moral Ecology of South Africa's Township Youth*, Johannesburg: Wits University Press.

Taylor, C. (2007), *A Secular Age*, Cambridge: Harvard University Press.

van Niekerk, M. P. (2004), 'The National Plan for Higher Education in South Africa and African Indigenous Knowledge Systems: A Case of Conflicting Value Systems?', *South African Journal of Higher Education*, 18(3):115–26.

Walls, A. F. (1998), 'Africa in Christian History: Retrospect and Prospect', *Journal of African Christian Thought* 1(1): 2–15.

Walsh, F. (2003), 'Family Resilience: Strengths Forged through Adversity', in F. Walsh (ed.), *Normal Family Processes*, 399–421, New York: The Guilford Press.

6

A Longitudinal Account of the Factors Shaping the Degree Paths of Black Students

Bongi Bangeni

Introduction

In this chapter I provide an account of the factors shaping the degree paths taken by six black students who were first registered at the University of Cape Town (UCT) in 2002. While preceding chapters offer insights into students' negotiations within their undergraduate disciplines and social environments, this chapter tracks their progress from undergraduate spaces of engagement into the postgraduate domain. The participants in the study had completed their schooling at under-resourced township or rural schools and were classified as needing additional language support upon entry into the institution. They were registered for general programmes in the Humanities and graduated with a Bachelor of Social Science degree in 2004, having completed their degrees within the required three years. The chapter focuses on six of these students. In 2005, two of the six registered for honours degrees in Criminal Justice, an interdisciplinary programme comprising mostly of law courses from the Law Faculty's Institute of Criminology. Two students registered for the three-year, postgraduate Bachelor of Laws (LLB) degree, while the last two registered for postgraduate diplomas in Marketing and in Human Resource Management respectively, within the Commerce Faculty.

In this chapter I illustrate how these students' degree paths were shaped by a number of factors. First, none of the six students was accepted into the degree they had listed as their first choice when they applied to the institution, due to inadequate matriculation points. This closing up of access continued after graduation as they did not gain entry into the honours degrees of their undergraduate majors either, again after falling short of meeting the entrance requirements. The second factor which influenced their degree paths was the extent of their personal investment (Norton 2000) in their first choice of degree. This fuelled their determination to find ways of accessing these disciplines after they graduated. Thirdly, the data show how the influence of their immediate families and home communities significantly impacted on their choice processes. The last factor concerned the challenges they faced accessing the job market after graduation, which resulted in some of them having to register for postgraduate studies. The data attest to how this lack of access in their first year necessitated a number of strategic moves which took them on unanticipated routes in the course of their academic journeys. For some of the students, these unanticipated routes served to open up access to alternative ways of thinking, believing and engaging which impacted on how they interacted within their postgraduate disciplines. As this chapter will show, a qualitative longitudinal perspective allows for an understanding of the ways in which particular affordances and constraints regarding the choices students make come to shape their engagements with disciplinary knowledge, institutional culture and the professional identities they have to take on within the applied disciplines in which they seek membership. I conclude with a number of reflections on the implications of the findings for the graduation rates of black, undergraduate students and their access to postgraduate studies.

The importance of exploring access and success at the postgraduate level in South Africa

Several studies within the field of academic development have described the nature of concerns around access and success for black students in South African higher education (HE), focusing mainly on the transition from school to university. These concerns include challenges with reading, writing and engaging with knowledge which are significantly different from those they encountered at school (see Thesen 1997; Paxton 2003; McKenna 2004; Boughey 2005; Zulu 2005; Bangeni and Kapp 2006; van Pletzen 2006; van Schalkwyk, Bitzer and van der Walt 2009). While this body of research has resulted in a better understanding of the challenges encountered by these students as they enter HE, it does not provide insights into their experiences after obtaining their undergraduate degree or the implications of these struggles for their degree paths as a whole.

The Council on Higher Education (2013: 15) maintains that only one in four students in South Africa's contact institutions graduates within three or four years. Black students seem to be at a significant disadvantage in this respect.

This disadvantage is evident in the University's official reporting on teaching and learning within the faculties. An analysis of the undergraduate throughput rates during the research project's data collection period indicates that although there were 'marked improvements in the success rate of African and coloured students between 2000 and 2006, there were still marked differences in undergraduate success rates by race' (UCT 2008: 13). These differences in success rates affect the pipeline to postgraduate studies directly. It is significant to note that in the 2005 Teaching and Learning Report, African and coloured students made up only 13 per cent of the postgraduate enrolment (UCT 2005). Investigating the factors that shape these students' degree paths therefore becomes necessary at a time when concerns about the low throughput rates among black students and their access to postgraduate studies in South Africa abound. This chapter responds to this need through an appraisal of the factors shaping students' access to honours degrees and postgraduate diplomas, also known as 'capping' diplomas, which students register for to complement their undergraduate qualifications.

The notion of *choice* in black students' degree pathways

A fundamental concept in the body of research that explores students' degree paths in HE is that of *choice* (see, for example, Reay, David and Ball 2005). These studies reference the choices that are available to students from working-class backgrounds as they navigate their degree paths in HE institutions and more importantly, describe the strategizing which accompanies the decision students have to make during their studies. Reay, David and Ball (2005) consider how the descriptors of social class, race and gender circumscribe the options available to students from working-class backgrounds in the UK, in the process of choosing which institutions to attend. In explaining what this process entails for what they term 'non-traditional' students, they argue that 'Choice for a majority involved either a process of finding out what you cannot have, what is not open for negotiation and then looking at the few options left, or a process of self-exclusion' (ibid. 85). These authors define choice as 'a social process which is structured and structuring' (ibid. 160), largely informed by one's social position and educational background. Adopting this perspective therefore problematizes the notion of *choice*, as it compels one to consider its constrained nature, here profoundly expressed by one of the participants in their study: '[having] a choice of one' (ibid. 85).

The above perspective on choice is evident in Ball et al. (2002: 51) who conceptualize choice 'as alluding to both power and constraint'. Following Ball et al. (2002), my use of the term in this chapter takes into account both these aspects of choice: the agency displayed by students in responding to these choices and the constraining effect of institutional structures on their ability to choose. Thus a consideration of the factors that serve to promote or hinder students' agency as they make their way through the institution becomes important. For the research participants in my study, agency links up with the kinds of investments (Norton 2000) that inform the decisions they make. Norton uses the term *investment* to signal individuals' multiple desires, ambivalences and complex social histories, and argues that one's investment is likely to be 'complex, contradictory and in a state of flux' (Norton 2000: 10–11). My study illustrates the ways in which students' investment in their first choice of degree shaped the strategic moves they made throughout their academic careers.

The act of choosing a degree is significantly shaped by identity. The chapter takes into account poststructuralist notions of identity (see the Introduction; Bhabha 1994; Sarup 1996). Here, identity is understood to include the students' identities as English additional language (EAL) speakers, with English spoken as a second or third language. The notion also includes their identities as postgraduate students in transition from undergraduate studies where they majored in Psychology and Sociology, classified as 'soft pure' disciplines (see Becher 1989) which focus on facilitating an understanding and interpretation of disciplinary theory and key concepts, to the professional disciplines of law and marketing which are characterized by a strong leaning towards contextual knowledge which emphasizes the application of theory to professional contexts and practical experience. Identity thus comprises disciplinary identity, linguistic identity which is tied to their racial identities, and an emerging professional identity. In describing students' degree paths I illustrate the ways in which their personal, linguistic and emerging professional identities come to shape the process of choosing, as well as engaging at both undergraduate and postgraduate levels of study. From a South African perspective, the constrained nature of choice is evident in a number of contexts within the HE sector among mostly black students from disadvantaged schooling and home backgrounds. As I will describe later in the chapter, all six students in my study were refused entry into either their first choice of undergraduate degree or into the honours degree of one of their undergraduate majors. This meant that they had to make strategic choices in attempting to address their respective desires and life situations within and outside of the institution.

The concept of choice and its links to identity are also explored in relation to Hetherington's (1998) notion of *space*. Hetherington suggests that identity involves identification with particular places. This implies that 'there are certain spaces that act as sites for the performance of identity' (ibid. 105) where individuals choose which aspects of their identity to foreground depending on the power relations at play. Likewise, Blommaert's (2010) notion of *space* points to the regulated and political nature of spaces. He argues: 'Movement of people across space is ... never a move across empty spaces. The spaces are always someone's space, and they are filled with norms [and] expectations' (p.6). My interpretation of the term 'space' is, first and foremost, the disciplinary spaces within which the students interact. However, this definition is not confined to the immediate learning space but also encompasses physical environments in the form of the buildings and the symbols within them and the spaces of their home environments and communities. In describing their transition into postgraduate studies, the students in my study commented on these spaces and juxtaposed them with those in their former undergraduate disciplines, in a bid to make statements about how they felt positioned by their new environments. This points to how the notions of choice and agency are linked to time. Klemenčič (2015: 13) maintains that the notions of agentic possibility are temporally embedded, implying that they are shaped through considerations of past habits of mind and action, present judgments of alternatives for action and projections of the future.' It was in looking backward to undergraduate and home spaces within which they had engaged, and in looking forward to anticipated professional careers and the world of work, that the participants were able to attach meaning to the choices they had made and to take action. So considerations of how and why certain aspects of identity are foregrounded in particular spaces and at particular times, and instances where agency is enabled, become important. Below I describe the honours space and its position within the postgraduate domain.

The ambiguous position of the honours degree within the postgraduate domain

The characterization of spaces as contested and therefore political necessitates an examination of the nature of the postgraduate space in which the participants' strategizing occurred. The honours degree occupies a tenuous space within the postgraduate domain. Its official classification as a postgraduate qualification distinguishes it from the undergraduate degree. However, this distinction is mostly an artificial one as the coursework masters is perceived to represent an entry into the 'postgraduate proper', with the general perception in South Africa being that the honours degree constitutes the fourth year of undergraduate studies. This has certainly influenced the Council on Higher Education's (2013) motivation for a four-year degree that would see the honours degree incorporated into the undergraduate bachelor degree. The underlying implication of the above is that the honours degree does not fit seamlessly into the neat categories of either 'undergraduate' or 'postgraduate' but could be said to constitute an ambiguous space. Its ambiguous nature is apparent in how the Criminal Justice honours course, along with the postgraduate diplomas and the postgraduate LLB, have been explicitly set up to accommodate students from other faculties. The Criminal Justice honours and the Marketing diploma are geared towards social science graduates and non-commerce graduates respectively, with the postgraduate LLB similarly sourcing its students from the humanities graduate pool. While this reflects the institution's strategic attempts at facilitating additional access into postgraduate studies, it has implications for how students engage within this space.

Methodology

The longitudinal narrative in this chapter is made possible by drawing on data yielded by two qualitative research projects, one which tracked the participants over the course of their undergraduate studies and the other which explored their transition into the postgraduate domain. In addition to the data yielded by the undergraduate research project, three main sources of data were yielded at the postgraduate level. For both projects, students submitted their essays with feedback from their lecturers and tutors and wrote reflection papers in which they described their engagement with their various disciplines in their undergraduate years and, for the second project, their transition into their postgraduate disciplines after graduating. Semi-structured interviews were conducted with each participant over the course of their undergraduate and postgraduate years. Interview questions were revisited in subsequent interviews in order to address students' changing subjectivities.

To date, the degree pathways of black South African students have been theorized within the context of the high attrition and dropout rates in South Africa's HE system (see, for example, Scott, Yeld and Henry 2007; Letseka et al. 2010). As important as these studies are for understanding patterns in recruitment and retention rates within this context, they have tended to offer insights which are mainly based on quantitative cohort tracking studies. What is missing is the student voice that allows one to understand the individual and collective experiences that underpin these statistics. Studies such as those of Petersen, Louw and Dumont (2009) illustrate that students' challenges are not only academic in nature but also multifaceted and therefore necessitate enquiry which goes beyond quantitative methodologies. In this chapter I therefore focus on the undergraduate and postgraduate interviews, as well as on students' reflection papers, as it is in these data sources that students give meaning to the factors that shaped their degree paths and the choices they made. The questions in the interviews and reflection papers sought to gain insight into the following: the reasons behind the students' decisions to proceed to postgraduate studies, their understandings and perceptions of their new discourse communities and the dominant discourses and literacy practices therein, the extent to which they felt they belonged in their new disciplines and reasons behind these feelings, and lastly their views on their EAL status and the extent to which they felt this impacted on their academic engagement at the postgraduate level. In the next section I describe the students' investments in the identities linked to their first choice of degree.

Investing in the identities of psychologist and lawyer

In the first postgraduate interview, which was conducted towards the end of the first semester, I questioned the students on the reasons behind their decision to register for postgraduate studies. The data presented in this section illuminate the ways in which the students' degree paths and choice of postgraduate degrees were largely shaped by their investment in their undergraduate aspirations to study law and psychology and to qualify as psychologists and lawyers. The students in the Law Faculty, Harold and Andrew who were registered for honours in Criminology, as well as Babalwa and Noluthando who were studying towards LLB degrees, spoke of this investment in clear terms in their postgraduate interviews.

Andrew's investment in the discipline of psychology and the extent to which he was determined to continue with it after graduating was evident in his undergraduate years. In his first undergraduate year he registered for a degree in Social Work in order to gain entry into psychology after not having met the Psychology Department's competitive entrance requirements. When asked in an interview in his second year whether he enjoyed social work, he stated, 'It was enjoyable but psychology was my main interest' (undergraduate interview 3, 2003). His determination to proceed with psychology after graduating was so strong that in his second-year interview, he spoke of how he would consider moving to another institution if he could not register for honours in Psychology at the UCT.

As his undergraduate studies progressed, Andrew's interviews reflected how he was gaining confidence in himself and in his abilities as a humanities student. His identity as a psychology student became increasingly important to him. This is reflected in the following statement which he wrote in his undergraduate reflection paper (see also Kapp and Bangeni 2011):

> I have come to realize over these past three years that it is one thing to be in a discipline and another 'to be' the discipline. And each day I find more and more evidence within myself that I am at that point where I moved from being in my discipline to where I am my discipline. This is evident in my speech, thought, and in the ways I approach things; whether in an academic context or informal setting. (reflection paper 2004)

Within the field of education, Bourdieu (1990) extends his notion of *habitus* to include an academic *habitus* and within that a 'disciplinary *habitus*' (see Klüver and Schmidt 1990). In this chapter, the notion of a disciplinary habitus offers a lens through which to characterize the ways of thinking, feeling and believing which the research participants brought from their undergraduate disciplines. These dispositions then came to influence how the students made sense of their choices in the process of coming to terms with new discourses and ways of thinking and believing that characterize their postgraduate disciplines, as is evident in Andrew's statement.

Andrew's best friend Harold had similar reasons for continuing with his studies after graduating in that he also hoped to access postgraduate studies in psychology. His decision to register for postgraduate studies was also based on what he vaguely described as the need to 'finish what I had started' (postgraduate interview 1, 2005). At the beginning of his first postgraduate interview he elaborated on his reasoning in the following way: 'I felt it's not done until I … I just had this vision, and I thought that if I just go out there, if I went out there to get the money first without my honours, feel the money and be able to afford, I'll lose the initial touch, that thing of what university is all about.'

Like Andrew, Harold came from a working-class background and like Andrew, was the first in his family to register for a tertiary qualification. He identified Afrikaans as his home language even though his family members spoke English and Afrikaans equally. Originally from the province of KwaZulu-Natal, he initially registered for a Bachelor of Arts degree but changed his registration to a Bachelor of Social Science in his second year, where, like Andrew, he majored in Psychology and Sociology. His investment in psychology was evident in a statement he wrote in his undergraduate reflection paper: 'Personally I have found that I score better in my psychology essays due to the fact that I see myself becoming a clinical psychologist in the end and I therefore put more work and emphasis in that course' (undergraduate reflection paper, 2004).

Both Harold and Andrew graduated in 2004 with majors in Psychology and Sociology but did not qualify for honours in Psychology. They then registered for honours in Criminal Justice, which they hoped would facilitate access to psychology: 'So getting a degree in Criminology is going to allow us to go back into the original discipline we wanted to do' (Andrew, postgraduate interview 1, 2005). Harold echoed Andrew's words in his interview:

> I was planning to do a postgraduate degree in Psychology and within Psych, I wanted Forensic Psychology, uhm, then after not getting through someone said I can do Criminology because there's no Forensic Psychology in South Africa. I thought okay it would be something interesting it would give me a criminology background into the whole thing which would then put me at an advantage when I do my Psychology later.

However, both students struggled with the world view assumed by the social practices within the Law Faculty and the lawyer identity they were expected to take on (see Bangeni 2009 for a detailed description of these struggles). The cultural elements of the discipline were substantially different from those of their previous learning contexts. This inevitably resulted in tensions between their past selves, their disciplinary habitus and the regulative practices constituting the new field. An example of this struggle is a comment made by Andrew where he directly addressed the implications of being in the Law Faculty for his writing: 'Everything is about the law. I feel that what I bring to the Law Faculty and what this environment requires from me, it's so far from psychology. It's law-structured, it has been set, it has been structured, there is no room for debate ... and this affects how I am able to express myself in my writing' (postgraduate interview 2, 2005). This struggle resulted in Andrew and Harold questioning the discipline's knowledge-validation practices as they attempted to make sense of the professional identities and corresponding world views fostered by the discipline. Both students explicitly rejected the lawyer identity, vehemently stating that they could not imagine themselves as lawyers. But despite this struggle with the epistemological orientation of their new context, they managed to graduate with honours degrees at the end of the year. Andrew's investment in psychology saw him register for a masters in Clinical Psychology at another institution. He then went on to practise as a clinical psychologist in his home town and to register for a Ph.D. in Psychology.

Harold and Andrew's trajectories reflect what Klemenčič (2015) defines as agency: one's *belief* in one's efficacy and that one's actions will bring about desired effects. Similarly, Bean (in Seidman 2005) maintains that self-efficacy beliefs are what ultimately determine the extent of an individual's investment. Both Harold and Andrew's undergraduate and postgraduate interviews reflected the extent to which their decision to register for postgraduate studies was heavily influenced by the need to prove they could succeed despite the challenges of their working-class background. In these interviews they spoke of the actions they took to realize their dream of ultimately studying for Psychology honours.

The data also illustrate the influence of family circumstances and influences on the students' degree pathways. Andrew's family circumstances remained a constant motivating factor in his undergraduate years, as he wanted to rise above the poverty, gangsterism and drug abuse that characterized the area in which he grew up. He made reference to this in explaining his decision to study further: 'One thing which inspired me was that I wanted recognition you know, I wanted to break off from where I come from. Despite the circumstances that you are faced with but the reality is that you want to be something' (postgraduate interview 1, 2005). A majority of the participants in both projects were from communities that are characterized by poverty and crime. While they felt relief at having managed to escape these circumstances, in their undergraduate interviews they described how they were invested in graduating, finding employment and returning to their communities to 'give back' (see Bangeni and Kapp 2005). The decision to register for postgraduate studies instead of finding employment, therefore, had implications for their families and immediate communities.

The other law students, Noluthando and Babalwa, both registered for the three-year postgraduate LLB degree after having graduated with Bachelor of Social Science degrees. Noluthando, a multilingual speaker of Xhosa and

Setswana, was raised by her Xhosa grandmother in the Northern Cape. Her father was a businessman and her mother a domestic worker. She did most of her schooling at a relatively well-resourced, private Catholic school in an area where the majority of students were black. After matriculating, she was persuaded by a friend to apply to the UCT and did so even though she felt she would not succeed due to its reputation as a leading African institution. Noluthando's initial months were marked by frustration as she had intended to register for the LLB degree in her first year but was not accepted into the Law Faculty due to her marks:

> When I came here I thought that I was going to be introduced to law in my first year of study. Then to my surprise I learnt I had to get 60 per cent to get to the Law Faculty. They did not accept me for the BA Law but for the general BA. I found this very frustrating because I did not come here to study social sciences. (undergraduate interview 1, 2002)

Noluthando's frustration with the institution and her placement in the Faculty of Humanities extended to how she perceived institutional culture. In her second first-year undergraduate interview, in response to a question on how she perceived the culture of the institution, she expressed her disapproval of what she referred to as its 'white culture'. Like the other participants in the undergraduate study, she struggled with the clearly visible class differences among the student population. She did, however, state at the end of the interview that she was adapting to being in the Humanities Faculty and acknowledged the value of the Social Science courses she was studying. She majored in Political Studies, which she thoroughly enjoyed. Below, she explains the reason why she registered for postgraduate studies:

> I always wanted to do law especially when I was applying at first year. And then I was accepted in the humanities and I didn't want to do it but then I thought it was quite okay because it was the first year. I was just going to get a certain percentage and go on [to Law] but then I didn't. I couldn't get the required 60 per cent so I was like, I would come back and after grad I would do law. So here I am now. (postgraduate interview 1, 2005)

The decision to study law was strongly influenced by her grandfather, who was a lawyer. Her entry into the Law Faculty, however, was not what she expected it would be. Her postgraduate status seemed to bring with it pressure which was largely due to family expectations. This was evident in her description of her family's reaction to the fact that she had graduated and was now a registered student in the Law Faculty: 'My dad is telling everyone that I'm a law student and my other family members as well are telling everyone the same thing. It creates expectations, so much pressure' (postgraduate interview 1, 2005). Like Andrew, Noluthando was, at this point, attempting to make sense of her disciplinary identity and the implications for her engagement with the literacy practices of the discipline:

> It [being a postgraduate student] feels good, but on the other hand postgrad is tough. I thought it was going to be easier since I was bringing all this knowledge from my undergrad but it's tough. I'm kind of floating. I don't know whether I know or I don't know. The kind of writing here just puts me in a very awkward position. (postgraduate interview 1, 2005)

The students' analyses of the postgraduate domain were not restricted to their immediate learning environments or the knowledge shaping these learning environments, but extended to include accounts of the physical spaces which they occupied. Noluthando supported her view of the faculty as 'white and male dominated' by referring to the dean's office with its row of portraits depicting past deans and influential people in the Faculty, who are mostly male and white: 'The Faculty is snobbish, competitive, white male dominated, and "stuck-up"'(postgraduate interview 1, 2005). This description illustrates how she perceived the institutional culture to be inscribed in the institution's physical spaces in ways that positioned particular students as outsiders. Noluthando's characterization of the faculty resonates with Sander's (2011) description of law school education in the United States and its agenda as being essentially controlled by white middle-class males.

Noluthando's postgraduate interviews were characterized by a deep anger and resentment at her new discipline. In her interview she referred to what she perceived as high dropout rates in the Faculty: 'The Law Faculty is very harsh; people drop out. In the first semester, a whole lot of people drop out. The pressure! There's too much pressure.' In discussing the Faculty dropout rates, she made reference to the low percentage of black graduates: 'It's very difficult for black people who have English as a second language to graduate in the Law Faculty, it's very difficult' (postgraduate interview 1, 2005). Babalwa also commented on the racial profile of the Faculty in her postgraduate reflection paper where she highlighted the fact that most of the black students in the Faculty are from Southern African Development Community countries, with less than 5 per cent being South Africans. While the students mostly foregrounded social class in explaining their undergraduate experiences and their position within the institution, it appears that they foregrounded their racial identities heavily in explaining their engagement in the space of the Law Faculty and its institutional culture.

Once she was a postgraduate student, Noluthando spoke of her undergraduate studies in positive terms in comparison to her new environment. At this stage of her transition it seemed that her initial resentment of having to study in the social sciences for her undergraduate degree had been replaced by an appreciation of all that she had learnt. She noted that accessing the LLB degree via the Humanities did, in some ways, prepare her for studying in the Law Faculty and that she was 'very humbled' by the way the Humanities had shaped her way of thinking and writing. In her postgraduate reflection paper she compared the Humanities and Law Faculties, pointing out that there was 'intellectual freedom' in the Faculty of Humanities, which she felt was not encouraged in Law. This perceived lack of debate, along with what Noluthando described as inaccessible teaching methods, seemed to affect her ability to be agentic in her new learning context. While she had initially found it important to approach her lecturers, her perception of the institutional culture within the Faculty restricted her engagement with her lecturers: 'There's one lecturer who is very closed up. She doesn't want to go outside of the textbook in her teaching. Once you challenge her, she gets very defensive, as if she's saying "I've been here so I know." I finally decided not to question her, whether I understood or not.' Noluthando did not submit any of her postgraduate writing to the research project. In her second interview she claimed that she was deeply dissatisfied with her marks and had, as a result, torn up most of her marked essays. She left the institution after being excluded for failing her first LLB year.

Babalwa's reasons for making the decision to proceed to postgraduate studies after graduating were similar to Noluthando's in that she also had aspirations to study law in her first year. Like Noluthando, she did not obtain the required points to gain entry into law in her first year and took the decision to access law via the Humanities. Babalwa grew up in a township in Cape Town and attended a township school where she did her primary education through the medium of Xhosa. She only encountered English as the language of learning at high school, which was a relatively well-resourced school situated closer to the city and attended by African and coloured learners. In her first interview with me she was not forthcoming about the factors that influenced her to apply to the institution, simply stating that she thought 'it was the best option' (undergraduate interview 1, 2002).

Over time Babalwa came to appreciate studying in the Humanities and selected Political Studies and Sociology as her majors. The reflection paper that she wrote in her third year in 2004 was very insightful and aptly captured her academic journey and her perceptions of notable changes in her academic persona. These included her ability to question. Her trajectory in the course of her undergraduate studies initially saw her questioning the epistemological foundations of her disciplines, especially philosophy. In this reflection paper she wrote: 'I am frustrated that here in the Humanities there is no right answer.' She made the same comment in her second first-year interview which took place in the second semester. 'There is nothing concrete. There is no concrete answer as compared to mathematics and science; you have to think all the time' (undergraduate interview 2, 2002; see also Kapp and Bangeni 2009). However, she ultimately came to appreciate this as it allowed her to see that there were alternative ways of viewing contentious issues as far as culture and religion were concerned. This empowered her to challenge values and traditions which she perceived as sexist within her community and in church practices, a skill which she believed would facilitate her engagement in law: 'I think this has prepared me well for studying law when I graduate' (undergraduate reflection paper, 2004).

Even though she was very optimistic about studying law, the data from Babalwa's postgraduate interviews and reflection paper reveal how she, like Noluthando, struggled with the discipline. In describing her new environment, Babalwa spoke of the implications of the transition for the literacy practices she had acquired in her undergraduate courses and those she now had to engage in: 'Unfortunately for me, I entered a new academic discipline which means that I have to unlearn what I learned in my previous degree. So, in terms of writing and engaging with the discipline it has not been an easy transition for me' (postgraduate interview 1, 2005). It is clear from the above quote that Babalwa felt that her entry into her new discipline rendered the knowledge that she had gained in her previous disciplines insignificant and therefore unworthy of retaining. Her postgraduate reflection paper was also striking in that she focused her description of the law discipline on its professional aspects. In responding to a question which sought to find out what students appreciated about their postgraduate disciplines she wrote:

- It [law discipline] prepares you well for the practice; it has codes of conduct to follow that are consistent throughout the country;
- it requires discipline and respect and for the individual to uphold the qualities and qualification for attorney or advocate;
- it prepares you to serve the public with dignity.

Klemenčič's (2015) notion of *looking forward* is applicable here. Babalwa focused her description of the Law Faculty on the profession. This particular characterization of the discipline, while appearing to contradict her feelings of disillusionment, was not surprising given her investment in studying law and practising in the field. Like Noluthando, Babalwa was excluded from the Faculty after failing her first year. After leaving the institution she maintained that she planned to continue to study for her LLB degree at a distance education institution. She managed to register but did not complete the degree as she was appointed as a junior researcher at a research institution. In time, her interests took a different route, and she graduated with an honours degree in Sustainable Development in 2010. When she informed me of this achievement she had not lost sight of her initial objective and still planned to complete her LLB degree as soon as she found the time and financial support to do so. While this chapter does not provide a detailed description of the factors which led to Babalwa and Noluthando's exclusion from the Faculty, the findings of research on novice writers in law by Bangeni and Greenbaum (2013) suggest that postgraduate students who enter the Faculty without a legal background struggle with the discipline's literacy demands to the same extent as first-year students straight from high school.

In this section I have illustrated the ways in which the students' trajectories from undergraduate studies into their postgraduate disciplines were characterized by a significant amount of strategizing. The choices which they made were, to an extent, dictated by shortcomings in academic performance as they were unable to access their first choice of degree due to not having attained the required admissions' scores. The data presented here illustrate the ways in which these choices played out in their negotiation of postgraduate spaces and the attendant discourses. In the next section I present the experiences of the remaining two students who were registered for postgraduate degrees in Commerce: Sizwe in Marketing and Dudu in Human Resource Management. Unlike the law participants, their degree paths were marked less by investments in first choice of degrees and more by strategic attempts to access the graduate job market.

Accessing the job market

In their postgraduate interviews, Sizwe and Dudu gave varied responses as to why they decided to proceed to postgraduate studies. Unlike the law students, whose reasons were largely tied to an investment in their first choice degrees, Sizwe and Dudu's responses were mainly financial in nature, and as I had anticipated, reflected strong leanings towards an anticipation of future careers in the field. Like Andrew and Harold, Sizwe was not accepted into the honours degree he chose due to his marks. Having failed to secure a job for which he had applied, he registered for the postgraduate diploma in Marketing. This was, according to him, the quickest way to gain entry into an increasingly competitive job market:

> They [International Relations] said they need 70 per cent or 65 per cent average and I didn't get that, I just managed to pass. If I didn't get accepted into International Relations I was going to work in the government sector but I got a letter from the department which said I'm not accepted. That's how I ended up doing marketing. It's not something I planned. I didn't have a job and needed to get one so I thought I should register for the Marketing diploma to improve my chances. (postgraduate interview 1, 2005)

This reasoning was backed by the convener of the Marketing diploma. When I asked for his opinion regarding the reasons behind students' decisions to register for the diploma he said:

> You can study poetry, for example, in Humanities and it might be great for three years but it's unlikely to get you a good job. So there are students who realize that and they come through to us. It's not necessarily true that the market can accommodate all the students which we output umm … but I like to think we are quite competitive in terms of the programmes we offer and our students do get jobs and do pretty well in the workplace. (interview with the programme convener)

Sizwe's pressing need to find a job after obtaining his degree can be traced back to his home life. He grew up in a hostel in one of the local townships located on the outskirts of the city. In South African townships, hostels were created during apartheid to accommodate African migrant workers. Sizwe's father worked at the dockside in the city and his mother made and sold dresses from home. He attended a school in the community that was within walking distance of the hostel. Sizwe excelled at school, particularly in history, and was awarded a certificate by the Western Cape Education Department for being the top student in the subject in the province, an acknowledgement that convinced him and his family that he should access HE, despite the family's dire financial position.

When Sizwe was accepted at the University he had, like Noluthando and Babalwa, selected law as his first choice but had to register for a Social Science degree instead due to inadequate matriculation points. His plan to register for Law courses in his second year did not materialize after he failed a course in his first year. This prevented him from obtaining the required 63 per cent average, which would have enabled him to do so. As a consequence, he changed his registration from a BA Law to Public Policy and Administration (PPA) in his second year, selecting History and Political Studies as his majors. Like Noluthando and Babalwa, Sizwe found value in studying the social sciences and his majors. He especially loved political studies, even volunteering to tutor first-year students in his university residence in his second year. Sizwe made a number of strategic moves in his undergraduate years. One of these was his decision to join the Investment Society, a society on campus that advises students on investing. After graduating, this strategizing extended to his decision to register for the Marketing diploma. Sizwe graduated in 2007 after having failed one of his mathematics courses which he completed at a distance education institution. He then worked for a local non-governmental organization.

Dudu's reasons for proceeding to postgraduate studies were linked to her quest for further knowledge and as a means of preparing herself for the workplace:

> I wanted to get the skills that I didn't get in this particular field and that's why I had to register [for postgraduate studies] to get that. And I'm getting that so far. It was not like I just wanted to get to postgrad, I wanted to enhance the knowledge I have so that when I get to the workplace I don't get there blank. Yeah, that's what I can say. (postgraduate interview 1, 2005)

While Sizwe's reason was mainly instrumental, Dudu's was also influenced by how her family and community perceived the act of pursuing postgraduate studies. In her first postgraduate interview Dudu referred to her graduation party which she had invited me to attend:

> Now people back there know I have graduated. Now they will expect me to go on. And the mere fact that people acknowledge me it comes back to me as well. I have to make sure that I study further and that I pass because people will be like she was postgrad and didn't make it. So it's not responsibility to me only but to people out there. Not only at varsity but at home as well. Yeah and the community as well because people know that I'm doing postgrad. Well they thought I was working but they know I'm doing postgrad they expect me to pass. (postgraduate interview 1, 2005)

The above was evident at the party when the guest speaker said that Dudu had set an example for other young people in the community to follow. This was echoed by the other speakers who all emphasized the importance of 'going as far as you can go' (field notes 2004), and who obviously expected that of Dudu.

In the above quotes, Klemenčič's (2015) notion of *temporal agency* in terms of looking back and looking forward is evident in Dudu's use of the phrase 'people back there' when referring to her community, signalling a space with which she no longer seemed to identify. This phrase seems particularly significant when juxtaposed with her family and community's plea to her to 'go as far as you can go'. It would seem that this not only referred to their desire for her to further her education but also suggests a desire to see her move on from the space of the township. Ball et al. (2002: 52–3) explain how the act of choosing an HE institution is informed not only by cognitive factors which are linked to a student's performance but also by 'social classifications of self and institution'. In the light of this statement, it is important to consider data that offer insights into students' constructions of the institution and the physical space it occupies in the city's landscape. It is striking how the participants who were from townships in Cape Town, including Sizwe and Dudu, described the University when they explained their decision to apply to the institution. In one of her interviews, Dudu spoke of how her family referred to the UCT as '*Entabeni*', a Xhosa word which means 'up on the hill'. While they use this term to refer to the University's physical position at the foot of Devil's Peak and its high visibility in the city's geographical landscape, it also, perhaps more significantly, suggests how township residents perceive it and the quality of education it offers, as being out of their immediate reach. As first-generation students from working-class backgrounds, both Dudu and Sizwe cited this perceived unattainability as a motivating factor in their decisions to access HE and to apply to the institution. Being at the UCT therefore signalled upward mobility both literally and figuratively: literally moving from the township to the top of the hill, and figuratively by gaining access to the affordances of a good-quality education and the impact of this on their academic and domestic lives.

Dudu, like Sizwe, was born in Cape Town and grew up in one of the city's townships with her mother. She was educated at what she referred to as a well-resourced coloured school situated on the periphery of one of the suburbs. She applied to the UCT 'to fulfil my mother's wish. I just did not have this thing where everyone wanted to study at UCT but my mom wanted me to go to an institution that had all the resources so I came.' She majored in Psychology and Sociology as she wanted to be a psychologist 'to help people you know'. However, she did not manage to access Psychology honours either and registered for a diploma in

Human Resources instead. In her second postgraduate interview she spoke of how she planned to leave Cape Town after completing her postgraduate studies: 'I have been in Cape Town all my life and I would want to be in an environment that challenges me, where I feel that my capabilities have been exhausted and I don't feel I've achieved that yet. I think Jo'burg would be challenging for me.' Thomson's (2009: 36) study of young people making the transition to adulthood in the UK classifies this phenomenon of 'moving out in order to move on' as a key marker of change and growth. It seems that both Dudu and Sizwe had this in mind when they spoke about the need to relocate. Indeed, after her second graduation Dudu managed to secure a job in HR in Johannesburg.

Dudu's and Sizwe's descriptions of the postgraduate environment reflect the ways in which the disciplinary habitus acquired within their undergraduate majors played a role in determining their approaches to learning within marketing and HR. The data from their postgraduate interviews reflect how they insisted on viewing the business cases they had to produce from the perspective of their undergraduate majors. While both were aware of the risks this entailed, they insisted on creating a space for the disciplinary habitus attached to their former disciplines, asserting that this enabled a more holistic way of engaging with the issues raised in these cases. However, like Harold and Andrew, they succeeded in adapting to the requirements of their professional disciplines, a process which, according to Klemenčič (2015), constitutes agency.

In the questions guiding the postgraduate reflection papers I ended by asking all six students whether they felt they belonged in their disciplines. Initially, Dudu stated that she did not feel a sense of belonging. She related this feeling to her identity as a former humanities student: 'I come from a humanities background and those were comfortable three years at humanities. I was settled there and now being at commerce is a challenging experience.' Later in the same interview however, she stated that she did feel at home in the Commerce Faculty. Her positive feeling about the new context was linked to her investment in studying Human Resources:

> Okay, I do partly feel that I belong. I think uhm, obviously HR has been my passion. So now I'm dealing with HR. The bulk of my work in my postgrad course is HR. So I feel at home in that sense. I'm dealing with my passion on a daily basis. That's what I intend doing after graduation. At the same time I'm exposed to different kinds of courses, numerically or whatever. They'll probably skill me like in a number of various skills which I can use when I get a job in this field. So, I probably feel at home in that manner as I'm very much into HR.

For Dudu, the extent to which she felt she belonged was linked to the affordances of the disciplinary knowledge for her engagement with the profession. Her postgraduate interviews reflected how she strived to achieve her goal of working for her 'dream company'. At the time of her second postgraduate interview she had just come from an interview for a position in the company's Human Resources department:

> Even if I didn't make it now but I think I did the best I did. If I didn't get it that won't be a limit. I'll pursue other companies then. The fact that I made through, getting selected from 150 applicants at UCT means I have what it takes. I don't mean to be demotivating but if you do believe in yourself like I do then yeah. Even in the interview when the lady asked me [where I see myself], I said I see myself as an HR director. And I wanna get there one day even if it takes me a number of years I'll achieve that goal.

The above quote highlights what Klemenčič (2015: 18) calls 'the projective dimension of agency [where] students construct new possible images of future selves and along with these projections, the ways to achieve them'. Dudu's closing statement in her final postgraduate interview sums this up cogently:

> Yeah I'm sure you can also see the difference in me from first year. I can say it all goes with learning, like in your experiences, academically mostly. You get to know what you want in life. Postgrad has shaped my life. It shaped my life so much in terms of my values and my passion like where I see myself in five years and what I want to do.

Similarly, Sizwe's response to my question about belonging was mainly expressed in terms of an imagined future self and anticipated financial rewards:

> I feel like I belong to my discipline. You know I've developed a business interest since I got to my discipline so I know for sure that when I have enough money I'll try to open up my own business. So those business issues we are dealing with and strategies have helped me. I can kind of come up with my own business and make money. I'll build on my interest in my discipline, since I now have business interests because of it.

Conclusion

In this chapter I have drawn on data which show the value of a longitudinal consideration of black students' experiences within HE and how they make sense of the choices that inform their degree paths. In most instances, the quality of education with which they enter the institution significantly limits their options. Even though the student sample is limited to six, the data show how students' degree paths are marked by strategizing which they have to do from their first year into their postgraduate studies due to a lack of access to anticipated degree paths. I have also shown how factors such as disciplinary habitus and levels of investment in the degree can assist in explaining students' various challenges regarding the extent to which they are effectively able to negotiate the transition from undergraduate to postgraduate spaces of engagement. The nature and extent of their individual investments had implications for how they negotiated their emerging professional identities. The law students' struggles with the values of their discipline, and their lack of investment in practising law, resulted in an explicit rejection of the professional identities attached to legal studies. On the other hand, Sizwe and Dudu, who were both able to imagine themselves in the marketing and management professions, embraced the professional identities carved out for them by their new context as they acknowledged its affordances for their careers.

The data show how investment functioned on another level, namely in the students' investment in the knowledge they brought with them from their undergraduate disciplines, particularly their majors. While these disciplines presented challenges, their investment in the knowledge that they brought to their postgraduate disciplines enabled them to be agentic in a number of instances. It enabled them to question and challenge the structures within marketing and law and informed their attempts to carve out spaces for other ways of believing and arguing.

The data also provide insights into the affordances of the contested honours year and the postgraduate diploma. While the educational benefits of an additional undergraduate year as suggested in the Council on Higher Education Report (2013) are obvious, the findings point to the platform afforded by the honours year for the reconciliation of embodied literacy practices and ways of thinking, with those valued in the postgraduate domain. The data show how the honours space functions as a middle ground between undergraduate studies and the postgraduate proper. They also allude to its mediative role as it facilitates a dialogue between the forms of knowledge students bring with them from former undergraduate spaces and those valued within postgraduate disciplines and their corresponding professions. In highlighting this mediative role the data underscore the significance of honours degrees and postgraduate diplomas as transitional postgraduate studies, as spaces in which students can make sense of the knowledge they bring from undergraduate studies in preparation for entry into the postgraduate proper or the workplace. It is therefore crucial for academic development and disciplinary specialists to work together to assist students in reconciling the knowledge they bring with them from undergraduate disciplines with new forms of knowledge and discourses. This is especially important for the opening up of access into the postgraduate proper for black students who were classified as being at risk when they entered university.

References

Ball, S. J., Davies, J., David, M. and Reay, D. (2002), '"Classification" and "Judgement": Social Class and the "Cognitive Structures" of Choice of Higher Education', *British Journal of Sociology of Education*, 23(1): 51–72.

Bangeni, B. (2009), 'Negotiating between Past and Present Discourse Values in a Postgraduate Law Course: Implications for Writing', *Southern African Linguistics and Applied Language Studies*, 27(1): 65–76.

Bangeni, B. and Greenbaum, L. (2013), 'An Analysis of the Textual Practices of Undergraduate and Postgraduate Novice Writers in Law', *Per Linguam*, 29(2): 72–84.

Bangeni, B. and Kapp, R. (2005), 'Identities in Transition: Shifting Conceptions of Home among "Black" South African University Students', *African Studies Review*, 48 (3): 1–19.

Bangeni, B. and Kapp, R. (2006), '"I Want to Write about the Dalai Lama without being Penalised": Literacies in Transition', in L. Thesen and E. van Pletzen (eds), *Languages of Change*, 67–83, New York and London: Continuum Publishers.

Becher T. 1989. *Academic Tribes and Territories: intellectual enquiry and the cultures of disciplines.* New York, USA: Open University Press.

Bhabha, H. (1994), *The Location of Culture*, London: Routledge.

Blommaert, J. (2010), *The Sociolinguistics of Globalization*, Cambridge: Cambridge University Press.

Boughey, C. (2005), 'Epistemological Access to the University: An Alternative Perspective', *South African Journal of Higher Education*, 19 (3): 638–50.

Bourdieu, P. (1990), *The Logic of Practice*, Stanford, CA: Stanford University Press.

Council on Higher Education, (2013), *A Proposal for Undergraduate Curriculum Reform in South Africa: The Case for a Flexible Curriculum Structure*, http://www.che.ac.za/sites/default/files/publications/, accessed 28 November 2013.

Hetherington, K. (1998), *Expressions of Identity: Space, Performance, Politics*, London and New Delhi: Sage Publications.

Kapp, R. and Bangeni, B. (2009), 'Positioning (in) the Discipline: Undergraduate Students' Negotiations of Disciplinary Discourses', *Teaching in Higher Education*, 14(6): 587–96.

Kapp, R. and Bangeni, B. (2011), 'A Longitudinal Study of Students' Negotiation of Language, Literacy and Identity', *Southern African Linguistics and Applied Language Studies*, 29(2): 195–206.

Klemenčič, M. (2015), 'What is Student Agency? An Ontological Exploration in the Context of Research on Student Engagement', in Klemenčič, M., Bergan, S. and Primožič, R. (eds), *Student Engagement in Europe: Society, Higher Education and Student Governance*, 11–29, Council of Europe Higher Education Series No. 20, Strasbourg: Council of Europe Publishing.

Klüver, J. and Schmidt, J. (1990), 'The Disciplinary Realisation of Cognitive Education', *European Journal of Education*, 25(3): 305–17.

Letseka, M., Cosser, M., Breier, M. and Visser, M. (2010), *Student Retention and Graduate Destination: Higher Education and Labour Market Access and Success*, Cape Town: Human Sciences Research Council Press.

McKenna, S. (2004), 'A Critical Investigation into the Discourses used to Construct Academic Literacy at the Durban Institute of Technology'. Published Ph.D. thesis, Rhodes University, Grahamstown.

Norton, B. (2000), *Identity and Language Learning: Gender, Ethnicity and Educational Change*, London: Longman.

Paxton, M. (2003), 'Developing Academic Literacy in Economics in a South African University', *Literacy and Numeracy Studies*, 12(2): 1–14.

Petersen, I., Louw, J. and Dumont, K. (2009), 'Adjustment to University and Academic Performance among Disadvantaged Students in South Africa', *Educational Psychology*, 29(1): 99–115.

Reay, D., David, M. E. and Ball, S. (2005), *Degrees of Choice: Social Class, Race and Gender in Higher Education*, Stoke-on-Trent: Trentham Books.

Sander, R. H. (2011), 'Class in American Legal Education', *Denver University Law Review*, 88: 631–82.

Sarup, M. (1996), *Identity, Culture and the Postmodern World*, Edinburgh: Edinburgh University Press.

Scott, I., Yeld, N. and Hendry, J. (2007), 'A Case for Improving Teaching and Learning in South African Higher Education', *Higher Education Monitor* No.6, Pretoria: Research Paper Prepared for the Council on Higher Education.

Seidman, A. (2005), *College Student Retention: Formula for Student Success*, Westport: Praeger Publishers.

Thesen, L. (1997), 'Voices, Discourse and Transition: In Search of New Categories in EAP', *TESOL Quarterly*, 31(3): 487–511.

Thomson, R. (2009), *Unfolding Lives: Youth, Gender and Change*, Bristol: The Policy Press.

University of Cape Town (2005), 'Teaching and Learning Report: A Report on the 2005 Academic Year', https://www.uct.ac.za/downloads/news.uct.ac.za/publications/ teaching_learning_2005.pdf. Accessed 13 June 2013

University of Cape Town, Institutional Planning Department (2008), 'A Report on Institutional Development, 2000–2008', http://www.uct.ac.za/downloads/news.uct. ac.za/publications/institutional_report0008.pdf. Accessed 13 June 2013.

van Pletzen, E. (2006), 'A Body of Reading: Making "visible" the Reading Experiences of First-Year Medical Students', in L. Thesen and E. van Pletzen (eds), *Academic Literacy and the Languages of Change*, 104–29, London and New York: Continuum.

van Schalkwyk, S., Bitzer, E. and van der Walt, C. (2009), 'Acquiring Academic Literacy: A Case of First-Year Extended Degree Programme Students', *Southern African Linguistics and Applied Language Studies*, 27(2): 189–201.

Zulu, C. (2005), 'Academic Reading Ability of First-Year Students: What's High School Performance or Prior Exposure to Academic Reading got to do with it?', *Southern African Linguistics and Applied Language Studies*, 23(1): 111–23.

7

Enabling Capabilities in an Engineering Extended Curriculum Programme

Tracy S. Craig

Introduction

The Academic Support Programme for Engineering (ASPECT) was founded in 1988 to increase access to engineering studies at the University of Cape Town (UCT) for students from disadvantaged backgrounds and to provide academic support for those students (Sass 1988; Meyer and Sass 1992; Jawitz 1994; Jawitz and Scott 1997). The legacy of apartheid is such that graduation rates of students from disadvantaged backgrounds are still low. The need for the Programme to provide academic (and other) support to students from a previously disadvantaged educational system has been recognized as an important part of the University's agenda of access and transformation, providing educational opportunities and resources to ameliorate inequalities in our society. The students who enter the Programme at the beginning of their first year at the UCT are South African black students. ASPECT students (in general, not exclusively) enter under special admissions circumstances. In general, the students have been successful, despite coming from poorly resourced home backgrounds and schools with a weak academic record. They are frequently the first member of their family, school or larger community to be accepted at university (Pym and Kapp 2013; Craig 2013; Kapp et al. 2014).

The aim of ASPECT is to provide the necessary academic foundations which the students did not receive at school and to support students through the school-university transition, which is especially tough for first-generation, rural students with inadequate preparation from school (Pearce et al. 2015). Walker (2003: 171) points out that 'in a class-stratified society widening participation is a matter of justice' and Nussbaum (2006: 387) agrees when she states that 'nothing could be more crucial to democracy than the education of its citizens'.

The Programme's role is to provide marginalized students with crucial access to studies which can have a transformative effect on the individual, their family and on their greater communities.

The ASPECT model offers a decreased course load and additional support, with a particular focus on mathematics and physics. The students do the same courses as the mainstream students, at the same pace, but fewer of them at a time, resulting in spreading the four-year degree over five years. The model is one of 'more time, more tuition' (Kloot, Case and Marshal 2008: 803). Students in the ASPECT programme have a different experience to those in the mainstream programme in a number of ways: the ASPECT first-year class is smaller than the mainstream classes, roughly 80 in ASPECT to 500 in the mainstream, which allows the students and lecturers to get to know one another better and allows for varied class activities involving more interaction, active learning and group work. I am one of the mathematics lecturers on the Programme and while the primary focus of ASPECT is on supporting students' academic transitions, we recognize that the transition requires psycho-social support as well. For example, the ASPECT administrative assistant is far more than a secretary, filling a maternal role for students far from home and usually the first to hear of family, financial or other stressors.

In this chapter I use the lens of Amartya Sen's capability approach (see below) to identify the capabilities the Programme expects to enable, and compare them to the capabilities articulated by fifteen ASPECT students who participated in the longitudinal study. I examine the agreements and silences and observe that while certain key capabilities are being enabled as hoped, others are not well aligned across the Programme expectation/student experience divide. The success of ASPECT, as one small part of a much larger national programme of transformation and social justice in higher education, hinges in part on the successful enabling of capabilities which provide students with the potential to choose a life of value. I argue that the efficacy of ASPECT would be increased by a two-pronged approach, that of extending academic support further than first year and redesigning ASPECT as a well-defined learning community. This approach might address some of the perceived shortfalls while benefitting from existing strengths.

The capability approach

The capability approach is generally associated with Amartya Sen, a Nobel Prize-winning economist and philosopher. Sen developed the capability approach as a way of thinking about and evaluating human well-being and matters of social justice. Sen defines capability as 'a person's ability to *do valuable acts* or *reach valuable states of being*; [it] represents the alternative combinations of things a person is able to do or be' (Sen 1993: 30, my italics). In Sen's theoretical framework, achieved outcomes are termed *functionings*, while capabilities are the potential to achieve these functionings. Capabilities are opportunities to achieve while functionings are the actual achievement (Walker 2006; Walker and Unterhalter 2007).

Walker and Unterhalter (2007:8) suggest that 'the [capabilities] approach leads us to ask questions such as ... Do some people get more opportunities to convert their resources into capabilities than others?' In the South African context, as in many other places in the world, disparity of opportunity is undoubtedly the case. Despite countrywide access to basic education, the quality of that education can be extremely poor (Walker 2006; Christie 2010). Not only do social and political circumstances lead to unequal opportunities, but 'schooling can and in some cases does contribute to capability deprivation, often through reproducing existing inequalities' (Tikly and Barrett 2011:7). Students who gain entry into ASPECT are recognized as having the internal resources which could be converted into capabilities. The Programme aims to provide an environment where the students leave with well-developed capabilities and after that it is up to them to choose to realize their capabilities as functionings as much as educational and societal structures will allow.

Methodology

Following Walker (2006) I draw on Robeyns's (2003: 70–71) five criteria for listing capabilities:

1. 'The list should be explicit, discussed, and defended.'
2. We should clarify the method used to generate the list.
3. The level of abstraction of the list should be appropriate for our objectives with respect to our use of the capability approach.
4. Policymakers should first draw up an ideal list, then a pragmatic list.
5. The list should include all important elements with no element reducible to another element.

Since it is not my purpose in this chapter to develop or critique policy, Robeyns's fourth criterion is not applicable here. I draw up and discuss an explicit list;

however, I do not defend it as an ideal list, nor can I be sure that the same list would have arisen through an analysis of a different data set.

The method used to generate the list of capabilities discussed in this chapter was produced by first recognizing and acknowledging the definition referenced earlier of a capability as an ability 'to do valuable acts' or an ability 'to reach valuable states of being' (Sen 1993: 30). Thereafter the annual interview transcripts of the engineering students participating in this study (up to five interviews per student) were examined for references made to 'acts' or 'being' enabled or constrained by the Programme. Parallel to engaging with the interview data, the available formal Programme documentation (a 2008 brochure sent out to prospective students and the 2009 Programme Review document, internal to the institution) was examined for references made to 'acts' or 'being' enabled or constrained by the Programme. Each of these data sources revealed expressions of capabilities as defined above, with areas of overlap and elements arising primarily from one source only.

When references to capabilities in the Programme documentation and in the data in the student interviews are extracted, the following 'abilities to be' or 'to reach valuable states of being' begin our list:

1. to be a university student;
2. to be a member of a valued community.

The abilities 'to do valuable acts' that can be recognized expand the list to include:

3. to transition to university studies;
4. to learn work habits and study skills;
5. to transition into second year and beyond;
6. to graduate in five years.

The capabilities listed here are expressed in general terms, clustering similar elements together, in order to adhere to Robeyns's fifth criterion, that the 'list should include all important elements with no element reducible to another element'. The list is sufficiently abstract for our purposes and includes all important elements recognized by the described method. Having drawn up this explicit list, the capabilities can be discussed, comparing and contrasting the voices of the students with that of the formal Programme documentation.

This chapter draws on interview data from fifteen engineering students who participated in the longitudinal project and who joined the ASPECT extended degree programme as first years in 2009. The longitudinal approach with annual interviews provides successive 'snapshots' of the student's lives (Thomson 2009: 14), allowing one to gain insight (in this case) into the participants' subjective experience of having been part of the extended degree programme. Interview questions covered pre-university experiences, experiences of ASPECT across the years, academic progress and managing challenges, finances, experiences of mathematics and language, social life and hobbies, personal highlights and low points, and future aspirations. Data were collected from multiple interviews for the majority of the fifteen ASPECT students who participated in the longitudinal project. Of the participants, nine have graduated, one is still completing the degree, four were academically excluded and one left the university before completion. In the student quotes used in this chapter the attributions are (Pseudonym, interview year) where the year is a number between 1 (2009) and 5 (2013).

Access: Embarking as a university student

ASPECT gives the students in the Programme the capability to be university students, the first capability on our list. The access role of ASPECT is crucial, because certain school-leaving learners have the resources which can be converted into capabilities during their year in the Programme, allowing them to choose a life of value, that is, to become an engineer. The Programme Review document foregrounds the access purpose of the Programme, access which in many cases would not have been possible without the existence of the Programme:

> The primary role of ASPECT has thus been to provide access and academic support for black and coloured students that enter into the Engineering and Built Environment [EBE] faculty from poor schooling backgrounds and to give them the best preparation for the further years of engineering studies (ASPECT Review 2009: 4); and
> The 'access' mission of the programme remains valid and there are still sufficient students who do graduate who would not have been admitted if it were not for the existence of ASPECT. (ASPECT Review 2009: 22)

Every year some of the students in the class begin their degree in the mainstream class and shift across to the ASPECT class. Those students had already gained access to the University, but were struggling with the mainstream demands and were concerned about their chances of completing the year. 'In Nussbaum's conceptualization, this student has the internal capabilities to handle academic work, but the (external) conditions in the institution to enhance her capabilities are missing or constrained.' (Walker and Unterhalter 2007:11). By choosing the extended degree programme, these students gain, through their own agency, where agency can be defined as 'the space where the individual acts with intentionality' (Case 2013: 31), the opportunity to enhance their capabilities and increase their chances of success. Walker (2005:105) points out that 'notions of agency are central to the capability approach. At the boundary of functionings and capabilities is the matter of choice, where a person exercises his or her agency, having the requisite set of capabilities.' Tsego is one of the students who made such a shift. Her metaphoric comment on the support offered by the Programme illustrates her conception of ASPECT as a site that would provide support that would facilitate her agency: 'ASPECT not only gave me a life vest, they made me swim as well because if you are in mainstream and you see that you are drowning, no one is there to say like – come out, like swim – or something like that but ASPECT did that, they were like – here is a life vest – swim' (Tsego, interview 4).

The capability of being a university student, in particular to be an engineering student, gained by access through ASPECT is a crucial point in the student's academic journey. Once physically present on the UCT campus, with access to lecturers and tutors, the library, electronic resources and fellow students, the student is now in an advantageous position to convert personal and internal resources into capabilities and thereafter academic functionings. The student has the 'capability to aspire' (Walker 2006:17). Walker (2005:109) recognizes that 'the issue for those of us working in education is that schools, colleges and universities contribute, for many people quite substantially, to the formation of their capabilities to function.' Once enrolled in the ASPECT programme, it is the task of the ASPECT staff to support the students in converting their resources into the capabilities required of them, of allowing the students to achieve the potential recognized in them by acceptance into the Programme.

Beyond embarkation: Transitioning to university studies

The capabilities the ASPECT programme hopes to develop in the early stages of first-year studies (as expressed in the brochure and review) are to transition to university studies (3 on our list) and to learn work and study skills (4). Developing the capability to transition to university studies is understood to be supported by a variety of processes including, but not limited to, explicitly teaching topics superficially covered in the school syllabus (an example in mathematics would be log laws), explicitly focusing on problem-solving in mathematics and physics, and paying attention to students' financial and accommodation needs. Developing the capability to learn work and study skills is addressed by the staff in the ASPECT programme in an ongoing manner both within and outside class. Within mathematics and physics classes, the teaching staff endeavour to instil good study skills specific to those disciplines. Outside those classes, the students are taught generic skills such as time management and technical report writing.

The review document articulates ASPECT's aim to facilitate students' transition to university as follows: 'ASPECT strives to provide a supportive environment that is sensitive to students' academic, social and emotional needs in an attempt to address the difficult transition from school to prepare them for tertiary education' (ASPECT Review 2009: 4). This aim appears to accord with participants' experiences. Most students do manage to transform their capability to transition into the achieved outcome of managing the first-year load. In their senior years, the students commented positively on ASPECT's role in closing the gap between school and university by providing individual support in their first year:

> You know that is one of the difficult years for people because they have to adapt to everything but I found it quite differently because through the programme, ASPECT, you had all the support that you needed academic-wise, even though I was not that social person but academic-wise but you had everything that you needed, [staff member], all the other ASPECT staff helping you through everything else (Chris, interview 4); and
>
> I think it was, ASPECT helped me a lot, … but because in ASPECT they do things differently compared to mainstream, I mean it helped me to change my strategy before it was too late … being in ASPECT helped me to close that gap between high school and university. (Senzo, interview 5)

A particular point which students foregrounded (without being asked) was recognition of the value of the decreased load model. Coping with the demands of university studies is made possible by the decreased load, which allows more time per subject and time to develop a more rounded lifestyle, with interests outside academic studies:

> Well first of all I would say [to incoming students] join ASPECT because obviously the academic load will be reduced significantly so that will give them

> enough time to adjust to the whole conditions at the university to be able to, for the next year you can progress (Chris, interview 3); and
>
> I felt relieved [upon joining ASPECT], because now I had more time to like do other things instead of just study, like I get time to go to the gym, I get time to get extra lessons for things like piano, I play the piano. (Tsego, interview 1)

A mismatch between the expectations of the Programme and the experience of the students is apparent in relation to the communication course. The course recognizes the centrality of language to learning in engineering and the struggles that students for whom English is an additional language are likely to have:

> The communication course is primarily concerned with written and oral communication in a professional and technical setting (ASPECT Review 2009: 8); and
>
> The [communication] course aims to develop first-year students' academic literacy in the context of the engineering curriculum and profession. Thus it focuses on nurturing sound academic writing and reading skills, as well as an awareness of and competency in a range of genres in engineering, including the academic essay, needs analysis, investigative report, poster and oral presentation. (ASPECT Review 2009: 22)

However, while the value of the communication course was often not recognized by the students at the time, some of the students continued to draw on the support of the lecturer in the years that followed, returning to ask for help with written course assignments, bursary applications and letters of various kinds. In five years, only one mention was made of the communication course, by a student asked, 'Would you say you have changed your approach to your writing compared to first year?': 'We did a course in first year which taught us a lot of the basics and setting out reports and all of that and from there I have used the same' (Leonard, interview 3). The communication course is foregrounded in the Programme documentation for good reason: engineers need to be able to write and present technical reports. The course carries fewer credits than the concurrent mathematics and physics courses, perhaps suggesting (erroneously) to the students that the course is not to be valued. It is also possible that students avoided mentioning (or thinking about) the communication course due to the very language difficulties which the course was designed to address.

The people: Being part of a valued community

The Programme documentation acknowledges the community aspect of the Programme, but does not discuss it as a major feature. Rather, the strengths of the Programme are considered to be primarily academic and references to community, though present, are muted: 'Many students find the ASPECT office a home away from home and are there frequently just to talk with [administrative staff member]' (ASPECT Review 2009:8); and: 'Students soon feel at home in the ASPECT community' (ASPECT Brochure 2008: 1). This contrasts with the students' responses, where a sense of community was strongly foregrounded and that sense of community persisted beyond first year. Academic advantages were certainly recognized by the students, but came across as secondary to the sense of community, which is 2 on our capabilities list. Apparent in the interview data is the value the students placed on the support they found by being part of the ASPECT community.

The participants emphasized the community aspect of the Programme repeatedly, up to interviews in year five. The community (staff and students) formed in their first year was valued by the students for a variety of reasons: first for the new friends made, second for being assured of continued curriculum support after first year, third for feeling that they are in a privileged position over mainstream students and fourth for valuing the diversity of the class and finally for having the opportunity to 'give back' as a mentor in later years. On the first point, in her second year Tsego described the communal aspect of ASPECT as the highlight of her first year:

> I have made a lot of good friends because in my ASPECT class it was this almost small group whereby we got to actually know each other more because we spent more time together and did a lot of things together like we did go out, to the beach maybe or maybe to have something to eat or something like that and *ja*, it worked out pretty well and we developed a study, we studied a lot of things together and that helped as well. (Tsego, interview 2)

The participants generally included staff members in their description of ASPECT as a 'family': 'It was like we had this whole family thing going on, you know we had a small class and *ja* [Afrikaans for 'yes'], it was, you could relate to the lecturers, you could pop by their office, they were always smiling and friendly, that type of thing' (Rethabile, interview 4).

Secondly, as members of the community, students can rely on continued support from the staff, lecturers and administrative staff, beyond their first-year direct involvement, as the two extracts below demonstrate:

> I mean working very hard is one of those but again there is one lecturer that I also go and see in ASPECT, that is also keep motivating me to work hard because sometimes mathematics is hard and then you can drop your head a bit, but she is always saying you have to work hard and stay focused (Chris, interview 2); and
>
> Like [administrative staff member], she is so helpful, like even this year I can go to her and ask her anything and when I had problems with registration, this semester, last semester, I would always just go to her, even though I went to the Civil Department, they didn't always know what was going on whereas I would go to [administrative staff member] and she would do everything for me. (Fatima, interview 2)

The students experienced a shift in perception during that first year, resulting in the third reason to value being in ASPECT. To begin with the students often felt uncomfortable being placed in the extended degree programme, all of them having been top achievers in their secondary schools. Towards the end of the first quarter of the academic year, students transfer across from the mainstream programme and the perception changes to being part of an exclusive and desirable community:

> I was asking myself what is wrong with this ASPECT and then they gave us a mentor from ASPECT as well and then he told us 'No, don't worry about much, the class will be full, people from mainstream will come to us.' ... And then actually what he was saying was true because there are some people who got rejected because the class was full, who want to go, who were willing to go ... to ASPECT, and then they end up doing, like, a decant course and when you are doing a decant course you are already in a five-year programme because there are courses that you can't do when you did not finish maths and physics (Senzo, interview 2);
>
> The lecturers are much better, you kind of like, they set you up, you know, it helps a lot actually, and I think a lot of mainstream people also realise that. (Lesego, interview 1)

Fourth, the community was valued for being diverse: '*Ja,* because I was in ASPECT, I think I met a lot of people from all over the place, so I have been exposed to different religious backgrounds, different people from different ... social classes' (Fatima, interview 2); and, 'In ASPECT there are different, you have different cultures, I am Xhosa, there are also Pedi guys, Sotho guys, Tswana guys, Venda and also a Chinese guy, *ja* so I can say sometimes we try to learn each other's languages, so it's fun staying here' (John, interview 1).

Finally, in their senior years, the students also valued being able to give back to the community by becoming mentors for the students following in their footsteps:

> It's going well because I'm also telling those students, I'm also giving them advice of how to maybe cope with their courses like explaining to them because some people may think ASPECT is for students maybe who are not serious about education, things like that, their education is at a low standard than others but ASPECT is a good thing, maybe some people think maths that is done in ASPECT is different from the maths that is done on the mainstream, as well as the physics, actually I do tell them that it's the same. (John, interview 2)

The capabilities enabled and developed by being an ASPECT student, in the first year specifically, are, in the view of the staff, to transition to university studies, to learn valuable work and study skills and to become part of a valued community. The first of those capabilities (3 on the list) was recognized by the participants and discussed in some detail in their interviews. The students appreciated and benefitted from the decreased load, both academically and otherwise, and positive assessment data provide quantitative verification, justifying their confidence in the transition process. The study skills gained by the students (4 on the list) are emphasized more by the Programme documentation than by the students themselves. This is not to say that the students have not gained those skills – they may well have – but they were not foregrounded in the students' perception of the capabilities gained by being a member of ASPECT. The fact that students did not mention the communication course is cause for concern, however, and this could be addressed by increasing the credit value of the course, making the need for the skills more explicit, or integrating the communication skills into the other courses. The valuable state of being a member of the ASPECT community (2 on the capabilities list) is mentioned in the Programme documentation, but not nearly to the extent that the students mentioned it.

The Programme also tries to develop the capability to transition to second year and further, beyond the immediate reach of the ASPECT staff members, but with the necessary skills for coping. Some students, such as Senzo and Simphiwe, gained those skills. Others did not seem to, such as Fatima and Siphilisiwe. In addition, structural challenges beyond the control of the students and the ASPECT staff can prevent the smooth conversion of capabilities into functionings.

Continuing the journey: Transitioning into second year and beyond

In their second year at the university, ASPECT students have a mixed curriculum of first- and second-year subjects. They are required to take more courses and they are no longer provided with additional academic support. They are now in larger classes, with fewer contact hours per subject than before. The work is often more cognitively demanding than in first year. The close-knit community of first year begins to break apart as students take courses specific to their engineering disciplines. All of these changes make for a substantial adjustment which is frequently troublesome and hinders the conversion of the capability into the achieved functioning of transitioning. Constraints such as 'classroom pedagogy and management' or a lack of 'cultures of concern with learners' difference' might render the implementing of the capability as a functioning very difficult (Walker and Unterhalter 2007:10).

The year of immersion in the ASPECT system, with all its support structures, is intended to develop the capability (the potential) to transition to second year successfully, yet the functioning (actual achievement) of coping with second-year demands was not experienced by all the students in the study. The capabilities have possibly been enabled but cannot be put into practice (Walker 2003). The participants' views, as recorded in their interviews, and the Programme's declarations of intent are in accord about this capability being crucial to success:

> Although ASPECT is only a first-year programme the intention is to prepare students for further years of study and to graduate (ASPECT Review 2009: 16);
>
> The aim of ASPECT is to improve on the number of black and coloured student graduates as well as the graduation rate of these students in the EBE faculty. This is achieved by providing the students that enter the programme with the best possible preparation to succeed in the following years in their engineering studies, through excellent teaching, building a supportive learning community, recognition of the level of the preparedness and being attentive to students. (ASPECT Review 2009: 4)

It is frequently the case that ASPECT students struggle to cope with the changes as they shift from the supported first year to the less supported second year (see also Pym and Kapp 2013). The capability to handle the workload and larger classes of mainstream studies failed to transform into successful functioning and the participants' experience did not live up to the optimism of the Programme expectations:

> It [ASPECT] helped, but then when we got to second year … you know how you hold a baby when they learn to walk, right, and then once they start walking just let them walk on their own. So I felt like, in second year, ok, so now, baby, you have wings, now fly, but some of us couldn't fly (Tsego, interview 3);
>
> I feel like there is so much support during first year and then after that it is like – *ja*, do your thing, I don't know like sometimes it feels like you somehow still need the support like throughout, so …. (Rethabile, interview 4)

A few of the students reported that the transition to second year was aided by having observed first-year mainstream loads, but that the tough transition then just shifted to third year.

> Although we were ASPECT, we still interacted with other students who were in mainstream, so we could see how pressurised they were and we knew that it was coming, so it was kind of, either you prepare for it or you just have to see how you move through it when your pressure comes, you are prepared I think, in second year (Tsego, interview 5);
>
> Well, I guess the lowlight was discovering that ASPECT was kind of just a start-off, it was just a little push in the right direction and then after like the first two years, now we must cut the apron (Tsego, interview 5);
>
> So first year courses were mostly a recap or a spin-off of matric work, so maths and science and etc., but last year [third year] was all new work and so they keep the same pace but it is all new so it was difficult to get a handle on it. (Leonard, interview 4)

The data point to the possibility of there being too much support in first year. Couple this 'over support' with a student perception (whether justified or not) of a lack of concern on the part of the staff towards the abrupt transition and we inevitably have students who stumble and fall. Pym and Kapp (2013:273) recognize the danger of too much support in the first year at university, arguing that it 'encourages passivity and dependence, thus stripping students of the agency which enabled them to attain access to tertiary studies despite their home and school circumstances'. Yet, decreasing support in first year is not an inevitable response to the difficulty of transitioning from a support-heavy environment to a support-light one. The dilemma is that it is the self-same support which enables students to succeed in their first-year studies.

Tsego's motif of 'ASPECT as crèche' is a good example of a theme repeated vertically through the data: 'You know how you hold a baby when they learn to walk … ok, so now, baby, you have wings, now fly' (interview 3); 'Here is a life vest – swim' (interview 4) and 'Now we must cut the apron' (interview 5). Such instances provide us with a sense of narrative coherence in Tsego's 'life history' (Thomson 2009: 13) while simultaneously underlining the perception of too much support followed by a sudden disappearance of support.

The struggles of the students to cope with the pressures of advanced years within the degree are known to the ASPECT staff and were acknowledged in the review:

> A one year foundational experience has not proved to be adequate to erase the effects of years of inadequate preparation. Many have been excluded in the first few years of being with the mainstream. Some criticism levelled at the ASPECT model has attempted to suggest that the students fail in second year because there is too much support in first year and then it is suddenly withdrawn. 'Spoon-feeding' is often mentioned. (ASPECT Review 2009: 21)

In addition to trying to instil work and study skills which will allow students to transition to the increased workload and cognitive demands of second-year courses (capability 5), the Programme aims to provide help in the practicalities of the transition by providing ongoing curriculum advice and a structured navigation plan. A student entering the faculty via the ASPECT programme has their five-year plan mapped out for them. Approximately a third of all students who register for a mainstream engineering degree complete in the minimum time of four years (Scott, Yeld and Hendry 2007). Most students fail one or more courses and have to repeat the courses they fail. If a course which is a prerequisite for subsequent courses has to be repeated, the degree is extended. Entering the university through ASPECT sets the student up to complete the degree in five years with an explicitly designed curriculum structure to make that possible. The students in the study recognized the distinction between their five-year structured programme, with continued curriculum advice throughout their stay at the UCT, and the five-year experience of a mainstream student who has failed something and struggles to reconcile their timetable and make up lost credits. This is reflected in the comments below:

> Honestly speaking, I feel like it is of an advantage because like most of the people … like they have either maybe repeated a course or something, like eventually they also have to do it for five year, so at least I have something structured (Rethabile, interview 2);

I think if I didn't choose ASPECT I would still be doing 5 years in ChemEng again … because maths first year … *sho hey* … … So, *ja*, maths was giving me problems. So I went to ASPECT then I passed it. I don't think that if I had stayed in mainstream I could have … I could have passed it. … Now they're like me, who am in ASPECT … they'll finish with me in 5 years. So I don't feel bad. (Nwabisa, interview 3)

The struggles of students to graduate with an engineering degree are an area of great concern, both locally and nationally. It is crucial that students who enter universities through special entry programmes are given the skills to progress further than just the first year of studies. Widening participation in higher education through access is a wasted benefit if transitioning through the more advanced years of study is not similarly supported (Badat 2013).

Journey's end: Graduating

Of the fifteen students taking part in the study, five graduated in 2013 in minimum time (five years) and three graduated in 2014 and one in 2015. At the time of writing, one student continues in good academic standing and five left the university during the period of study. The graduation rate of the students taking part in the study is currently 60 per cent and could rise as high as 66 per cent. These figures are rather higher than typical, with an approximate 35 per cent eventual graduation rate expected from the extended programme's historical data.

Recall that most of the participants in the study would not have been accepted into the University at all (and hence have a graduation rate of 0 per cent), or were struggling so much in their first six weeks of first-year mainstream studies that their chance of passing even first year was small, let alone graduating. For at least some of these students the capability to graduate has been converted into an actual graduation. Structuring the degree to extend over five years, with the first two years of mainstream study effectively spread over three years, is the primary characteristic of the Programme and is understood to be the reason why students can achieve the 'valuable act' of being able to graduate: 'The ASPECT programme's model of intervention can be classified as a model of "extended" curriculum. The curriculum is planned so that the four-year engineering degree should ideally take five years to complete' (ASPECT Review 2009: 6). In certain cases, students in ASPECT who consider themselves capable of 'fast tracking' their degree and completing in four years can register for more courses than recommended. The ASPECT curriculum advisors generally advise against such a choice. Leonard is one student who chose to take on extra courses in an ultimately unsuccessful bid at graduating early. In his first year, he expressed ambivalence about being part of ASPECT:

> In ASPECT, the teaching is better, one on one, like if you have any problems you go, they make sure you understand it but on the other hand I want to finish in four years, so ASPECT was a good thing for me, but now that I've, I'm in the motion of doing well and working I'm focusing on finishing in four years, so like I'm doing Engineering Statics now, which is not an ASPECT [first-year] course, so I wanted to take more courses in the beginning and they said if I do well in the semester, then I'd be able to, so now I'm going to fast track my degree. (Leonard, interview 1)

This quotation reflects the fact that while the Programme is designed to extend the degree and is expected to increase the chances of functionings such as transitioning and graduation, students view the extended time as a constraining feature, hampering their chances of an earlier graduation.

Conclusion

It is a feature of good governance to provide citizens with opportunities for good-quality education. Under most circumstances, but particularly under circumstances of great social inequality or class stratification (Walker 2003), it is a matter of social justice that the available educational opportunities be designed to widen participation to all sectors of the population. Tikly and Barrett (2011: 11) argue that there are three dimensions of a good-quality education from a social justice perspective:

1. The inclusion dimension, concerned with access and opportunities;
2. The relevance dimension, concerned with meaningful learning outcomes (see also Wood and Deprez 2012);
3. The democratic dimension, concerned with 'issues of participation and voice' and drawing 'attention to the fundamentally political nature of the debate about education quality'.

In the South African context, and in other countries with similar socio-economic inequalities, it is not enough that universities with good schools of engineering, medicine and other fields of study exist. The inclusion dimension (and indeed the democratic dimension) of a good-quality education demands that at least some of those universities, if not all, explicitly create opportunities for previously marginalized sections of the population to gain access to fields of study considered relevant and valuable, such as engineering.

One way in which universities across South Africa have chosen to address the inclusion dimension is to create access routes into university for students who are judged to have the capacity to succeed at university, yet cannot achieve so-called mainstream access, for a range of reasons related to socio-economic structures and the lingering effects of South Africa's apartheid history. Over the last twenty years, there has been some significant success (Badat 2013) with respect to social justice, access and success in higher education. ASPECT forms part of the University's process of addressing this issue through admissions and through access to resources. As such, the Programme is located within a 'pedagogy of consequence' (Unterhalter 2010) where inequality is recognized and addressed in a context of differentiated fields of disciplinary knowledge. While programmes like ASPECT partially meet social justice aims, high dropout rates and low graduation rates persist among black students. The Education White Paper of 1997 expressed a concern that remains valid today, that 'ensuring equity of access must be complemented by a concern for equity of outcomes' (Department of Education 1997:16, 2:29).

The capability approach, with its focus on converting resources into capabilities and thereafter (ideally) into functionings, offers a means of assessing the effectiveness of pedagogies and the structures within which they are located for fostering well-being and the ability to choose a life of value. 'We need to know what we are trying to make and to be able to judge whether we have made it well' (Walker 2003:169). Since ASPECT forms one small part of the local and national agenda of transformation and social justice in education, it is important that we know 'what we are trying to make' and 'whether we have made it well'. The approach taken in this chapter towards judging the efficacy of the ASPECT programme was to compare and contrast the envisioned capability development as expressed in the Programme documentation with the experienced capability development as expressed in student interviews across five years of engineering studies. A positive conclusion reached through this method is that the access role of the Programme is being successfully recognized and realized as are the first-year pedagogic processes related to transitioning from school to university study.

While access to higher education is a necessary part of good-quality tertiary education, it is not sufficient (Walker 2003; Badat 2013). A major area of concern relates to the identity of ASPECT as primarily a first-year programme and the pronounced differential between the amount of support available in first-year ASPECT on the one hand, and second-year studies and beyond on the other. Many students claim that the support provided in that first crucial year is instrumental in guaranteeing their success, yet 'nowhere is education an uncomplicated "good"' (Walker 2003:169) and that same support is blamed for making the proceeding years more challenging than they might otherwise have been. Addressing this apparent dilemma, of support being simultaneously crippling and enabling, can be tackled by shifting focus and dealing with the differential instead. One such treatment is to extend ASPECT support beyond first year into, for instance, second-year mathematics (Craig and Campbell 2013) and possibly other courses. This approach holds the amount of support in first year steady, while allowing the support to taper off, rather than disappear abruptly, in second year. A parallel approach is to integrate the reading, writing and presenting skills of the communication course into engineering courses, a process underway at the time of writing. The integration of communication skills into disciplinary studies increases the perceived relevance of those skills and avoids students seeing them as an 'add on'.

Working through the data for this longitudinal project, it has become clear that the community feature of ASPECT is very important to the students, more important than the Programme officially recognizes. The emphasis on community throughout the 'snapshot' interviews (Thomson 2009: 14) provided narrative coherence both horizontally and vertically within the data set. The research on 'learning communities' indicates that participation in a robust learning community has positive effects not just academically, but emotionally and socially. A 'learning community' is defined as a cohort of students who take two or more courses together, and who are generally involved in out-of-class activities together (Pike, Kuh and McCormick 2011; Goldman 2012). Learning communities can have a residential component and frequently include peer mentoring. Research has shown that participation in a learning community is linked to higher levels of student achievement, learning and success (Pike, Kuh and McCormick 2011; Goldman 2012; Hatch 2013). The link between community participation and positive academic effects is indirect, with participation resulting in student engagement which in turn results in improved 'grades in college, desired learning outcomes, satisfaction with college, and persistence and graduation' (Pike, Kuh and McCormick 2011: 301). This evidence supports the argument that the development of an appropriate identity (in this case as a novice engineer) leads to engagement and hence positive academic results (Cobb and Hodge 2005; Cobb, Gresalfi and Hodge 2009; Craig 2013). The creation of a tight-knit learning community in the first-year cohort is due in part to the actions and input of the staff but far more to the agency of the students themselves, who recognize the value of the academic and psycho-social support they receive from their peers.

A promising avenue to explore is whether extending the ASPECT activities to include out-of-class (possibly non-academic) activities would have an indirect positive effect on issues such as the multiple transitions the students experience or on study habits. Pike, Kuh and McCormick (2011) cite Szelényi et al. (2007), who found evidence to suggest that the positive relationship between learning community participation and a successful transition to college was stronger for low socio-economic status students, as ASPECT students generally are. The work done on 'wellness' at the University of Stellenbosch near Cape Town has interesting parallels, with wellness defined by 'six domains of human existence, namely, the intellectual, social, emotional, physical, spiritual, and occupational domain' (Botha and Cilliers 2012: 244).

Agreement between student voice and Programme documentation suggests that 'to be a university student' and to 'transition to university studies' are fully developed functionings. The data do not show clearly whether the participants 'learnt work habits and study skills'. 'To transition into second year and beyond' is the capability least enabled and least likely to achieve status of a functioning, with obvious implications for 'to graduate in five years'. I argue that the weaknesses in the system thrown into relief by the analysis discussed in this chapter can be addressed by a two-pronged approach of direct academic intervention (extension of support slightly beyond first year and integrating communication skills into disciplinary studies), as well as indirectly by explicitly fostering a learning community in ways which, ideally, will have positive effects, academically, socially and emotionally.

The longitudinal project has provided a unique opportunity to trace students' journeys through their degree and to foreground their voices: the satisfaction in being granted access to university studies, the struggles to adapt to first-year studies, the second-year transition and beyond, the emotional ups and downs, the good times and the bad. The capability approach has provided a language with which to discuss the aims of the Programme and to recognize the successes and the shortfalls. The ASPECT extended curriculum programme plays its own small part in providing social justice in South Africa and, with research such as discussed here, will improve its offerings to afford students the freedom to choose a life of value.

References

Academic Support Programme for Engineering in Cape Town (2008), 'ASPECT Brochure', unpublished internal UCT brochure, available from author.

Academic Support Programme for Engineering in Cape Town (2009), 'ASPECT Review', unpublished internal UCT review, available from author.

Badat, S. (2013), 'The Limits of Access, Success and Social Justice in Post-1994 South African Higher Education: Building the Learning and Teaching Capabilities of Universities', *Keynote address, Second Biennial Conference of the South African Society for Engineering Education,* 10–12 June, Cape Town, South Africa.

Botha, L. and Cilliers, C. (2012), '"Adolescent" South Africa (18 Years since Democratization): Challenges for Universities to Optimize Wellness as a Prerequisite for Cognitive Development and Learning in a Diverse Society', *Journal of Cognitive Education and Psychology,* 11(3): 241–55.

Case, J. M. (2013), *Researching Student Learning in Higher Education: A Social Realist Approach,* Oxford: Routledge.

Christie, P. (2010), 'The Complexity of Human Rights in Global Times: The Case of the Right to Education in South Africa', *International Journal of Educational Development,* 30: 3–11.

Cobb, P. and Hodge, L. L. (2005), 'An Interpretive Scheme for Analysing Identities that Students Develop in Mathematics Classrooms', http://www.udel.edu/educ/whitson/897s05/files/Cobb_ID.pdf , accessed 29 July 2016.

Cobb, P., Gresalfi, M. and Hodge, L. L. (2009), 'An Interpretive Scheme for Analysing the Identities that Students Develop in Mathematics Classrooms', *Journal for Research in Mathematics Education,* 40(1): 40–68.

Craig, T. S. (2013), 'Conceptions of Mathematics and Student Identity: Implications for Engineering Education', *International Journal of Mathematics Education in Science and Technology,* 44(7): 1020–29.

Craig, T. S. and Campbell, A. (2013), 'Vector Calculus for Engineers – The Academic Development Model', *Community for Undergraduate Learning in the Mathematical Sciences (CULMS) Newsletter,* 7: 21–5.

Department of Education (1997), '*Education White Paper 3: A Programme for the Transformation of Higher Education*', Government Gazette No. 18207.

Goldman, C. A. (2012), 'A Cohort-Based Learning Community Enhances Academic Success and Satisfaction with University Experience for First-Year Students', *The Canadian Journal for the Scholarship of Teaching and Learning,* 3(2) Article 3: 1–19.

Hatch, D. K. (2013), 'Student Engagement and the Design of High-Impact Practices at Community Colleges', unpublished Ph.D. thesis, University of Texas, http://repositories.lib.utexas.edu/handle/2152/21775, accessed 29 July 2016.

Jawitz, J. (1994), 'Developments in the Academic Support Programme for Engineering in Cape Town (ASPECT)', in Adey et al. (eds), *State of the Art in Higher Education Volume 1, Proceedings of the 9th Biannual SAARDHE Conference*, 372–9, Cape Town.

Jawitz, J. and Scott, L. (1997), 'Who Does Not Succeed in Engineering at the University of Cape Town? What Can One Tell from the Retention Rate?', presented at the 1997 *Frontiers in Education Conference*.

Kapp, R., Badenhorst, E., Bangeni, B., Craig, T. S., Janse van Rensburg, V., le Roux, K., Prince, R., Pym, J. and van Pletzen, E. (2014), 'Successful Students' Negotiation of Township Schooling in Contemporary South Africa', *Perspectives in Education* 32(3): 50–61.

Kloot, B., Case, J. M. and Marshall, D. (2008), 'A Critical Review of the Educational Philosophies Underpinning Science and Engineering Foundation Programmes', *South African Journal of Higher Education*, 22(4): 799–816.

Meyer, J. H. F. and Sass, A. R. (1992), 'Engineering Students from Educationally Disadvantaged Backgrounds: Assumptions, Research Conclusions, and Curriculum Responses', *International Journal of Engineering Education*, 8(5): 328–35.

Nussbaum, M. (2006), 'Education and Democratic Citizenship: Capabilities and Quality Education', *Journal of Human Development*, 7(3): 385–95.

Pearce, H., Campbell, A., Craig, T. S., le Roux, P., Nathoo, K. and Vicatos, E. (2015), 'The Articulation between the Extended (5-year) and Mainstream (4-year) Programmes in Engineering at the University of Cape Town: Reflections and Possibilities', *South African Journal of Higher Education*, 29(1): 151–64.

Pike, G. R., Kuh, G. D. and McCormick, A. C. (2011), 'An Investigation of the Contingent Relationships between Learning Community Participation and Student Engagement', *Research in Higher Education*, 52: 300–22.

Pym, J. and Kapp, R. (2013), 'Harnessing Agency: Towards a Learning Model for Undergraduate Students', *Studies in Higher Education*, 28(2): 272–84.

Robeyns, I. (2003), 'Sen's Capability Approach and Gender Inequality: Selecting Relevant Capabilities', *Feminist Economics*, 9(2–3): 61–92.

Sass, A. (1988), 'Academic Support in Engineering at the University of Cape Town', *South African Journal of Higher Education*, 2(1), 25–8.

Scott, I., Yeld, N. and Hendry, J. (2007), 'A Case for Improving Teaching and Learning in South African Higher Education', *Higher Education Monitor, No.6*, Pretoria: Research Paper Prepared for the Council on Higher Education.

Sen, A. (1993), 'Capability and Well-Being', in M. Nussbaum and A. Sen (eds), *The Quality of Life: Studies in Developmental Economics*, 30–53, Oxford: Oxford University Press.

Szelényi, K., Inkelas, K. K., Drechsler, M. J. and Kim, Y. C. (2007). 'Exploring social capital in the transition to college of students in living-learning programs from differing socioeconomic backgrounds'. In *Annual Meeting of the Association for the Study of Higher Education,* Louisville, KY.

Thomson, R. (2009), *Unfolding Lives: Youth, Gender and Change,* Bristol: The Policy Press.

Tikly, L. and Barrett, A. M. (2011), 'Social Justice, Capabilities and the Quality of Education in Low Income Countries', *International Journal of Educational Development,* 31: 3–14.

Unterhalter, E. (2010), 'Considering Equality, Equity and Higher Education Pedagogies in the Context of Globalization', in E. Unterhalter and V. Carpentier (eds), *Universities into the 21st Century: Global Inequalities and Higher Education. Whose Interests Are We Serving?*, 91–116, Basingstoke, Hampshire UK: Palgrave Macmillan.

Walker, M. (2003), 'Framing Social Justice in Education: What does the "Capabilities" Approach Offer?', *British Journal of Educational Studies,* 51(2): 168–87.

Walker, M. (2005), 'Amartya Sen's Capability Approach and Education', *Educational Action Research,* 13(1): 103–10.

Walker, M. (2006), 'Towards a Capability-Based Theory of Justice for Education Policy-Making', *Journal of Educational Policy,* 21(2): 163–85.

Walker, M. and Unterhalter, E. (2007), 'The Capability Approach: Its Potential for Work in Education', in M. Walker and E. Unterhalter (eds), *Amartya Sen's Capability Approach and Social Justice in Education,* 1–18, Palgrave Macmillan: New York.

Wood, D. and Deprez, L. Z. (2012), 'Teaching for Human Well-Being: Curricular Implications for the Capability Approach', *Journal of Human Development and Capabilities: A Multidisciplinary Journal for People-Centred Development,* 13(3): 471–93.

8

The Impact of Previous Experiences and Social Connectedness on Students' Transition to Higher Education

June Pym and Judy Sacks

Introduction

While there has been a great deal of change in patterns of access and an increase in the amount of support offered to students in the South African context, as pointed out in the Introduction to this book, the legacy of apartheid is still evident in patterns of access and retention, as well as in institutional policies and power relations. In this chapter we will analyse the learning and social experiences of five first-generation students over a five-year period at the University of Cape Town (UCT). We describe how the participants positioned themselves in relation to their new environment, and the events and experiences they had when they first entered the institution and how they repositioned themselves in relation to experiences within the academy, changing notions of their academic pathways and anticipated careers. The participants who are the focus of this chapter are Chris (Engineering), Philisani (Science), Senzo (Engineering), Monique (Commerce) and Lyndsey (Commerce). All five students identified themselves as successful, confident, motivated learners in their school environments and their school trajectories reflect varying degrees of agency. However, their university learning journeys reflect significant differences in their degree of confidence and comfort, and in the ways in which they engaged, negotiated difference, responded to challenges and used resources.

We draw on Bourdieu's (1984) notions of *habitus*, *field* and *capital*, on the work of Reay, Crozier and Clayton (2010) on the transitions of working-class students in the UK and on a conceptual framework developed by Watson et al. (2009) to analyse the changes in values, attitudes and behaviours of the five participants, as they learnt the accepted codes, behaviours and practices that characterized their disciplinary and social contexts. The qualitative longitudinal analysis of the data highlights the complexities and shifts in their trajectories over the course of their undergraduate degrees as they re-evaluated their sense of self in relation to their peers, their disciplines and the institution. Their narratives foreground the ways in which individual dispositions, past and present experiences and social relationships played a role in the participants' shifts in positioning and conceptualization of their future. The longitudinal analysis reveals the heterogeneous and situated nature of students' experiences, problematizing statistical indicators that foreground atomized predictors which influence the success or failure of first-generation students. It also foregrounds the extent to which first-generation, working-class students have to engage in invisible identity work in order to succeed.

The significance of habitus and capital for the transition of first-generation students

Bourdieu's (1984) notions of *habitus* and *capital* have been used extensively in higher education research to provide an analytical lens for exploring the complexity of an individual's transition from one social context to another. Bourdieu (1991:57) defines habitus as 'our ingrained unconscious way of being that embodies beliefs, values and ways of doing' and provides a lens for viewing and judging the world. Bourdieu (1984) argues that these dispositions are largely informed by one's family and class position. An individual's exposure over time to the particular social influences of their family, school friends, culture and community informs their habitus, which becomes internalized and unconscious. Bourdieu (1990) argues that these dispositions have the potential to direct an individual's actions in social fields, thus serving to constrain or facilitate agency depending on the nature of the field and the cultural capital valued within that field.

In their research on working-class students' experiences of higher education in the UK context, Reay, Crozier and Clayton (2010: 111) use the concept of *institutional habitus* to describe accepted (generally middle-class) norms, standards and practices within universities that have been established over time, are taken for granted by insiders, but which are often invisible or opaque to students from under-represented groups. They show that institutional habitus exerted a powerful influence on how the learning identities of the students in their studies evolved and developed.

Bourdieu et al. (1999) argue that an individual's success within a given field is particularly dependent on the capital held by the individual. Students bring to university varying types of capital that can include social, cultural, language and symbolic aspects (Bourdieu 1986). Many of these resources are seldom recognized or required in the established higher education field. While there are differences between first-generation students, research has shown that for most of them, there is little that resonates when they first enter the university and that there is a great deal of adjustment and adaptation necessary to understand and establish themselves in this new context, because they do not necessarily have the capital deemed appropriate (Reay, David and Ball 2005; Haggis 2006; Christie et al. 2008; Pym 2013). Reay, Crozier and Clayton (2010) highlight a complex interplay between students' backgrounds, the educational environment and personal dispositions which impacts on the degree to which learners adapt to higher education and adopt appropriate learning identities. These authors have argued that students' ability to adjust to the academic and social demands of university depends on developing a particular habitus in relationship to the institutional habitus, as well as on the institution's willingness to shift practices and culture in relation to the diverse student intake. In other words, student success is not simply about assimilation into the institutional habitus, but also about institutional habitus changing to recognize the diverse range of student experiences (Reay, Crozier and Clayton 2010; Case 2013; Pym and Kapp 2013). Nevertheless, institutional habitus tends to be resistant to change. Watson et al. (2009: 666) describe the ways in which student challenges in their transition to higher education 'stem from its long-established culture, which generally remains oriented towards the traditional white middle-class student population'. This means that students have to negotiate their own habitus and that of the higher education institution.

Methodology

The five participants that are the focus of this study were purposively selected because they were first-generation students and because they brought specific and different habituses and capital to the institution, thus enabling us to compare and contrast their narratives. The students were admitted to academic development programmes in the Science, Commerce and Engineering Faculties. While these programmes all provide additional academic support in relatively small classes (as described in the Introduction to this book), they are fairly different in terms of their operations, structure and academic load. We drew on biographical questionnaires and five semi-structured interviews per student, conducted each year from 2009 to 2013. The analysis of the data focused on the nature and forms of the participants' habitus on entry and how various forms of capital were accumulated and exchanged as they negotiated home and university (Kelly-Blakeney 2014). Where the participants' agency and autonomy were strongly foregrounded, the generative capacity of habitus featured strongly in their narratives.

We drew on Watson et al.'s (2009: 671) diagram depicting students' transition to higher education to place our participants (according to their self-description) in the diagram, when they started in first year. We have used the identical Bourdieuian theoretical framework Watson et al. used, but have altered the naming of the descriptors to depict our context and research findings more accurately. Watson et al. (2009: 671) used the descriptors 'fish in water' and 'exclusion' on one axis and a 'natural fit' and 'marked incongruence' on the other, to indicate the range of adaptation in their study. We found these descriptors fairly extreme and for our purposes needed more nuanced contrasts. Whereas their study was focused on the students' first year only, our study tracked transitions over a considerably longer period. Lastly, they predominantly focused on linguistic capital, whereas we have broadened the study to include the multiple types of capital that impact on student transitions. We placed the participants in our study in the quadrant (Figure 8.1) that best described their habitus and the capital they held as they entered their first year. It is important to note that this placement is based on their experiences when they entered higher education. We will be noting if and where students' placement changes over time.

Figure 8.1 depicts student transactions: the horizontal axis represents the students' sense of belonging and fitting in and their level of contentment. The vertical axis represents the 'congruence between the established habitus of individual participants and the practices and expectations of the new field of HE they have entered' (Watson et al. 2009: 670). We used four descriptors: *outsider, adaptor, strategist* and *insider* to place students on the diagram. First, there is the *outsider*. This is the student who is socially isolated, does not understand the rules of the university and holds cultural capital that is not recognized by

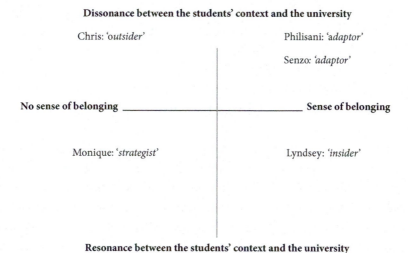

Dissonance between the students' context and the university

Chris: '*outsider*'   Philisani: '*adaptor*'

Senzo: '*adaptor*'

No sense of belonging _____ **Sense of belonging**

Monique: '*strategist*'   Lyndsey: '*insider*'

Resonance between the students' context and the university

Figure 8.1 Students' sense of fitting in when entering higher education (Adapted from Watson et al., 2009: 671, Figure 1, *Experiencing the transition*)

the university. The second type identified by Watson et al. (2009: 671) is the *adaptor*. This student feels relatively comfortable socially in the university, but is a stranger to the culture and academic demands of the university. In other words, this student seems to be coping. However, there could be a variety of issues relating to language, time management, cultural norms and previous conceptual development that could be undermining in different ways. The third type is the *strategist*. This is the student who feels that they do not belong socially, but who has the cultural capital to negotiate the rules and mores of the university. Finally, there is the *insider*. The insider feels comfortable being at university, is involved, feels a sense of belonging and has little adjustment to do regarding the 'ways of being' at the university and the academic expectations. While these positions are not absolute, they provide a useful framework within which to locate the very different dispositions students have as they enter university.

We placed each of the five participants in a quadrant on the diagram when they first entered the university and then tracked their 'journeys' to gauge whether there had been any movement in these positions during the course of their degrees. As Watson et al. (2009) did, we applied Bourdieu's (1977) conceptual tool of *habitus* to position these students at entry, into particular groupings in relationship to the academy.

We will describe and provide the rationale for the placement of the five students when they entered university and use this as a basis to describe and analyse how they negotiated their undergraduate years and the extent to which they shifted from the positions they took up as they entered university, as they progressed through higher education.

Chris's transition

Chris comes from a township in Pretoria. There are few educational or job opportunities for the residents of that township and Chris explained that many people turn to alcohol and drugs and do not complete their schooling. Chris is multilingual, speaking Tswana, Zulu and English. He lived with his parents, three sisters (one his twin) and two brothers. His mother died in 2003, when he was in Grade 7. Chris described his high school as under-resourced with a poor infrastructure. He talked about the staff and students as unmotivated, but explained simply that at school he and a friend 'we just had to do the job'. He seemed to be regarded as an academic achiever at school. 'I think for me to keep up the image was to really work very hard, for me, in terms of academics.' Despite his teachers' lack of effort and involvement, Chris managed to achieve high marks in his final school exams and was accepted at the UCT. He was the first in his family to attend university.

Chris was accepted into the mainstream engineering programme, but applied for and joined the ASPECT programme (an academic development first-year programme in the engineering faculty, see Chapter 7) when he arrived. His initial perceptions of the UCT were that it is a good institution at which to study engineering and that all the students work very hard. He found the transition from school to university very challenging and struggled with the academic pace. ASPECT stood out for Chris as a place of both academic and emotional support. Chris's cultural capital included his multilingualism, strong academic potential (he had been accepted into the mainstream engineering programme) and a steely determination to succeed. He ascribed this determination to the fact that his identity at high school and home was one of being self-sufficient as there were few people at school who supported him and no one at home who could relate to or help him with his school work. However, despite these attributes and seemingly strong identity, he felt acutely lonely and apart from the institution. His habitus was predominantly that of a loner as there was only one person he interacted with socially and as a study partner and he joined no societies or organizations.

Based on the narrative in his first interview in 2009, we placed Chris in the *outsider* quadrant. In this interview, Chris foregrounded his sense of disconnect from the institution and described a number of causes, including his discomfort with speaking English, the level of academic challenge and the pace of lectures. Our sense is that he was not particularly content with this degree of alienation but merely accepted it. Part of the challenge he faced as a first-generation student was the lack of cultural capital to make informed decisions about degree choice. Chris had chosen engineering, based on information from his brother's friends who advised him that the institution had a good engineering department and that the degree would afford him many job opportunities. In his first interview, he displayed little understanding of or passion for the degree or for a career in engineering. Yet, despite all his challenges in adapting to the new environment, Chris passed all his courses in the first year.

In his second year, Chris left the Engineering Faculty and moved to the Science Faculty and changed to a degree with mathematics major. When discussing the change, he said: '[I was] just enjoying mathematics and maybe a career in this field will be fulfilling. I'm not sure [about] engineering. … I just didn't have the vision to continue with it.' He expressed a passion for mathematics: 'First I know mathematics and I want to explore the fact.' Nevertheless, the move away from engineering was both academically and socially challenging. He continued to struggle with the pace of his courses and his time management. He also moved into a self-catering residence and spoke about the financial constraints affecting his studies, as he sometimes did not have enough money to buy food. Socially, Chris remained alienated from the other students. After leaving ASPECT, he identified himself as working alone: 'I mean working alone, sometimes it's difficult because I also don't have or too many friends if I can say that, so I am battling alone there and it is a bit difficult now…sometimes [I am coping], but sometimes I'm not coping.'

Nevertheless, Chris learnt to negotiate his way around a number of aspects of university life. He was confident enough to utilize various academic support resources, including the library, lecturers, tutors and the hot seat which provided support for mathematics. He also stated that he was becoming more comfortable understanding and using English and this was clearly evident in his increasingly long interviews which contrasted with the brevity of his responses in the first year. He joined a student-run, non-profit community outreach organization and the Student Christian Fellowship. Yet the sense of alienation he experienced in his first year in engineering seemed to continue in his second year in science.

Despite his increased involvement in student life, he reflected that he did not belong at the UCT. 'I have friends with whom I am very different from so I don't really like go out with them because they like to go out so I don't really like to go out. ... Most of the time you find that I am alone.' Chris considered that he had grown at the UCT. 'I mean you have to live by yourself here, there are no parents who say you must do this and this you have to make decisions, the only development I don't have now is time management and that is the only problem.' He managed to pass all his courses, and in his second year, on the basis of his results, was invited to join the Golden Key International Honour Society, an organization which connects high-achieving individuals.

In his third year, Chris returned to his Engineering course. He said that he was still unsure about his career path: 'I am still a little confused between engineering and maths. ... I am still chopping and changing. ... I like the mechanical [engineering] and I also like mathematics but I think mechanical is a good base degree to have but also I mostly want to do all my academic things in mathematics.' He commented that he had also struggled socially, being away from his peers in engineering and ASPECT. But once he was back in the anticipated comfortable, supportive ASPECT environment, this was not the uncomplicated move he had hoped for, as his cohort from first year had moved up without him. Academically, he still struggled with time management. He found the work 'demanding' especially his new Drawing course. Chris managed to cope but was unable to engage in a meta-level analysis of the processes that enabled him to succeed: 'Somehow I am managing to pass but I don't know again how, it just happened.'

In his fourth year, Chris continued to feel socially alienated and experienced difficulties with his courses. He considered leaving the UCT. 'I have been here for four years, this is my fourth year but I have never been like, you know, I have never felt at home.' Then several incidents occurred that changed his mind and caused him to start identifying and positioning himself differently. In the second semester, Chris had a strange episode on campus which dramatically changed the way he saw himself at the UCT and the way he perceived the institution itself. He fell asleep in the library one afternoon and woke up screaming. Students around him were very concerned and came forward and offered to help. 'They came to help me, so that is what I felt like, I think my perception that everyone was turning away from me was not the case, so everyone was, now they came to help me, like what is going on, so that is why I am saying like I have now felt like at home.' Despite still being challenged with his work (especially his Drawing course) Chris started to focus on his university life and stopped thinking about leaving.

Reay (2004: 434) recognizes that 'habituses are permeable and responsive to what is going on around them. Current circumstances are not just there to be acted upon, but are internalized and become yet another layer to add to those from earlier socializations.' Chris described himself as not particularly close to his family, even his twin. This sense of physical and emotional distance from his family was exacerbated by the fact that no one at home could identify with his experiences in Cape Town. He commented that his family did not know what he was studying at university and were not interested to ask: 'My family are not that, if I can say emotional or something like that.' Nevertheless, Chris seemed to have experienced several shifts in his way of thinking about himself and his relationships to others. In his fourth year, he spoke of how he felt he needed to open up to people more which showed a dramatic shift from his first three years: 'If you speak to people then you learn to understand people and people learn to understand you, so you must be open in a way, so I don't think I was that person three years ago and that is why I experienced this kind of problem in the first three years.' His initial habitus of isolation and coping alone shifted to an acceptance of the benefits of engaging with others.

Chris talked about his reasons for working hard at university. In addition to becoming a professional so that he could provide for a future family, he also felt the need to prove something to his family and community about studying:

> They don't really believe in education, so that is the first point that I am trying to prove that it doesn't matter where you come from, you can still do it from any situation or circumstance. ... They say school is something that is impossible, so I want to show it to them, that this thing is possible and obviously outside in my community as well.

Here he showed a stronger sense of identifying with the institution and recognizing the worth of a university degree.

Over the course of his undergraduate degree, Chris's sense of alienation receded and he seemed to develop an increasing sense of belonging that was facilitated by his church group and his developing professional identity as an engineering student: 'Every time I go to class I feel like an engineer.' His positive vacation work experience also cemented his chosen career path. At the end of his sixth year, he had one course outstanding and was on track to graduate. Although he took considerably longer than the expected period to complete his degree, his tenacity clearly helped to sustain him. Chris's trajectory on the grid moved from an *outsider* position, to that of an *adaptor*, one of increased belonging to and alignment with institutional habitus.

Philisani's transition

Philisani grew up in an informal settlement in Kwa-Zulu Natal. His home language is Zulu. His father died in his second year of high school. He changed schools several times because his mother moved to different cities. He attended overcrowded, under-resourced township schools, which he described as chaotic. At school, Philisani and those who wanted to focus on their studies had to 'ask for help, you did what you basically could do in order to get education, so it was more like standing up for yourself as one and finding out what you really wanted to do.' He chose to associate with students who were serious about their academic work and he was part of a study group. The schools he attended did not provide him with adequate academic capital in the form of critical thinking, research and writing skills for university. He described his schools as 'tough environments' where he had many 'dark days' but it was a 'growing experience and it also taught me how to get along with life'. As a high school student, Philisani displayed a strong sense of agency and a motivated approach:

> I was forced to be independent, if I can say it because I had to think about my future, I had to think about what I want, so I had to give it my full shot, I couldn't just sit around and not do anything because the time was running by. ... I had to take advantage of everything that I have in order to put myself out there so, it was very important for me to make sure of my future.

Philisani was always focused on his studies and showed determination and agency, taking advantage of whatever opportunities presented themselves in order to succeed. While his school and home did not provide him with the cultural capital and academic background required by the university, he brought a focused, goal-orientated approach to his work.

Both Chris and Philisani had developed varying degrees of agency prior to entering higher education. However, unlike Chris, Philisani was able to take advantage of the support available in the university to counter his own lack of capital in certain areas. This level of confidence meant that the transition was far less alienating. We therefore placed Philisani as an *adaptor* in the diagram. He registered for a degree in Computer Science, and his first year was completed through the General Entry Programme for Science (GEPS), an extended science degree programme. Like Chris, on arriving at the UCT, Philisani found the environment very different and he had to adapt and grow quickly. Adjusting to the academic demands was one of his biggest challenges as his school had not adequately prepared him for the first-year requirements. He had expected an unsympathetic atmosphere where no one would show an interest in him, but instead he encountered a system of tutors, lecturers and advisors in which he could access advice and help. He seemed to do this with relative ease by taking advantage of the structures in place and finding fellow students he could relate to and work with when he was struggling academically.

In contrast to Chris, Philisani asserted that he fitted in at the university. He foregrounded the fact that his social life at the university was familiar, because he had a wide circle of friends, mainly from the 'the same background' with whom he shared a sense of 'unity'. In his first year, Philisani joined various student organizations and the Student Emerging Leadership Programme. Although he did not bring the required capital to adapt to the academic requirements, his willingness to find help, get involved, take opportunities and his gregarious attitude seemed to enable him to adapt relatively easily to the university.

In his second year, Philisani said that he was studying hard and felt that he understood the work, but this was evidently not enough, as he was not passing. His solution was to visit the hot seats, but he particularly foregrounded peer support through forming study groups and he resolved to 'just speak to people about academics and not just be on my own and say I'm going to get through this, just go and seek out for help, research more about it'. Despite his struggles, Philisani positioned himself as a secure, self-assured student. He showed an understanding of the university's systems and forms of support. He stated that he felt at home at the University. 'It feels so good to be back at UCT because this proves something of me. ... So now I have the confidence to make sure that I produce. ... I know that if anything that goes bad, I know which people to go to now, I'm far more advanced with UCT, I know where to go seek for help.' Philisani also talked about how his experiences within the university had changed him. He described himself as being more independent and organized, his time-management skills had improved, he knew where and how to access resources, he took advantage of opportunities and he was more open and secure about speaking to new people. Interestingly, when he went home in the holidays, he interacted with his childhood friends who were studying at other institutions and he remarked that they seemed immature and he no longer had respect for them. This revealed a changing personal disposition as he shifted towards adopting the habitus of his new friends and redefining himself and his habitus within the broader environment at the university.

Although he failed half of his courses (including his major, Computer Science), Philisani was allowed to return for his third year. In his third interview, he ascribed his failure to the group support that he had so actively sought to help him with his studies, claiming that he had become 'lazy' as he had relied too heavily on them. Despite having failed some courses, he displayed a very positive attitude and almost refused to see that he was struggling and that his place at the university was in jeopardy. His sense of comfort and belonging seemed to override the seriousness of his academic predicament:

> So I feel like I'm, even though I sort of like wasted my time a bit because I failed the other courses, now I have to make up for them but I still have that motivation, that push you know and I know that I have the support, so I feel like I am home, I feel like I am ready. ... I wouldn't say I'm struggling but it does get a bit challenging sometimes, so the only thing that can push me is the motivation and the willingness that I have.

In his third year, Philisani was not as involved in university organizations, but he took on a job as the receptionist at his student residence. He continued to turn to his peers, lecturers and other forms of support for help with his academic work.

In his fourth interview, Philisani was very focused on graduating. He was motivated and spoke with urgency about finishing his degree and starting his intern programme with his sponsors. His graduation would mean a 'weight lifted off everyone's shoulders, especially my mom' as he would be able to contribute financially. He reflected that when he went home in the holidays there was a disconnect with his neighbours as they considered him arrogant. 'Because of the way I carry myself, like at home, you know, I don't do what they do, out in the street, always at home sitting around, not that it is a bad thing but then it is something that I wouldn't do.'

In all his interviews, Philisani displayed a strong commitment to the institution, both in his involvement and in his attitude. However, in his fourth interview he qualified his sense of belonging, foregrounding the stratified nature of the culture in the institution:

> If you are going to look at UCT in terms of the wide variety and you know, I say this all the time, each and every kind of person is at UCT and if you look in

the right places you are going to find yourself within UCT, so looking at it that way, … I do find myself, but then in terms of the dominant lifestyle, you know, the fancy rich and you know that whole opulence, not opulence but rich people lifestyle, not in that way, *ja* [Afrikaans for 'yes'].

Although his outlook remained optimistic and his goal was to graduate, Philisani also spoke about the fact that every year after writing exams he considered other universities as he felt insecure about his results.

For four years, Philisani demonstrated agency, a willingness to access support structures and ask for help and a positive, motivated attitude. Unfortunately, after struggling with his courses for four years, he was excluded and could not return to complete his studies. It is difficult to determine exactly where the disjuncture lies, but there is a dissonance between the facts that Philisani managed to pass for three years and adapted to the university environment on the one hand and his final academic results on the other. A more careful analysis of how he followed up on poor results, his time management, how he utilized the support he obtained, his contributions to his study group and other specifics might reveal which rules of the academy he failed to learn. Philisani quickly acquired some of the social capital and the mainstream habitus which could have lulled him into a sense of complacency regarding his academic work. It was only when he reflected on his results that he began to doubt his competence. Although placed as an *adaptor*, his sense of belonging and motivated approach were not sufficient for him to adapt to academic demands.

Senzo's transition

Senzo was born and lived in a rural part of the Eastern Cape. His home language is Xhosa. He lived with his grandparents and two nephews and they were all supported by an uncle. He went to boarding school from Grade 9 to Grade 12, where he frequently experienced crime and violence. His time at school was marked by absent teachers and in desperation Senzo taught himself the mathematics curriculum. His final mathematics result was 83 per cent. At school he exhibited a great degree of agency and hard work and was extremely goal orientated.

Like Philisani, we placed Senzo in the *adaptor* quadrant. He was accepted into electrical engineering through the ASPECT programme. In spite of the newness of the university environment, Senzo did not find the transition overwhelming.

His initial impressions of the University were very positive: 'It's the coolest place, meeting people who are friendly, *ja*, everything was fine …. No discrimination here, all people like want to be in one way.' Although he did not participate much in extra-mural activities, he had a few friends from his school and seemed to find a place for himself early on. The hardest aspect of the transition for Senzo was his mathematics course as he was presented with material that he had never seen before. In addition, communicating in English was a challenge as he was used to speaking and learning in Xhosa. Senzo took advantage of the student mentor assigned to him as his main source of support. He also turned to fellow students for help and started a study group.

Senzo's second interview reflected his growing academic and social confidence. He found he related well to other students, especially those in his residence; he continued with his study group and found it easier to function in English. When he went home in the holidays, he was happy to reconnect with his old friends, some of whom were studying at other institutions. He spoke about some of them asking for his help with mathematics and he was proud to be perceived as the person who could help academically. He consistently displayed faith in his own abilities and a sense of agency: 'Believe in yourself, if you don't believe in yourself, like you have to trust yourself because if you don't trust yourself there is nothing else that is going to go, everything is going to stop the way it is, *ja*, it's just to believe in yourself.'

In his third year, Senzo maintained this confidence. He asserted that he had no role model and restated that one had to believe in oneself. He still received support from those around him and from his family at home. He described himself as comfortable and happy at the UCT and said that he managed by working. 'It's basically it's to work … do your work properly. And then most of all, just try and believe that you can do it … everything. And then when it comes to social, you just have to make sure that there's … the decisions you make are still going to help you.'

In his fourth interview, Senzo described himself as the same as a stress ball: not because he felt pressurized, but because he saw himself as able to adapt to different situations and remain strong. That year, he limited the time he spent at home to only two weeks, and he felt that his family did not know him as well anymore. He felt he had changed but that his family constructed him as 'still the same person that they used to know'. As with Philisani, there was a change in Senzo's habitus as he negotiated the institutional habitus. In his fourth interview, he re-evaluated and re-assessed many of his earlier views and reflected on the ways in which his personal disposition and relationship to the institutional habitus had shifted. He admitted that earlier he had self-doubt and a lack of confidence, and he described the most difficult part of being a student: 'When you get here and you start being connected like see different faces every day and all are doing engineering and you know they come from high school with the better marks, maybe even better marks than the ones you have and then *ja*, that's .... Yes, you become less confident about yourself.' He acknowledged that when he first arrived he was not confident, but also stated that that kind of comparison and competition is good, 'if I hadn't looked at that, I doubt I will be where I am today'. Senzo made a definite move towards taking up the identity of a university student: 'I was just going to school and do whatever I had to do because my [grand]parents sent me to do that and when I first got here and then things started to change, you get introduced to new stuff and then that is when you become interested about all the study environment and that is when it changed.' Senzo worked as a mentor in his department and spoke proudly about the students he helped and the improvements they made. He also spoke confidently about graduating and his plans for registering for a master's degree while working. 'I mean this is my fourth year now and I haven't failed anything, so that should tell me something about myself.'

Another example of a change in Senzo's perspective was in his fifth interview where he remembered that he was a high school student who did not study hard and who did not care. This is a very different picture from the one painted in his first interview. He reflected on how the University gave him study skills and the attitude to focus and remain goal orientated. For him, the status of the University worked as a great motivation. 'It is difficult to get here, when you are here you make sure that you don't get excluded, you have to work hard all the time'. He described himself as a risk-taker with regard to his attitude towards his studies:

> because when I started doing this course, advisors told me that it is going to be hard on me, there is no way you are going to be able to pass all these courses, because some of them are even clashing, ... but I still went ahead, so I think I am a risk-taker, but that is me, if I want to do something I just do it.

By his fourth year, Senzo had clearly positioned himself as a UCT student, taken up the institutional habitus and moved towards the *insider* quadrant. He went on to tutor others and to graduate in a shorter-than-expected time despite being warned by lecturers that he was taking on too much. He learnt not only what was expected, but also how to deliver these requirements successfully. He defined himself in terms of and aligned himself with the values of the university and saw it having an ongoing place in his life in the future.

Monique's transition

Monique is from an urban suburb in Johannesburg, where she lived with her two working parents. Her home language is Sesotho. Monique attended a well-resourced school where English was the language of teaching and learning. She had wanted to attend the UCT from an early age and she drove herself through high school with that aim. Her reputation at school was that of a diligent, serious student and she identified herself as motivated and focused.

We placed Monique in the *strategist* quadrant. Although her school provided her with some of the academic capital she needed for university, her habitus did not easily adapt to her new environment and socially it was a difficult transition for her. In her first interview, she described the move to Cape Town and the University as a 'big adjustment' emotionally as she was leaving her home and family for the first time. In her first year, she reflected that she had to 'find out who I am away from all those things that used to define me'. Without her parents and familiar structures, she felt she had a lot of questioning to do and had to constantly evaluate 'why I was doing what I was doing'. Monique was not accepted into her first choice of degree in Quantitative Finance. She applied to read for her Bachelor of Business Science through the Academic Development Programme. Although her high school was well resourced, her teachers 'didn't go on strike' and she was taught in English, Monique felt 'inadequate' and less intelligent than other students. Like Chris, Philisani and Senzo, Monique felt that her secondary schooling had not adequately prepared her for her tertiary studies and found the amount of work and the pace at which it was covered overwhelming. 'Because [at] varsity, the pace and the way they do things is completely different to school.' During her first year, she felt alienated and did not feel as though she fitted in at the University.

In her second year, the university environment started to become more familiar to Monique and she started to feel at home in the institution, 'to a certain extent'. She described herself as being less stressed and panicked, because she knew what to expect. She was also finding her way around the academic field and had better strategies when it came to learning. In lectures, she did not try to write everything down, but listened more and took notes with greater selectivity. Socially and academically, Monique felt less threatened by her peers. In her first year, she was intimidated by them, and felt less competent academically and socially, and could not turn to them for help. But in her second year, fellow students formed part of her emotional and academic support. 'I have solidified my relationships with my friends so I can tell them when things are getting difficult for me, I don't feel like I'm all alone.' She felt comfortable studying and doing academic work with her peers, helping them and accepting help from them. She stated that unlike in her first year, she no longer perceived the UCT as 'the enemy'. She felt

> more responsible for who I am and who I decide to become, my actions and my consequences and outcomes. ... I think it was just aligning myself with people that want to do well, people that are ambitious, hardworking and they want to succeed in life, so when you are around people like that it forces, not forces but encourages you to also strive to be better.

In her third year, Monique took proactive steps to become involved with various aspects of campus life. She joined several societies, sat on committees and tutored for one of the residences. She felt her involvement in all these extra-mural activities aided her time management and forced her to work productively. She described herself as being 'more confident' in the academic sphere, and when she was unsure of something, she approached lecturers and took advantage of hot seats and tutors. She acknowledged all these support systems and even wondered why she had never accessed them before.

When she returned home for the holidays, there were significant shifts in terms of Monique's interactions with her family. Previously, she had been happy to accept her parents' ideas and beliefs and would not have challenged them. However, as her ways of being and thinking as a university student become more dominant she challenged her parents' authority:

> But I find that ... how the relationships have changed now, is I like arguing more and ... I'm now more confident about my arguments and even the way I structure my thoughts is stronger than before. Because, when arguing or debating with my family, my parents would say one thing and I'd just shut up, you know, but now I have different ways of thinking and even challenging their arguments that I've learned through varsity and interactions with other people here, so I've grown in my confidence in that way.

She also described her relationship with her friends from home as changing:

> They still feel the same and to me, I think that's part of the problem … the fact that it's still the same. I don't find them as interesting [laughing] as before, so … and I don't feel as comfortable around the people I called my close friends, whereas everyone else I wasn't as close to, I feel more comfortable around them.

In her third year, Monique positioned herself primarily as a UCT student. The discourses she drew on and her frames of reference were no longer those of her home and family. This shift was very clear when she discussed how she felt at home at the UCT and entitled to be there 'because there are people that I can relate to and on most days I feel as if I do have … like I have the right to be here as much as everyone else does'. This statement shows a notable move from her feelings of insecurity and inferiority in her first year.

At this stage, Monique seemed to have adapted and taken on some of the institutional habitus. She did not forgo her initial home habitus, and her values, centred on her church, her family and a strong respect for her background, are very evident. However, her sense of where she fitted in, her closeness to her university friends and a bigger world view had shifted and in some cases, transformed her sense of who she was: 'Like I've had a lot, questioning a lot of things that I do and why I do them and, because a lot of things you did then because your parents said so and here you don't really have to do them anymore, so it's like okay, why am I doing what I'm doing?' Monique's sense of self-esteem, autonomy and agency grew with time and experience.

In her fourth year, Monique changed degree streams from a Bachelor of Business Science degree to a Bachelor of Commerce, Chartered Accounting degree. While she had started her degree with the idea of doing a conventional job in business, she now no longer saw herself as limited or constrained by her degree:

> I know what I want to do, I don't exactly know what order it is going to happen in. I would love to go into management consultancy, I'd love to work in finance, some form of investment banking, I am not exactly sure what though and then eventually I want to have an NGO [non-government not-for-profit organization] that focuses on development of women and children and I want to have a coffee shop, I don't know how it is going to work out, because of the timeline but those are my future aspirations.

Monique changed streams and took five years to complete a three-year commerce degree. In her fourth year she had only one course outstanding to complete her honours degree (Financial Analysis and Portfolio Management). We moved her from the initial placement of *strategist*, a stranger with feelings of insecurity and inferiority, to that of an *insider* who felt a sense of involvement and belonging. As her degree progressed she developed a more nuanced sense of academic expectations and learnt strategies such as study and social collaboration and time management and she grew in confidence. She became increasingly interested in pursuing a variety of extra-mural activities. Monique was involved with her residence house committee, tutoring and several other societies. This boosted her self-esteem and improved her time management. She made the discourse of the University and its ways of thinking and seeing the world her own. Adapting to the institution and actively involving herself beyond the formal learning environment helped her acquire the institutional habitus. Her resilience helped move her from being fairly isolated, working alone and being self-reliant to being more integrated with her peers and within the University.

Lyndsey's transition

The last student we discuss is Lyndsey. She speaks English at home and lives with her mother and brothers in her grandparents' house in a working-class community in Cape Town. Although all her female cousins attended the UCT, she was a first-generation student. She always knew she would apply to study at the University. She attended a well-resourced, private high school (on a scholarship) whose academic habitus was similar to that of her first year at university. She registered for a Bachelor of Business Science degree and, in contrast to the other participants, felt well prepared for her first-year courses with regard to time management, independent study, writing and academic pressure. Her transition to university seemed relatively smooth and in her reflections on the culture, she said: 'everything is normal' and 'everyone fits in', in the extended degree programme. We placed her in the *insider* quadrant as a result.

In her second year, Lyndsey continued to integrate into student life. She repeated how her schooling had prepared her with regard to independent thinking, time management and taking responsibility for her studies. She did acknowledge that socially it was not always easy, but being in the extended degree programme made making friends much easier. 'So it's quite difficult to make friends and lots of people come to UCT in cliques already, so socially

I mean it's not the best, but I mean I'm not really here to socialize so much and I have a lot of friends and we like a good group of friends, so it's fine.' Unlike the other participants, Lyndsey lived at home for the duration of her undergraduate degree and never joined any societies or organizations associated with the University. Although she never explicitly talked about struggling academically, Lyndsey did talk about asking friends for help or going to her tutor or the hot seat. She reflected on how she had changed since being at the University. 'I think you have to change as you age, not maybe change fundamentally who you are but you experience different things and you grow in different ways. ... But I think like at this age you are still trying to figure exactly who you are and what you want, *ja*, it is a journey.'

In June in her fourth year at university, Lyndsey graduated with a commerce degree and then continued studying as an occasional student, earning credits to qualify for a postgraduate course in Accounting. In her third interview she had not referred to any difficulties, but with hindsight, she revealed in her fourth interview, that the exceedingly demanding circumstances meant that she struggled academically for the first time:

> Like in third year it becomes much more intense than in any of the other years ... and you keep working but you are just not getting to where you want to be, like that was the toughest part for me last year because you get demotivated because it is not like you are not working, you are working every day and you are working weekends and you have study groups and the test comes and you are just not seeing an improvement, so I think the most difficult thing was like to separate that from yourself because people get, like people in our faculty committed suicide last year, like people, it gets them down.

It also became apparent in her final interview that despite seeming to adapt easily and to feel a sense of belonging in the institution, her sense of belonging was not entirely positive. Like the other participants, she felt a connection and affinity with her membership of the Academic Development Programme, rather than with the UCT:

> I think if there is one thing third year gave us like as a group of students, we felt like victimized together, like we were all in the struggle together and even when it got bad we all just kept going back, but I have never really felt like, like Stellenbosch students are always so proudly Maties [informal name for University of Stellenbosch students] and stuff, I don't feel that way really at UCT, I have never really felt that way.

Lyndsey was familiar with and quickly grasped the requirements and practices of academia and from the beginning of her studies had a sense of academic processes due to her school background. She started with a strong sense of fitting in to the University environment. Over the years her sense of connection with the institution decreased. However, despite having experienced some difficulties with the academic expectations and her lack of connection to the greater university community, she was still able to retain her position as an *insider*. Lyndsey completed her Bachelor of Commerce degree and went on to read for a postgraduate Diploma in Accounting. She is now doing her articles with an accounting firm and completing her professional accounting examinations.

Reflections

In this chapter we have described the changing trajectories of five students from their starting point in first year through their degrees. It is clear that these students' 'journeys' in higher education studies are complex, multifaceted and dynamic. For some students their familiarity with the institutional capital and habitus meant less identity work and time to become an *insider*. For others the unfamiliarity of the institution created barriers and necessitated energy to *adapt, strategize* or *fit in*. There are multiple aspects that impact on students' success. We have highlighted the issues related to students' changing sense of belonging, as well as their varying abilities to understand and negotiate the various forms of capital required in an academic institution.

Both Monique and Lyndsey benefitted from having acquired the cultural capital valued by the institution prior to entry. Their different narratives motivated us to place Monique as a *strategist* and Lyndsey as an *insider*. Their cultural capital enabled them to graduate and proceed to postgraduate studies. Lyndsey succeeded academically, negotiated the system and made friends, but she reflected that by the end of her degree, she did not actually feel as though she had an institutional identity. Her cultural capital and habitus did not ensure a sense of belonging and broader involvement and investment in the University, but it did afford her a relatively unproblematic academic journey and she thus remained an *insider*. Although initially Monique felt more alienated than Lyndsey regarding the language and ways of being at the University, with time she exhibited increased agency and became more connected to her peers and surroundings. This clearly enhanced her sense of belonging. By her final year she moved from being a *strategist* to that of being an *insider* due to an enhanced sense of social and academic belonging.

Philisani and Chris did not feel that they understood or were familiar with the academic expectations and culture of the University. However, they had contrasting experiences regarding their sense of personal and social connection with others. Philisani, whom we positioned as an *adapter*, continually appeared very confident in his new surroundings, as well as connected in a variety of ways to people and student organizations. This expressed confidence and his evident social capital did not change over time even though he was eventually excluded after four years. Chris, on the other hand, was an *outsider*, a 'fish out of water' from the beginning. The ways of the University and his personal circumstances made him feel like an isolate. A shift in this experience came about in his fourth year when a particular personal event made him feel that people cared and he recovered some sense of self-worth and identity. He continues to pursue an engineering degree after six years.

Interestingly, Senzo arrived without the necessary academic capital, but his strong belief in himself and his capabilities and a developing sense of belonging allowed him to adapt successfully. Unlike Monique and Lyndsey he had far less previous home and schooling to prepare him for the particularities and demands of academia. He continually spent energy and time adapting his identity to fit in academically. His activities such as tutoring and mentoring facilitated a movement from *adapter* towards being an *insider* and a feeling of pride in being part of the institution. Thus, Chris, Monique and Senzo all shifted from their initial positions towards an increased *insider* identity. Philisani seemed to *adapt* and fit in; however, he never grasped the academic rigour and expectations in order to graduate and move towards the *insider* quadrant. While Lyndsey did not shift from an *insider* position, her identity trajectory was equally complex.

Bourdieu's observation that capital begets capital (cited in Watson et al. 2009: 672) is true at face value. Any capital or habitus that the student brings and is valued by the institution is an advantage to a student but the lack thereof does not imply failure at the institution. To illustrate, Watson et al. (2009: 679) highlight language as a high-value form of cultural capital in the higher education field that 'has a bearing on understanding the "rules of the game", maximizing the potential of learning opportunities and the ability to demonstrate "legitimate" forms of knowledge and understanding'. Lyndsey and Monique had a great advantage as they were taught in school contexts with English as the language of learning and teaching. At school they had also been inducted into some of the academic literacy practices and ways of thinking that characterized their higher education disciplines. However, Philisani, Senzo and Chris did not have this particular capital when they entered higher education. In their cases, English was taught as an additional language and although the language of learning and teaching was officially English, in reality they had very little exposure to the language and limited induction into academic literacy practices. And yet with time all three students' English language ability improved, increasing their confidence. Although they struggled initially, both Chris and Senzo managed to negotiate and meet the academic demands.

From this study of these five students, it is apparent that there is a complexity of factors at play when students adapt to being in an institution such as the UCT. It is clearly not easy to infer that students who enter higher education with some synergy with the University are more likely to succeed. Likewise, students who feel a sense of social belonging and feel connected with themselves and others are not necessarily able to negotiate the demands of university education. What the findings suggest is that it takes more energy and identity work for the students who do not have the institutional capital and habitus. This means that students who have different social, cultural and linguistic capital to the institution obviously have more emotional demands and learning curves to negotiate than those who have the required capital and are familiar with the norms, values and ways of being in the institution.

Conclusion

This study illustrates the socially situated nature of student success. While academic ability is important, a range of factors impact on students' negotiation in higher education: personal dispositions, their sense of belonging and social connectedness, and the ability to access support and negotiate life's circumstances. These can all contribute to adjustment issues and play a role in a student's journey through higher education. The study of these five students has shown that there is more emotional and psychological work involved if students do not possess the habitus and capital that is required by the University. Adapting and coping therefore takes time and involves overcoming particular difficulties.

Student success means not only the ability to graduate, but also the ability to develop a sense of self-efficacy, confidence and social justice. For example, although Philisani did not graduate, it could be speculated that because he exerted great agency while studying and took advantage of his time at the UCT, he developed a range of competencies in his four years there. Monique started her degree with a specific commerce career orientation. Through her experiences at the UCT and with the skills she acquired, she broadened the scope of her future self to encompass pursuing a social justice agenda.

While we have not focused on the institutional habitus, it is important that we do not simply foreground the students' capacity to negotiate and fit in to the University. This can quickly become a way of assimilating students as effectively as possible into the dominant culture of the University. Rather, as Haggis (2006:521) asserts, 'more subtle aspects of higher education pedagogical cultures may themselves be creating conditions which make it difficult, or even impossible, for some students to learn'. This means that for both the learning environment and in the broader institution as a whole, ways need to be explored that will enhance students' sense of belonging, as well as of valuing their different capitals. At a pedagogical level, it means being sensitive to and focused on language, using scaffolding, highlighting relevant case studies and context and exploring a variety of ways of establishing inclusion and engagement. It also means a broad focus on graduate attributes (such as critical thinking and social engagement) throughout the degree in order to nurture the holistic development of the student. At a broader institutional level, the University must review its taken-for-granted practices, ways of being, celebrations, norms and world views, to shift the institutional habitus to recognize and embrace the varying forms of capital that students bring, thereby enhancing inclusion by valuing the diversity of the student body.

This chapter provides an imperative to move beyond locating problems of adjustment *within* the student to engaging seriously with the underlying cultural assumptions, values, aims and purposes of higher education (Haggis 2006). There is clearly a great deal of structural work to do to create an environment that will help to minimize the time and emotional energy expended on the identity work necessary for students to comprehend the 'rules of the game'. 'Fitting in' can sometimes be counterproductive to students' well-being and ability to study, resulting in a failure to exert agency. Equally the University is missing out on rich opportunities to rethink and reformulate its practices and culture in relation to students' experiences. Putting the onus on the University to acknowledge the forms of capital that the students bring and for the institution to accept some responsibility for the transitions students make to higher education, could open up new ways of negotiating learning and identity.

References

Bourdieu, P. (1977), *Outline of a Theory of Practice*, Cambridge: Cambridge University Press.

Bourdieu, P. (1984), *Distinction: A Social Critique of the Judgement of Taste*, London: Routledge.

Bourdieu, P. (1986), 'The Forms of Capital', in the *Handbook of Theory and Research for the Sociology of Capital*, 241–58, J. G. Richardson, New York: Greenwood Press.

Bourdieu, P. (1990), *The Logic of Practice*, Stanford, California: Stanford University Press.

Bourdieu, P. (1991), *Language and Symbolic Power*, Cambridge, Massachusetts: Harvard University Press.

Bourdieu, P., Accardo, A., Balazs, G., Beaud, S., Bonvin, F., Bourdieu, E., Bourgois, P., Broccolichi, F., Champagne, P., Christin, R., Faguer, J. P., Garcia, S., Lenoir, R., Euvrard, F., Pialoux, M., Pinto, L., Podalydes, D., Sayad, A., Soulie, C. and Wacquant, L. J. D. (1999), *The Weight of the World*, Cambridge: Polity Press.

Case, J. M. (2013), *Researching Student Learning in Higher Education: A Social Realist Approach*, London and New York: Routledge.

Christie, H., Tett, L., Cree, V. E., Hounsell, J. and McCune, V. (2008), '"A Real Rollercoaster of Confidence and Emotions": Learning to be a University Student', *Studies in Higher Education*, 33(5): 567–81.

Haggis, T. (2006), 'Pedagogies for Diversity: Retaining Critical Challenge Amidst Fears of "Dumbing Down"', *Studies in Higher Education*, 31(5): 521–35.

Kelly-Blakeney, E. (2014), 'Response to HEA consultation paper: Towards the development of a new National Plan for Equity of Access to Higher Education 2014–2017', unpublished paper, St. Angela's College Sligo.

Pym, J. (2013), 'Introducing the Commerce Education Development Unit and its Work', in *Surfacing Possibilities: What it Means to Work with First-Generation Higher Education Students*, 1–13, Pym, J. and Paxton, M. (eds), IL: Common Ground.

Pym, J. and Kapp, R. (2013), 'Harnessing Agency: Towards a Learning Model for Undergraduate Students', *Studies in Higher Education*, 38(2): 272–84.

Reay, D. (2004), 'It's all becoming a Habitus: Beyond the Habitual use of Habitus in Educational Research', *British Journal of Sociology of Education*, 25(4): 431–44.

Reay, D., David, M. E. and Ball, S. (2005), *Degrees of Choice: Social Class, Race and Gender in Higher Education*, Stoke-on-Trent: Trentham Books.

Reay, D., Crozier, G. and Clayton, J. (2010), '"Fitting In" or "Standing Out": Working-Class Students in UK Higher Education', *British Educational Research Journal*, 36(1): 107–24.

Watson, J., Nind, M., Humphris, D. and Borthwick, A. (2009), 'Strange New World: Applying a Bourdieuian Lens to Understanding Early Student Experiences in Higher Education', *British Journal of Sociology of Education*, 30(6): 665–81.

Conclusion: Exploring the Implications of Students' Learning Journeys for Policy and Practice

Bongi Bangeni and Rochelle Kapp

This book has traced the lived experiences of a group of black students in order to understand how they gained access to higher education, how institutional and societal structures and discourses enabled and/or hindered their progress, and how and why they persisted. While we have no easy answers to these questions, travelling alongside the participants, teaching them, hearing their stories of challenge and success and analysing their writing have rendered us a more nuanced sense of the labyrinth that students traverse as they negotiate learning and identity. Our research shows that learning and identity are intertwined. Negotiating meaningful access to learning is inextricably connected to negotiating an intersection of race, class, linguistic, gendered and religious subject positions in relation to home, school and university. In this chapter we identify key research findings and consider the implications of these insights for higher education research, policy and practice globally. We do so by revisiting the questions we foreground in the introduction: How do we facilitate meaningful access to institutional and disciplinary discourses? How can we recognize and draw on the resources that students bring into the academy? How can we transform discourses and structures that impede, exclude, marginalize and silence?

Our study has focused on the ways in which the participants viewed the world, reasoned, rationalized, strategized, took decisions and used resources in order to progress and/or construct a narrative (sometimes multiple narratives) of progress. They drew on past home, school and academic experiences to make sense of the present, to explain their academic performance and ways of being, to assess their progress and to construct a future (see also Tema 1986; Boughey 2010; Klemenčič 2015). The longitudinal perspective along with the different theoretical lenses adopted by individual authors has enabled us to highlight the temporal and spatial nature of these constructions. The institution and the participants privilege a narrative of progress, of triumph over adversity, which constructs student transition in singular terms and views the journey as direct, linear and fixed in time. As the contributors in this book have shown, this view is more often than not at odds with students' experiences. The journey is not linear and entails many unscheduled detours and stops. Precipitous moves from steady progress to failure (and vice versa) from one year to the next are a reality. Students' experiences are situated. What is valued and expected and what constitutes and enables progress and success varies across space and time. Thus students are able to be agentic at certain times, in certain spaces but not in others. This is a crucial issue for how the field of higher education conceptualizes the issue of student access and retention. The implications of this understanding of the journey and the spatial and temporal nature of student agency are explored below.

Research across the globe has shown that students from traditionally under-represented social groups generally have to exert considerable agency in order to negotiate access to higher education (Herrington and Curtis 2000 and Reay, David and Ball 2005). A key finding in our research is the way in which agency in participants' working-class home and neighbourhood environments was often 'sponsored' (Herrington and Curtis 2000: 369) by individuals or community organizations outside of school who played a major role in motivating and guiding students and providing intellectual, linguistic and/or spiritual resources which enabled them to feel a sense of belonging and connection, to envisage a future beyond their immediate environment and to take action to make this a reality. The centrality of the role of the 'sponsor' in facilitating agency draws attention to the mismatch between ways of knowing and using language in black, working-class school contexts and higher education academic literacy practices. Participants', sponsors' and teachers' notions of post-school pathways, higher education and the world of work were often nebulous, limited and unrealistic. This book illustrates how high school discourses and decisions made at high school level continue to impact on students' pathways on entry, at senior levels and even after the successful completion of the first degree. While there are important, recent development projects designed to foster connections between higher education institutions and working-class schools, these initiatives are often limited in scope, sporadic, decontextualized and reliant on individual goodwill. They also tend to be located outside of school, which means that teachers are left out of the conversation. This finding points to the need for a much more systematic, integrated, sustained approach to facilitating meaningful epistemic and structural access to higher education institutions through schools' development work which draws on the considerable resources within universities to foster teacher development and peer mentoring/tutoring relationships that help to bridge the chasm that exists between the discourses and literacy practices of working-class schools and those of universities. Traditionally, higher education and school-based research have tended to occupy separate spaces. This finding points to the need to bridge this divide in order to better understand the affordances and challenges of the discourse practices in both contexts.

Globally, higher education has focused increasing attention on academic and psycho-social support within the first year as a major retention strategy. While the first year is foundational and clearly plays a crucial role in retention, the longitudinal focus of our research problematizes the notion that intense support and reduced load in the first year prepares students adequately for progression to their senior years and indeed, whether such an outcome is possible given the situated nature of learning. Chapters 2, 3, 6 and 7 all raise important questions about the nature of academic support that students receive in the foundation year, the forms that this support should take as the year progresses and the articulation between first year and subsequent years. The need for sustained, varied approaches to academic and psycho-social support over the course of the undergraduate degree is underscored by the descriptions in this book of how students experienced various forms and levels of failure and exclusion at different stages of the transition from school to university, during the course of their undergraduate degrees and in the transition to postgraduate study.

The data illustrate the ways in which student learning was often impeded by limitations of choice within degree structures; by lack of explicitness about intended pedagogy, its purpose and context; by lack of knowledge about how processes of knowledge construction within the discipline are connected to language, literacy and numeracy practices; and by a lack of coherence within and between courses. In general, the participants seemed to experience courses within disciplines as discrete entities and struggled to articulate conceptual connection. The lack of alignment between courses became an increasing challenge when the conceptual and literacy demands increased in volume and complexity in the senior years. These findings imply the need for flexible degree pathways (see Council on Higher Education 2013), sustained support that is tailored to suit students' needs at various times of the transition and greater explicitness and alignment between intended pedagogy, pedagogy and assessment within and across curricula (Christie 2008; Mann 2008).

While international research has recognized the centrality of identity to learning, in general, higher education practices still tend to construct identity as marginal to epistemic access. The data show the ways in which students felt positioned, silenced and rendered passive by disciplinary discourses which seemed to assume assimilation, offering very limited scope for debate and alternative positions. Both chapters 4 and 5 describe the ways in which disciplines constructed undergraduate students as outsiders to knowledge production. Lecturers made assumptions about students' prior knowledge and experience, but seldom engaged them on the subject. Assessment tasks were summative and often prescribed the possible subject positions available and the register in which they were expressed. Negative feedback resulted in students mimicking the discourse, adopting instrumental and reproductive subject positions in order to pass. Thus, the generative potential of learning from, and engaging with the tensions caused by clashes between home and institutional values and practices was missed. While there has been considerable critique of the Anglo-centric content of curricula in South African universities, it seems from the data that a great deal of the participants' sense of alienation stemmed from the ways in which they were positioned as marginal outsiders to academic engagement rather than to the curriculum content per se. When curriculum content focused on local issues that were central to the participants' lives or on deeply held norms and values, these were often not subject to debate. The notion that they would create a distant authorial persona and re-cast their working-class identities and language practices into a form acceptable within academia was assumed. Simultaneously, the participants' family and neighbourhood communities expected them to retain home discourses and identities while their increasing fluency in English, and in the 'cultural capital' valued within the institution (Bourdieu 1991: 230), often positioned them as outsiders within their home environments (see chapters 2, 4 and 8). This positioning had a material reality as well. Both the institution and the students' families assumed that they were adequately funded by state and institutional financial aid systems. They were constantly made aware that they were living well in comparison to their poverty-stricken families and family needs constituted a major source of stress and pressure. The data show the ways in which the participants' hopes, desires and choices were constrained and thwarted by financial constraints, fear of failure and expectations both at home and within the institution. Thus, the participants were engaged in constant emotion-work as they absorbed and resisted the discourses of the academy, negotiating the ambivalence caused by trying to connect and identify with contradictory discourses and expectations within home and the institution. As chapters 4 and 5 show, this too had a space-time dimension as they increasingly constructed situated ways of being, valuing and using language.

While there has been much critique, particularly in recent South African student protests about the ways in which special admissions and extended degree programmes have the potential to reinforce stigma and deficit constructions, the data provide a complex, entangled picture of participants' experiences, attitudes and perceptions. The participants described the extended degree programmes as safe spaces which enabled learning, growth, recognition and engagement, as well as sites which limited, infantilized, marginalized and constrained their choices (see chapters 2, 3 and 7). The rationale for being placed on an extended degree programme was discussed publicly on entry in first year, but never revisited. The chapters have emphasized how adjustments to being on the programmes happened over time and at different times for individual students. While a few participants retained anger at their placement, most rationalized their placement on the programmes through a process of looking back to how their high school experiences contributed to their academic standing and comparing their progress favourably in relation to their peers in mainstream programmes.

We argue that the institutional silence about the psychological and social aspects of students' transitions exacerbated students' sense of being constructed as deficit and 'other' (Pym and Kapp 2013: 274). An awareness of how students negotiate a sense of self in the process of negotiating multiple subject positions is therefore important in addressing factors which cause engagement and disengagement. For many participants who excelled within their school contexts and demonstrated high levels of agency, the experience of being placed on an extended degree programme, being excluded from meaningful engagement and/ or of failure rendered them passive, vulnerable and silent. On the other hand, chapters 2, 4 and 8 paint vivid pictures of the ways in which it is possible to enact agency through repositioning, reclaiming and reconfiguring problematic spaces, languages and discourses which have the potential to silence. Significantly, these agentic acts took place outside of the curriculum space. Many of the participants spoke about how much they enjoyed the research interviews because they provided an opportunity to reflect on their learning and growth seldom afforded within the institution. The challenge is for higher education institutions to provide enabling environments within the classroom and formative tasks where students can reflect and engage critically with content which they may find unsettling. The longitudinal perspective illustrates the importance of context and of a consequent situated perspective on student learning for understanding higher education and retention. Crucially, it foregrounds the need to harness student agency and to enable persistence through sustained, systemic intervention in multiple spaces over time. This represents a significant challenge to the ways in which higher education policy and practice has conceptualized student access in terms of discrete, first-year support.

The research for this book has been a learning journey for the contributors. It has provided an invaluable opportunity for us to reflect on our identities, our teaching practices and for a close, often uncomfortable examination of the models of teaching and learning and student support within extended degree programmes and the mainstream. In exploring strategies for the development of pedagogical tools in selected learning spaces and for the transforming of curricula, it is important for higher education research and practice to look at the ways in which institutional discourses of change, transformation and access impact on students and staff and the meanings students attach to their participation in higher education. The meaningful objects which students brought with them to their interviews in the final year of the project offer insights into the nature of their investment in their journeys to and through university: the student card which represents various forms of access; the photograph which signifies a student's desire to access a discipline which is out of reach; a definition of the term 'success' which one student defined to mean acceptance into higher education and by implication, a tertiary qualification. These are reminders to us as educators of the hopes and dreams of our youth and of our responsibility to ensure that facilitating meaningful access and retention continues to be at the core of our institutions' social justice agenda.

References

Boughey, C. (2010), 'Academic Development for Improved Efficiency in the Higher Education and Training System in South Africa', Report for the Development Bank of South Africa, Midrand, South Africa: Development Bank of South Africa.

Bourdieu, P. (1991), *Language and Symbolic Power*, Cambridge, MA: Harvard University Press.

Christie P. (2008), *Changing Schools in South Africa: Opening the Doors of Learning*, Johannesburg: Heinemann.

Council on Higher Education, (2013), *A Proposal for Undergraduate Curriculum Reform in South Africa: The Case for a Flexible Curriculum Structure*, http://www.che.ac.za/sites/default/files/publications/, accessed 28 November 2013.

Herrington, A. and Curtis, M. (2000), *Persons in Process: Four Stories of Writing and Personal Development in College*, Urbana, IL: National Council of Teachers of English.

Klemenčič, M. (2015), 'What is Student Agency? An Ontological Exploration in the Context of Research on Student Engagement', in Klemenčič, M., Bergan, S., Primožič, R. (eds), *Student Engagement in Europe: Society, Higher Education* and *Student Governance*, 11–29, Council of Europe Higher Education, Series No. 20, Strasbourg: Council of Europe Publishing.

Mann, S. (2008), *Study, Power and the University*, Maidenhead: Society for Research into Higher Education and Open University Press.

Pym, J. and Kapp, R. (2013), 'Harnessing Agency: Towards a Learning Model for Undergraduate Students', *Studies in Higher Education*, 38(2): 272–84.

Reay, D., David, M. and Ball, S. (2005), *Degrees of Choice. Social Class, Race and Gender in Higher Education*, Stoke on Trent: Trentham Books.

Tema, B. (1986), 'Academic Support: Its Assumptions and its Implications', *South African Journal of Higher Education*, 2(1): 29–31.

Index

Note: Page numbers in italics refer to figures

Academic Development
    Programme   7, 174
academic discourse
    circumscribed nature of   84–5
    resisted and absorbed by
        students   92, 184–5
    students' identification with   86,
        88–9, 116
    students' mimicking of   84, 184
    within ideological frameworks   106–7
academic habitus   116
academic load   139–40, 143
academic staff
    disquiet over changes   6
    few black academics   7
Academic Support Programme for
    Engineering, *see also* extended
    degree programmes
    access to university   137–8
    allows access to university   137–8, 149
    background/aims   133–4
    community aspects   141–3, 150
    and students' transitions   138–40,
        143–7
action, *see also* agency of students
    acting alone   41, 56, 71, 73, 160, 161
    helping other students   47
    students' difficulties in adopting   50
    as type of meaning   36
adaptor students   158, 159, *159*, 164–70
advanced mathematics
    pass rates   32
    students' views on   32, 39, 43–4,
        49–50, 51
    transition challenges   54–5
African churches   97
African students
    enrolment rates   1, 111
    graduation rates   111

labelled as 'coconuts'   82, 85–6, 93 n.1
    tensions between curricula and
        religion   95–6
Afrikaans   66, 79, 117
agency of students, *see also* action
    and adaptation   127
    and capability approach   138
    and choices/constraints   63, 112
    and learning communities   151
    little attention paid to   2
    must be harnessed by universities   186
    outside the curriculum space   185
    from passive to active student   44–5
    projective dimension of   128
    promoted by religious
        organisations   87
    refusing to accept rejection   67
    and responsibility towards others   47,
        56–7
    role in students' success/failure   18
    in school environment   24–5,
        26–7, 164
    and self-belief   24, 118, 168
    and social practices   35
    'sponsored' by others   182
    temporal/spatial nature of   75,
        113, 126
    uneven and complex   55–6, 182
alienation
    Bhabha's notion of 'unhomed'   86
    and ethnicity   83
    from family/neighbourhoods
        85–6, 184
    mitigated by religion   100
    not experienced by some   68
    outsider students   160–1, 161–2,
        163, 184
    and student uprisings   1–2
alone, acting   41, 56, 71, 73, 160, 161

apartheid
  effects on UCT   6
  geographic/racial separation   68,
    82, 83–4
  opposed by religious organizations   97
assessment, *see also* feedback
  of essays   91
  school examinations   22
  summative nature of   184
attrition, *see* dropping out

Backstage   88
belonging, sense of
  adaptor students   *159*, 166–7, 176
  enables finding a balance   57
  and future self/career   128
  insider students   159, *159*, 173, 174
  obtained through religion   95
  outsider students   *159*, 162, 163
  strategist students   *159*
  in transition to other
    disciplines   127, 128
  ways of enhancing   178
Bhabha, H
  concept of identity   97
  notion of postcolonial subjectivity   5
  notion of 'unhomed'   86
Biology classes   104, 105
black academics   7
black students
  drop out rates   61–2
  enrolment   1, 111
  graduation rates   32, 110–11, 133, 147
  percentage of student population   7
  from SADC countries   120
  school pass rates   19, 31
  women students   61–2
boundaries
  multicultural   68, 84
  in neighbourhood communities   65
Bourdieu, P   116, 156, 157, 159, 176

capabilities
  and agency   138
  and ASPECT programme   136,
    143–5, 147
  assessing effectiveness of
    pedagogies   149
  criteria for   135–6

Sen's approach   134–5
and students' transitions   138–40,
    143–7, 151
capital, *see also* cultural capital
  Bourdieu's concept of   156, 157, 176
  mismatch between student/
    institutional   177
careers
  choice of postgraduate studies
    123–8
  lack of clear goals   69–70, 72–3, 162
  and work experience   163
choice
  and capabilities   138
  constraints on   111–12, 183
  of degree   161
  of HE institution   126
  shaped by identity   112–13
  as a social process   111
Christianity   96, 101, 102, 103
clothes, brand names   87
'coconuts'   82, 85–6, 93 n.1
code-switching   21, 88
coloured students
  enrolment rates   1, 111
  graduation rates   32, 111
  home languages   79
communication course (ASPECT)   140,
    143, 150
community organizations
  involvement of school
    children   25, 26
  'sponsoring' of students' agency   182
completion rates, *see* graduation rates
coping mechanisms   26, 27, 72
Council on Higher Education   110,
    114, 129
critical debate
  needs to be fostered   178
  not taught in schools   104, 164
  students' impatience with   89
  students' limited use of   89, 90–1
  and students' religious beliefs   107
cultural capital
  and agency   156
  and alienation of students   4, 84
  and degree choices   161
  lacking in first-generation
    students   157

language as form of 176–7
and types of student 158–9, 160,
    175–7
culture, *see also* institutional culture
cross-cultural mixing 68, 83–4, 88,
    142–3
notion of common culture 83
curricula
ASPECT programme 146–7, 147–8
emphasis on critical literacy 21
revision of maths curriculum 32
and students' alienation 184
and students' religion 101–6, 106–7
and students' religious beliefs 95–6

data for case studies
ASPECT programme 136–7
female Muslim student 64–5
Humanities students 80–1
mathematics students 36–7
overview 8
postgraduate students 114–15
study of previous experiences
    18–19, 158
study of role of religion 98
degrees
ability to make informed choices 161
failure to study chosen degree 42, 48,
    109, 119, 121, 124, 170
investment in first choice of
    degree 110, 112, 115–23
need for flexible pathways 183
students' perceptions of 39, 163
designated identity 69
disciplinary habitus 116, 127, 129
disciplinary identity 112, 120
disciplinary spaces 55, 113, 120
discourse, *see also* academic discourse,
    concept of 18
discourse analysis
ASPECT case study 136, 138, 139–47
female Muslim student 65–73
Humanities students 81–91
mathematics students 37–52
and meaning-making 36–7
postgraduate students 115–28
study of role of religion 98–9, 101–6
study of students' previous
    experiences 160–75

dropping out
black male students 62
black women students 61–2, 72–3
postgraduate law students 120
and role of religion 25

engineering students, *see* Academic
    Support Programme for Engineering
English
'Africanisation' of 88
ASPECT communication course 140,
    143, 150
both access and gatekeeper 5
as cultural capital 176–7
difficulties in maths 38
dominance of at UCT 82
effect on school-university
    transition 20–1
and failure to achieve higher
    marks 91
increasingly spoken by students 87–8
level/speed of in classes 81
medium of instruction in schools 21
students' investment in 24
enrolment 1, 32, 111
essays
lecturers' negative feedback 84
limited critical debate 89, 90–1
written in schools 22
Ethics classes 103
ethnicity 83
extended degree programmes, *see also*
    Academic Support Programme for
    Engineering
extended time viewed as
    constraint 148
formation of social bonds 48
hinders students' ability to be
    independent 12, 50, 54, 145–6, 185
overview 8
students' ambivalence towards 185
students' choice to shift to 137–8
support needed beyond first year 54,
    92, 147, 150, 151, 183
extended mathematics programme
run over two years 32
students' views on 38, 40, 43, 49, 50
extended science programmes
enrolment figures 32

General Entry Progamme for
Science   165
students' views on   42–3, 47, 48–9
for students with potential   31
extra-mural activities   151, 171, 173

failing
attributed to struggles with English   91
black students   62
impact on students' degree
choice   125
influencing factors   18
mediated through religion   95, 99
and mimicking of academic
discourse   84, 184
and repetition of courses   45
results in leaving university   121,
123, 167
and study groups   165, 166
Fairclough, N   34–5, 36
family environments
alienation/separation from   41, 52,
85–6, 168, 184
challenging parents' authority   171
characteristics of   17
expectations for students   97, 119–20,
125–6, 184–5
female Muslim student   65–6, 67,
70–1, 72, 73–4
impact of working-class discourses   74
impact on students' degree choices   97,
110, 118
maths students case study   37, 41, 42,
47, 56
middle-class students   74
need to give back to   41, 52
need to maintain connections with   83
and notion of space   113
postgraduate case study   117, 118–19,
121, 124
previous experiences case study   160,
163, 164, 167, 170, 173
'sponsoring' of students' agency   182
feedback by lecturers
and appropriate academic
discourse   84–5, 184
on lack of critical debate   91
FeesMustFall   1–2
female students, *see* women students

feminism
recontextualisation of   71, 74
and religious beliefs   102
final year of study
increased usage of English   87
investment in academic
disciplines   88–9
lack of institutional support   92
more academically difficult   145, 174
students learn to question   89
and writer identity   89–90
free choice   63, 68, 73, 74
funding
and financial dropout   62
students' lack of   51–2, 71, 72, 161, 184
for UCT   6

gender studies   89, 102, 103
General Entry Progamme for
Science   165
goals, lack of direction   69–70, 72–3, 162
Golden Key International Honour
Society   162
graduation rates   32, 110–11, 133, 147

habitus, concept of   116, 127, 129, 156,
159, 163
His People church   87
home environments, *see* family
environments
home languages   21, 79, 82
honours degrees   111, 113–14, 129–30
Humanities students
overview of postgraduate case
study   109
overview of undergraduate case
studies   79, 92, 96
and religious beliefs   101–4
students' perceived value of
courses   119, 121, 121–2, 125

identification
as black multilingual student   41
of extended vs advanced courses   50
of extended vs mainstream
students   43
of lecturers   43
of 'other people'   37
as struggling student   49

as successful student   37, 38, 41,
    47–8, 53
as type of meaning   36
identity, *see also* learning identities;
    situational identities; social
    identities
  Bhabha's notion of   97
  central to learning   4, 62, 184
  and complexity of contexts   62–3
  and concept of choice   113
  designated identity   69
  disciplinary identity   112, 120
  and language   79–80, 82, 112
  and notion of space   113
  professional identity   110, 112, 118,
    129, 163
  reified by stereotypes   2
  social identities   25, 63, 98–9
  writer identity   81, 89–91
  youth identity   24
identity construction
  as 'negotiated experience'   82–3
  and notion of investment   18
  and peer relationships   25
  and religious beliefs   97
insider students   158, 159, *159*, 173–5
institutional culture
  of law faculties   120, 121
  little transformation of   7
  perceived as white   82, 83, 119
  and religious beliefs   106, 107
institutional habitus   156–7, 172, 178
interviews
  benefits of multiple interviews   64, 80
  concepts of background/
    foreground   36
  enjoyed by students   185
  not a source of 'essential
    truths'   9
  as social practice   35
  tools used to analyse   34
investment
  in academic disciplines   88–9, 91
  in education as tool for mobility   24
  in first choice of degree   110, 112,
    115–23
  and identity construction   18
  in undergraduate knowledge   129, 130
Investment Society   125

Kwaito   88

language
  and Bill of Rights   20
  and ethnicity   83
  as form of capital   176–7
  home languages   21, 79, 82
  and identity   79–80, 82, 112
Language in Education Policy   21
Law Faculty   117–18, 119, 120–1, 122–3
learning
  as a journey   2–3, 5, 175, 182
  need for alternative models   27
  rote learning in schools   22, 27
learning communities   150–1
learning identities
  constructed by teachers   23
  creating a strong identity   67–8
  fostered through affirmation   25
  and institutional habitus   157
lecturers, *see also* feedback by lecturers
  assumptions about prior
    knowledge   184
  frequent changes of   43
  help sought from   140, 142
  mismatch in understandings   3
  perceptions of white lecturers   38, 41
  reluctance to seek help from   41, 55,
    67, 91, 121
libraries   45, 48, 51, 161
life-skills programme   46
longitudinal studies, *see also* qualitative
    research; research on higher
    education
  allow temporal/spatial
    perspective   181–2
  foreground centrality of context
    4–5, 186
  interplay between agency and
    structure   62
  overview of case studies   7–8
  recontextualization in
    interviews   35–6
  school-to-university transition   34
  show situated nature of
    experiences   74, 156
  students' conflicting discourses   5
  understanding of students'
    choices   110

mainstream courses, *see also* advanced
    mathematics
    duration of   42
    require independent study   40
    shift across to extended
        programmes   48, 137–8, 142
    transition to   8, 47, 49
Marketing diploma   114, 124
masters degrees   114
mathematics, *see also* advanced
    mathematics
    extended mathematics   32, 38, 40, 43,
        49, 50
    school mathematics   22, 32, 38, 139
meanings, type of   36
mentors   47, 168, 169, 176
meta-awareness
    students' lack of   89, 90
    and transitions in discourses   19
meta-reflection   8, 11, 19, 107
middle-class students   74, 82, 157
mobility
    and academic discourse   85
    difficulties of class transition   64
    education as tool for   24
    as escape from working-class life   26,
        63, 66, 69
    promoted by religious
        organisations   87
    signified by attending UCT   126
mothers
    expectations of   126
    as key figures   46, 66, 99
motivation of students   7, 33, 62, 87, 169
multiculturalism   68, 83–4
multiple interviews   64, 80
Muslim student (Roshni)
    agency/action   67, 73, 75
    family environment   65–6, 67, 70–1,
        72, 73–4
    future goals   69–70, 72–3
    neighbourhood environment   65, 69
    relationships across boundaries   68
    views on religion   70, 102

neighbourhood environments
    alienated from students   86, 166
    expectations for students   125–6, 184
    'sponsoring' of students' agency   182

    students' descriptions of   65, 69
    students 'giving back' to   118
    views on education   163
non-academic activities   46–7, 151,
    171, 173
norms
    challenging of students' norms   107
    and dominant academic
        discourses   63, 106–7
    and institutional habitus   156–7, 178
    and measurement of excellence   92
    white/middle class   55

outcomes-based education   17, 32
outsider students   158–9, *159*, 161–4

parents
    authority challenged   171
    mothers   46, 66, 99, 126
    and upward mobility   64
participation
    in classes   67, 91
    in learning communities   150–1
part-time work   67, 69, 87, 166
pass rates   19, 31, 32
peer mentoring
    ASPECT programme   143
    and learning communities   150
    in schools   25
    by students   37, 47, 56, 168, 169, 176
Philosophy classes   85, 104, 122
postgraduate diplomas   111, 114, 129–30
postgraduate studies
    accessing the job market   123–8
    enrolment of black students   111
    honours degrees   111, 113–14,
        129–30
    and investment in undergraduate
        studies   115–23
    masters degrees   114
    overview of study participants   109–10
    postgraduate diplomas   111, 114,
        129–30
poststructuralism
    conceptions of identity   74, 97, 112
    views on language/literacy   79
prior knowledge   3, 122, 129–30, 184
professional identities   110, 112, 118,
    129, 163

qualitative research, *see also* longitudinal
    studies
  lack of gender analysis 62
  in maths education 33–4
  short time frame of 4
quantitative studies 115

racial classifications 12 n.1
racism
  towards students 81
  within students' families 84
religious beliefs
  and course curricula 95–6, 101–6,
    106–7
  and identity 25, 97
  perspectives on Muslim
    religion 70, 102
  provide moral compass 101
  reconfiguration of 46
  as a resource 10, 96–7, 98–100
  and sense of belonging 95
religious organizations
  dissonance between university/home
    practices 100–1
  dual role played by 106
  opposition to apartheid 97
  provide sense of direction 87
  source of social contacts 100
  students' questioning of 103–4
repeating courses 45
representations
  of academic studies 46
  of family/ friends' support 45
  of mathematics 38, 40, 43, 44
  of residences 46
  of self 81, 84
  of township schools 47
  as type of meaning 36
research on higher education 3–4, 5, *see*
    also longitudinal studies; qualitative
    research
residences 46, 87, 106
resources
  lacking in schools 19–20, 37,
    47, 160
  libraries 45, 48, 51, 161
  offered by community
    organizations 25, 26
  religious beliefs 10, 96–7, 98–100

retention of students 1, 61–2, 62–3,
    183, 186
RhodesMustFall 1–2
rote learning 22, 27
rural areas 22, 98

schooling, *see also* teachers; township
    schools
  and approaches to learning 3
  and capability deprivation 135
  SA's dual system 19
  social justice perspective 148–9
school mathematics 22, 32, 38, 139
school-to-university transition
  ASPECT programme 138–40
  challenges faced by students 110
  difficulties in maths 32, 33, 54–5
  difficulties with English 20–1
  divide between school/university
    discourses 27, 182–3
  lack of preparation for 170
  longitudinal studies of 34
  need for psycho-social support 134
  need to build inclusivity 55
  neither linear nor universal 5
  and students' capital 157
  and types of student 158–9
science students
  degree completion rate 32
  General Entry Progamme for
    Science 165
  need for academic support 31
  and religious beliefs 104–6
  school experiences 21–2
second year of study
  ASPECT programme 144–7
  increased student confidence 87, 170–1
  lack of critical debate 89
self-belief 168, 176
  and agency 24, 118, 168
self-esteem 24, 100, 172, 173
self-representation 81, 84, *see also*
    identity; identity construction
Sen, A. 134–5
situational identities
  rationalized by students 92
  and religious beliefs 106
  and sense of self 61, 74
  students' awareness of 89

Skovsmose, O 34, 36
social identities
    fluidity/complexity of 63
    and religious beliefs 25, 98–9
social justice 148–9
social networks
    adaptor students 171
    afforded by extended
        programmes 40, 48
    alienation from non-university
        friends 86, 172
    ASPECT programme 141, 142–3
    cross-cultural mixing 68, 142–3
    difficulty making friends 173–4
    dominance of English 82
    via religious organisations 100
social practices
    of Law Faculty 117
    and recontextualisation 34–5
spaces, disciplinary 55, 113, 120
special programmes, *see* extended degree
        programmes
'spoon feeding' 40, 146
stereotypes 2, 4
strategist students 158, 159, *159*, 170–3
stress
    dealt with alone 41
    juggling different lifestyles 72
    mitigated by religion 95, 99
Student Christian Fellowship 161
Student Christian Society 100
Student Emerging Leadership
        Programme 165
study groups
    in schools 25, 66, 164
    at university 165, 168
success, *see also* mobility
    and academic discourses 92–3
    influencing factors 18
    and institutional habitus 157
    interaction with top students
        25, 53
    seen as dependent on the
        individual 7
    socially situated nature of 177
    students' definitions of 45–6,
        51, 186
support courses, *see* extended degree
        programmes

support services
    needed in residences 106
    not used by students 100
    used by students 46–7

teachers, *see also* township schools
    absenteeism 20, 42, 66, 167
    encouragement for students 22, 24–5,
        37, 48
    negative discourses 22, 23, 66
    'scope' method of
        teaching 21–2, 27
    students' descriptions of 20, 22, 24
Thornton, R
    metaphor of boundaries 65, 68
    notion of common culture 83
throughput rates 32, 110–11, 133, 147
time
    linked to choice and agency 113
    notion of temporal agency 126
    and repetition of courses 45
    students' lack of 41, 44, 46, 49
    time management skills 139
townships 12 n.2, 69, 86
township schools, *see also* teachers
    characterised as 'corrupt' 66
    divide between school/university
        discourses 182–3
    lack of critical debate 104, 164
    poorly resourced 19–20, 37,
        47, 160
    in rural areas 22
    students' lack of discipline 23, 42
transformation
    students' belief in 84
    of UCT 5–6, 7, 92
tutorials 67
tutors
    students as 45, 176
    students' consultation of 41, 91

United Kingdom
    concept of institutional habitus 156
    erasure of student identities 7
    research on women/first-generation
        students 62
    student mobility 26
    students' degree choices 111
    transition to adulthood 127

universities
    institutional habitus   156–7, 172, 178
    institutional norms   55, 63, 92, 106–7,
       156–7, 178
    social justice perspective   148–9
University of Cape Town (UCT)
    historical background   6
    limited number of black academics   7
    racism towards students   81
    students' descriptions of   68, 126
    students' perceptions of   49, 83,
       86, 169
    uneven transformation   5–6, 7, 92
    whiteness of   82, 83, 119
University of Stellenbosch   151
upward mobility, *see* mobility

wellness   151
white lecturers   38, 41

whiteness
    distinguished from 'Englishness'   87–8
    of UCT   82, 83, 119
White Paper on Education   149
white students   1, 6, 32
women students
    discouraged by teachers   66
    dropping out   61–2
    and empowerment/equity
      discourses   63, 71
    gendered domestic roles   64, 67, 71,
      74, 89
    and social identities   63
work experience   163
writer identity   81, 89–91
Writing Centre   68

youth identity   24
YouTube videos   45